D1614500

A Management System for the Seventies

by the same author

Corporate Planning
Management Techniques

A Management System for the Seventies

John Argenti

London. George Allen & Unwin Ltd
Ruskin House   Museum Street

First Published 1972

© John Argenti, 1972

ISBN 0 04 658044 1

Printed in Great Britain
in 11 point Times Roman type
by Alden & Mowbray Ltd
at the Alden Press Oxford

Preface

I have written this book because I believe that many of the books (and also articles, films and lectures) on management suffer from two enormous defects. Firstly, although they claim to be about management they always seem to be really about business management. While there is much that is admirable in the way in which companies are managed there are several ugly blemishes inherent in that particular form of management that I would not like to see imitated by other forms of organisation and which should long ago have been eliminated from business management. Instead, they are perpetuated and disseminated by books on 'management'.

The second defect is that most books seem to be offering solutions to yesterday's management problems rather than tomorrow's.

This book, then, is designed to help anyone who is going to be managing any organisation (or any part of it, of course) in the next decade or so—I have tried to predict what problems managers will be facing during that period and to suggest a down-to-earth practical system of management designed to help them cope with these problems. This book is intended for managers (and intending managers) in *all* types of organisation—including managers in business, industry and commerce.

As you read it, spare a thought for Mrs P. J. Henley, my secretary, who typed the whole thing once, most of it twice and some of it four or five times.

JOHN ARGENTI
Pettistree Lodge, Woodbridge, Suffolk

Contents

Preface   *page* vii
1   A System, not a Theory   1
2   The Basic Elements of Management   9
3   The Basic Elements of an Organisation   12
4   MS 0 – a Basic Management System   18
5   Trends in the 1970s   41
6   Step 1 in the 1970s   53
7   Step 2 in the 1970s   78
8   Step 3 in the 1970s   115
9   Step 4 in the 1970s   150
10 The Hierarchy in the 1970s   171
11 MS 70   204
12 MS 70 in Practice   219
Bibliography   250
Index   252

Chapter 1

A System, not a Theory

In this book, we are going to try to design a completely new system of management that is specifically tailored to the conditions in which managers will be working during the 1970s. The aim is not, definitely not, to develop yet another theory of management nor to fiddle with academic details; the aim is to work out a down-to-earth practical step-by-step system of management. A system, then, not a theory.

This emphatic rejection of the idea of a theory of management is not to be interpreted as a rejection of the value of theory – being without one is like having nowhere to hang your clothes so that you have to dump them on the floor in an untidy heap. No, we must certainly have a sound theoretical framework and we are certainly going to use great chunks of several management theories in the early chapters of the book. But we already have enough theories of management; what we want now is to apply all this knowledge. The gap between management academics and practising managers still seems to be as wide as ever, perhaps because academics tend to examine minute parts of the subject in exquisite detail without spelling out clearly and simply how their conclusions affect day-to-day management. So no new theories – and certainly no attempt here to add any sophisticated frills to existing theories.

We are going to try to draw up a blueprint for the management of organisations in the 1970s. We are going to try to identify just what managers should do and how they should do it over the next few years to ensure that the organisation they work for continues to be efficient in spite of the trend, that every manager must have noticed, for the management of organisations to become more and more difficult. So we will try to see how organisations are managed today and then suggest what changes in their mechanism will be necessary over the next few years; the aim is to unscrew the lid of the management machine to inspect how it works today and to see what modifications we will have to make to it in order to bring it up to the standard required over the next decade.

Why should we want to do this? Well, one does not have to look far to see what an appalling mess many organisations are in today, and if management is going to become more difficult over the next decade, which it certainly is for reasons we will discuss later, it is obviously high time we had a fresh look at the whole management machine; it is so obviously creaking and groaning under the strain of so much new knowledge and so many new techniques that we must start again from scratch – it is no good just tinkering with it. If anyone doubts that some organisations are in a mess, let him consider the situation in many of the large cities in the world (a city is an organisation), let him work for a week or two in a car factory or a bottling plant, let him commit a technical breach of the law and see the machinery of justice at work, let him lose his investments in a well-known company. Now, we must never pretend that everyting that is wrong with the world can be put right tomorrow afternoon simply by redesigning the mechanism of management. Of course not, for indeed many organisations fail from nothing more reprehensible than a run of sheer bad luck, while others fail because the conditions that brought them into being now no longer exist and their demise is in the interests of all concerned. Some organisations enjoy wild success for the opposite reasons – a run of good luck or because the goods or services that they exist to provide suddenly become highly desirable. But, and it is a big but, there are many more organisations whose success, stagnation or failure is the direct result of the way in which they are managed, and in this highly organised society in which most people in the world live today none of us are immune from the effects of good or bad management. All of us belong to and are dependent on a number of organisations, some of which may have only a trivial effect on our lives; but with others it is a matter of life or death for us.

2

So crucially do we depend on some organisations, so huge a factor is the quality of management in their success, so difficult is the art of management becoming that we really must try to find out where managers are going wrong and what we must do to put it right. In this book, then, we will study how managers manage and where they go wrong. We will ask such questions about them as: 'Why did he do that?' and 'Then what did he do?' and 'When should he have done this?' But we are going to relate these questions to the whole management machine to see also where each manager fits in; it is really very like an engineer studying how a machine works to see where it is under strain and where it should be redesigned. We want to know, just as an engineer does, how that shaft turns to release that flap which hits the lever and ... but of course our management machine consists not of shafts and levers but telephones and computers and offices with people in them. What we want, then, is a blueprint which shows how an organisation will have to be managed if it is to be successful in the 1970s (and it will be a very different design to one we might have devised for the 1960s, or 1950s, as we will see later).

Is such a blueprint possible – after all, organisations come in all shapes and sizes and what is right for one may not necessarily be right for another? Wheelbarrows come in all shapes and sizes, too, but there are one or two absolutely basic and essential components that are present in all wheelbarrows: a wheel, a handle, a container and a leg. These four are essential to any wheelbarrow. (Some, it is true, have one wheel and two legs, others have two wheels and one leg, and so on through any permutation.) But a wheelbarrow has one other feature; these four essential components have to be fitted together in a certain way for otherwise it is useless; the wheel must not be placed above the container, for example. In exactly the same way we shall find that the management mechanism of all organisations – whatever their nature or size – consists of a certain number (five, in fact) of essential components each of which must be fitted together in a certain way, otherwise the organisation cannot be managed. So we are going to draw up a blueprint showing these basic five elements and the inter-connections required for the management machine of any organisation, and if we want to find out what is wrong with any organisation all we have to do is to compare the real organisation with the blueprint. Furthermore, the diagram should be valid for any organisation – a golf club in Japan, a fire service in Germany, a car factory in Detroit. And it should be valid for all managers throughout the organisation from top to bottom, from chairman to foreman, minister to clerk, general to corporal.

There are some very good reasons why we should try to design a system of management which is valid for any type of organisation. The first is that so much of the literature on 'management' is really about *business* management and while some features of management in business are excellent (the liberal use of figures by numerate managers for example) there are at least two huge areas* where business management is a sheer disgrace, and we certainly do not want to model our system of management on them. The second reason why we should avoid concentrating on purely business management is that the world is composed of many types of organisation, some of which are certainly no less important to us all than companies – charities, national governments, international agencies of all sorts, and so on. A system of management that is valid for any one of these is bound to be less useful than one that is right for them all. This, then, is what we are looking for; a system of management that is valid at all levels of management for all types of organisation and, furthermore, one that is specifically designed for the conditions in which managers will be working during the 1970s. It is the absence of this last feature that renders useless so much current study, research and literature on the subject of management. The trouble is that we live in a changing world, one that is now changing sufficiently rapidly for a proven recipe for success in management in one decade to become a ticket to stagnation in the next. Books and articles entitled, 'How We Manage at Bloggs & Co.' by A. Captain of Industry are usually based on the lessons the author learnt over two or more decades. Now some of these lessons will be valid for another year, some for a decade, some are eternally valid, but, unless one has a clear

* These are discussed in later chapters.

4

idea of the conditions in which managers will be working next year or in the next decade, one cannot say which of these lessons should be put into effect and which to ignore. The publication of a study on what features go to make a successful incentive scheme for workers packing eggs is all very fine – but not very useful if technological change or social conditions in the 1970s are going to render useless *all* incentive schemes in the egg-packing industry. It is useless for an academic to teach a class of potential managers that 'under these conditions one man cannot control more than eight subordinates', if he does not also add that these conditions are changing fast and before long advances in computer technology may allow this man to control eighteen subordinates. Or 'the most successful managers are highly autocratic'. Today, yes. But tomorrow? The point we are making is simply this; much of the management knowledge of today is valid today; some of it will still be valid tomorrow, but unless we know what tomorrow will bring we do not know how to select good advice from bad.

So we have two problems: any practical advice given us from practising managers may be out of date; and the advice we get from academics tends to be difficult to put into practice – the gap is wide, as we said above. So we really do need a new approach, and the one adopted in this book is that of casting aside present practical advice until we have tested it to determine whether it will be relevant to the 1970s, and if it will be, then we will weave it into our system. But if we cast aside *all* practical advice we are, surely, going to be left with nothing to build on? No, we shall still have the absolutely basic essentials of management – the five components we mentioned above – and these must be our starting point. So, beginning with this bare framework, we must then try to predict what conditions will be like for managing organisations in the 1970s, and thus clothe our framework with the garments appropriate to these conditions. We are approaching the problem of management in the 1970s in much the same way as an engineer would approach the problem of designing a wheelbarrow for use on the moon. He would start with the knowledge that a wheelbarrow has certain essential parts, then he would seek advice as to conditions on the moon, then, and only then, could he modify the basic design to meet these conditions.

So far as is known this is the first attempt to design a comprehensive system of management and it is certainly the first to be specifically designed for a decade ahead. It is going to be difficult for this reason alone; and also because management itself is a complex subject, which imposes the need of steering clear of the technical jargon that always seems to settle like smuts from a smoky chimney on to the pages of books like this. We shall, however, have to introduce some new technical words to describe some of the more important new concepts that this fresh approach will yield – for example we shall meet the Management Index and the Monitor, the Cell, the Sieve, Slack, Failure Plus, and (with apologies) Transdepartmental Projects. But these are relatively harmless terms compared with those that usually adorn new management techniques.* We not only want to keep the jargon light, we also want to keep the whole exposition simple and clear – because we want the reader to understand how the system is put together, so that if he disagrees with one or two parts of it he can see at once how to alter those parts more to his own liking and, very important, how to make the vital consequential changes to contiguous parts as well. Since the book is written for managers and the system is designed for use by them it is important that both should be readily digestible because their time is valuable.

The system will be built up in three main stages. In the first we shall identify the five essential components of management (Chapters 2 and 3). But, just as in the case of the wheelbarrow where we recognised that the parts had to be put together in a certain way, so, in Chapter 4, we shall put together these five components of management so that they form a complete system of management – but one so crude that it really has no practical value. It represents the absolute minimum system that would work in theory – it is so elementary that if one took away any component or altered any of the relationships between them it would cease to work even in theory; it would

---

* For those who thrive on sophisticated jargon with which to impress their friends we should point out that our system can be *very* precisely described as a Teleological Holism and it is designed to act by a Continuous Systemic Prophylaxis.

go as dead as a radio when a wire is cut. Since it is theoretically impossible to design a management system that is simpler than this we call it MS o (Management System, zero). It may be the simplest possible system but, as we will see, it is surprisingly complex and some quite interesting lessons can be learnt from it.

Then we turn to the second stage. This is done in Chapter 5 where we try to forecast the conditions in which managers will be working in the 1970s. We shall identify fifteen major trends in society, in technology, in economics and in politics that will have a major bearing on how managers manage during the decade.

Then, in the third stage we shall examine the effect of these trends on each of the five components of management. It is at this stage that we must start clothing our basic system (MS o) with garments appropriate to the seventies; this we shall do in Chapters 6 to 10 which form the main part of the book. By Chapter 11 we are ready to present the finished article, which we will call MS 70 – a Management System for the Seventies.

Finally, in Chapter 12, we shall discuss the practical use and implications of MS 70 and see how far we have achieved our aim. What is our aim? It is to design a system of management that can be applied in real live earthy situations by any manager at any level of seniority in any organisation. So, if any organisation finds itself in trouble it should be possible to compare*the actual way in which it is managed with our MS 70 blueprint and we should be able to say 'Oh, well! No wonder you have trouble – look, you have forgotten the bit that goes in there. Put that right, and you'll be O.K.'

Of course, to achieve that sort of thing, MS 70 would really have to be a miracle. It has got to be as valid for the job of a foreman in a company despatch department as for a prime minister – but this is just exactly what we are aiming for. We may not get there this time but it is surely something worth striving for in view of the really quite disgraceful way in which some organisations are run.

Is it all just too ambitious? Let us remind ourselves that if,

* The Management Index, which we will not meet again until Chapter 12 is designed to allow this comparison to be made.

sixty years ago, something had gone wrong with one of those new-fangled motor cars there would have been no one around for miles who could understand its mechanism well enough to repair it. But now if a car breaks down almost any passing schoolboy can diagnose the fault and, given a long enough piece of wire, can repair it. Man has been managing organisations for countless thousands of years, surely we ought to understand how they work by now.

Chapter 2

The Basic Elements of Management

In this chapter and the next our task will be to identify the basic parts of a management system, then in Chapter 4 we shall assemble them together and by turning the handle we shall test the mechanism we have built. In the previous chapter we mentioned that there would be five basic parts and it happens to be convenient to describe four of them in this chapter, leaving the fifth to be described in the next; the four dealt with in this chapter are relevant to management and the fifth is relevant to organisations – it will be seen at once how arbitrary this split is because one cannot have an organisation without management and one cannot practise management anywhere but in an organisation. To clarify the exposition, however, we are going to separate the inseparable just for the period of these two brief chapters. The extreme brevity of these two chapters also requires some explanation – we are trying to strip 'management' of all inessential details to get down to its bare bones and the bare essentials of most subjects are quite simple and can be described quite quickly. The reason we want to get down to the bare minimum is that, since we are trying to study management from a new angle, we want to exclude any preconceived ideas on the subject that are not part of the essence of management. It is part of the essence of a wheel-barrow that it has a wheel; it is not part of its essence to have a cast-iron wheel, that is just a feature of a nineteenth-century wheelbarrow. In exactly the same way we must try to exclude anything in our basic management system that is not part of the essence of management – we must avoid putting something in that is really only a piece of nineteenth-century management folk-lore. If we are going to get down to essentials, then, we must not be surprised if what we find is extremely simple – but we must also be sure that we have not so oversimplified the system that it does not work at all. We are aiming to describe a management system which has been so purged of inessentials that it is only just workable – take away one more part and it would fail to function. This is the minimum system we are searching for; we are going to call it MS o where 'MS' stands for Management System, of course, and 'o' (zero) implies that it is as simple and elementary a system as one can possibly design.

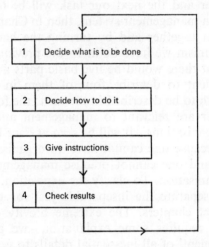

Fig 1: The four steps of the management process

Let us now try to identify the first four parts of the mechanism of management. The barest description of what managers do seems to boil down to this: they decide what is to be done, they decide how to do it, they give instructions, and they check results. That is all. These are the basic elements of management. There is only one other point to be made, namely that these four parts are linked together in the sequence in which they are stated above – that is to say, a manager must decide what is to be done before he can decide how to do it, he must know how it is to be done before giving instructions and he must give instructions before checking results. And, depending on what results he finds when he checks results, he can start the

10

process over again if necessary. So the management process appears* to be as in Fig. 1.

That is what managers do all day in those great glass and concrete boxes. If we could eavesdrop on a manager we would find him either deciding what to do, or deciding how to do it, or giving instructions to someone, or checking results. Furthermore, for any given management task he would do these things in that order – he cannot possibly decide how to do something unless he has decided what it is he is trying to achieve, he cannot give instructions until he has decided how the task is to be tackled and there is no point in checking results until the necessay instructions have been given. This is the order in which these steps must be taken and it makes no sense to carry them out in any other order, just as it would make no sense to assemble the parts of a wheelbarrow so that the wheel is placed above the container.

Fig. 1 represents the first four parts of MS o and shows how they are linked together. In the next chapter we shall discuss the fifth part.

* Many of the conclusions reached in these early chapters will be re-examined later – some of them will have to be revised.

Chapter 3

The Basic Elements of an Organisation

In the last chapter we said that management and organisation were inseparable – one cannot have an organisation without management and you cannot practice management anywhere but in an organisation – but in spite of this we tried to define 'management'. Now we are going to try to define what an organisation is, and again we must seek the simplest possible definition. It is this: an organisation is a group of people working together towards a common purpose. This definition contains two elements, 'a group of people working together' and 'towards a common purpose'. We shall have a great deal to say about the purpose of organisations later in the book, and it is not proposed to discuss it further here.

Let us instead turn to the other essential element in the definition, 'a group of people working together'. The first thing to notice about this is so simple that one hardly dares to mention it: an organisation consists of more than one person! In other words, one man pursuing a purpose is not an organisation, but two men pursuing the same purpose is. The fundamental distinction between one man and two or more is that where there is only one there can be no human relationship but where there is more than one – even if it is only one more than one – then there must be a relationship between them. We will call it the 'Relationship of Agreed Seniority'. This means that where two or more people are working together there is always an agreement of some sort between them that one of them is 'senior' to the others. This agreement means that the man who is senior to the others can give them instructions, that they agree to obey these and that the senior has the right to punish or reward his subordinates. This agreement exists in all organisations; sometimes it takes the form of a complex legal document setting out the terms of the relationship between a senior and his subordinates, sometimes the agreement is so informal and temporary as to be almost invisible, sometimes the agreement is wholly voluntary, sometimes it is enforced at the point of a gun. But is it always there. Inspect any organisation and you will find the relationship of agreed seniority, although in some small organisations one sometimes has to look quite carefully to find it.

In order to illustrate this relationship between people in an organisation let us take three examples which are intended to show how tenuous it can be and yet still exist. Take a retired bachelor living on his own who tends his own garden – he is not an organisation. But if he employs a gardener then together they are an organisation in the sense that they are working together for a common purpose (to keep the garden looking attractive) and the bachelor stands in the relationship of agreed seniority to the gardener – even if this is for only a few hours a week. The gardener recognises that if he carries out the bachelor's instructions satisfactorily he may be rewarded, if badly he may be punished or dismissed. The fact that this organisation is tiny (and also intermittent if he is a part-time gardener) does not alter the principle. Take another example: after a road accident a crowd has gathered. Someone starts giving instructions and some of the people in the crowd carry them out; although the whole incident is over in a few minutes, nevertheless during that time some members of the crowd, by agreeing to carry out the leader's instructions, have become an organisation. Notice that a crowd is not an organisation because the members of a crowd are neither working towards a common purpose nor have they agreed to recognise a senior from whom they are willing to take instructions. Now consider one further example: two brothers are running a business and while one is good at book-keeping the other is good at selling. It is highly probable that when both of them are working on the books the brother who is good at book-keeping will act as senior, but when both are out selling the other will act as senior. Here we have an organisation because two people are working together to make a profitable business, the only peculiarity in this case is that the relationship of agreed seniority is reversed from time to time. This, it is being suggested, does not alter the principle – that no organisation exists without it. Agreed seniority is one of the hallmarks of an organisation.

It will be recalled that in the last chapter we went to some lengths to ensure that our description of the management process was reduced to its bare essentials. We are trying now to do the same thing with our description of an organisation, that is to say, we are trying to arrive at a definition so wide that it includes every possible type of organisation – large or small, formal or informal, temporary or permanent – but excludes anything that is not an organisation, such as a crowd or a mob. The purpose behind these twin endeavours is to ensure that when the five parts of MS o are assembled together, it will form a management system that is valid for all managers at all levels in all organisations. This being the aim, it follows that each of the five parts that make up MS o must themselves be as general and as free from constraining detail as possible. The minimum description of an organisation, then, is that it is 'a group of people working together toward a common purpose' but we must now add that these people have between them the relationship of agreed seniority. This relationship implies that some of them have agreed to receive instructions from others and that they also recognise that they could be punished or rewarded by their seniors. We have also noted that this relationship can be permanent or temporary, formal or informal; by this we mean that the act of giving instructions can be formal ('You will proceed to the Sergeant's Mess at 1800 hours') or informal ('Fred, chuck over that spanner'). The punishments and rewards can also range from the formal and severe (being shot at dawn) to the informal and trivial ('Thanks, Tom'). The point being made here is that organisations come in all shapes and sizes but all of them are built on the same basic principles – although one may have to look very carefully at some of the small, informal organisations to see that they are in fact built of the same basic bricks as the large formal ones. We examined three small informal organisations above; let us now turn to the larger, more formal organisations where we shall find that the principle of agreed seniority is much more in evidence.

Take first an organisation consisting of two men. In ac-

THE BASIC ELEMENTS OF AN ORGANISATION

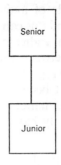

Fig 2: The relationship of agreed seniority

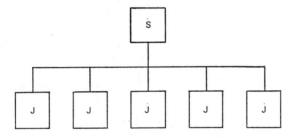

Fig 3: Agreed seniority between six people

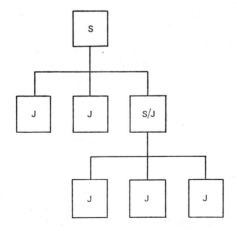

Fig 4: Three levels of seniority

cordance with the principle of agreed seniority, one of them
will be senior to the other and this can be shown as in Fig. 2. The
line joining the two men indicate that the relationship is
one of agreed seniority between them. Now take an organisation employing six men (Fig. 3). As the number of people in
an organisation increases it becomes at first difficult and then
impossible for the senior to handle so many subordinates and
two levels of agreed seniority have to be formed as in Fig. 4.

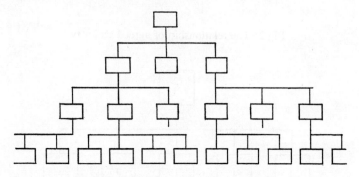

Fig 5: A typical family tree or pyramid

It will be seen at once that one of these men (J/S) is both a
junior and a senior at the same time, and this is a phenomenon
we had not met in the tiny organisations we have been discussing up to now. This new man is a manager. A manager is
a man who has both a boss and one or more subordinates. A
man who has no boss is not a manager; a man who has no
subordinates is not a manager. A manager has both a boss and
a subordinate – he is the meat in a sandwich of human relationships.

In an organisation consisting of less than about a dozen
people there will only be two levels of seniority, as in Fig. 3.
In larger organisations there will be three levels (as in Fig. 4)
or even, in very large organisations, as many as fifty levels. At
each level is a manager who stands in the agreed seniority
relation with the man above him and the man below him.
These chains of agreed seniority in larger organisations are
often known as a hierarchy of managers or sometimes as 'the

family tree' or 'the pyramid' because of its shape when drawn out as a traditional organisation chart as in Fig. 5.

It is this hierarchy that forms the fifth and final part of MS o. This hierarchy of agreed seniority is the essential backbone of all organisations (in very small organisations, there are only two vertebrae as in Fig. 3). No organisation can exist or has ever existed without the hierarchy of agreed seniority. It seems clear that when we defined an organisation as 'a group of people working together . . . ' we were being too vague for we now know that this group of people is not amorphous but has a definite structure. Perhaps we should redefine an organisation as 'a group of people formed into a hierarchy by the relationship of agreed seniority working toward a common purpose'. This definition is probably more correct than the previous one but it is too much of a mouthful for every-day use.

We have now the five basic parts of MS o. They are as follows:

The manager's job consists of: 1. deciding what is to be done
2. deciding how to do it
3. giving instructions to subordinates
4. checking results
All organisations consist of 5. people in a hierarchy of agreed seniority.

In the next chapter we shall put these five parts together to form a basic management system and show how it works.

Chapter 4

MS o – a Basic Management System

In Chapter 2 we discussed the process of management, and in Chapter 3 we discussed organisations – we separated these two concepts in order to simplify the discussions, but, as we have stressed before, they are logically inseparable. In this chapter we are going to join them together and discuss a basic management system for organisations; this means that we must intertwine the four steps of the management process with the hierarchy of agreed seniority. Although we have only these five building-bricks to play with we shall find that the act of merging the four elements of management with the one of organisation produces an incredibly complicated structure. It is one thing to pluck a manager out of a hierarchy and examine his job in isolation as we did in Chapter 2 but it is quite another matter to describe his job inside the hierarchy where he interacts with all the other managers. To make this point clearer, consider three managers at three levels of a hierarchy; if there was no interaction between them then we could easily draw a diagram showing each of them going through the four steps of the management process on their own and with no regard for the other managers in the hierarchy. Fig. 6 shows this situation; it consists merely of Fig. 1 repeated three times without any interconnections between the three managers, i.e. it does not show the agreed seniority relationship and is therefore incorrect.

In order to sort out the correct interconnections let us take a real-life organisation and follow its managers through a real-life decision. Imagine, therefore, a company with an organisation structure that has the Managing Director at the head of the pyramid, then several managers at the next level who report to him, one of whom is a Sales Manager. This

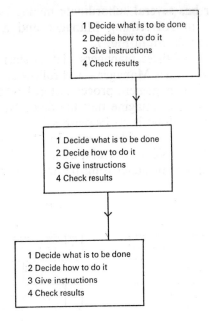

Fig 6: Three managers in a nonsense hierarchy

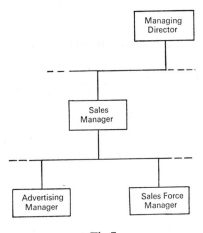

Fig 7

Sales Manager has several subordinate managers reporting to him including an Advertising Manager and a Sales Force Manager. This is shown in Fig. 7.

Now take one of these managers – let us start with the one in the middle, the Sales Manager – and follow him through the four steps of the management process. Step 1 is 'decide what is to be done': so let us imagine that the Sales Manager decides that what is to be done is to increase sales turnover. He has taken Step 1. Step 2 is 'decide how to do it' and here the Sales Manager would consider several possible actions: he might increase the amount of advertising perhaps, or recruit several

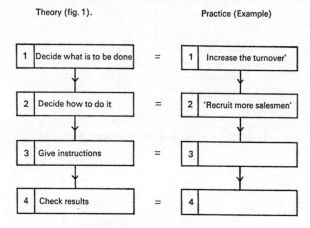

Fig 8: So far identical to Fig. 1

more salesmen, or improve the design of the product, and so on. Let us suppose that he decides that the best way of increasing turnover in the present circumstances is to take on some more salesmen. That is Step 2. So far we have met no snags and everything has gone according to Fig. 1. We can see from Fig. 8 that what the Sales Manager has been doing so far is identical to the diagram in Fig. 1. The next is Step 3 'give instructions' and, sure enough, it is clear that this is exactly what the Sales Manager is about to do – he will send for his Sales Force Manager and instruct him to recruit more salesmen. But now, for the first time, a second man (the Sales Force

Manager) has entered the picture, an event that was not provided for in Fig. 1. We must therefore modify Fig. 1 to show that when a manager gives instructions he invokes the principle of agreed seniority and this introduces a manager at a lower level in the hierarchy. This is shown in Fig. 9.

Now we come to Step 4, 'check results'. At once we see a difficulty that we had not noticed before because in Chapter 2 we were discussing one manager's job in isolation. But we must now see that there are two sets of results that the Sales Manager

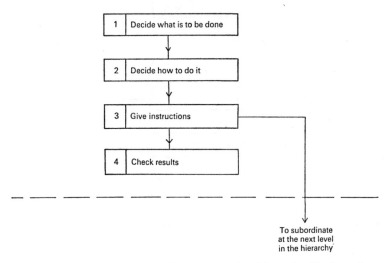

Fig 9: One of the links between the managers in a hierarchy (the boundary between the hierarchical levels is shown as a dotted line)

must check – his own (increase turnover) and his subordinate's (take on more salesmen). This is universally true for all managers – all managers have to check both on the progress that their subordinates are making, and on the progress of their own tasks. In order to avoid confusion in future we should draw attention to this fact by giving a name to these two results; we will call the task that a manager is set in Step 1 'the manager's task' and the task he sets to a subordinate in Step 3 'the subordinates' task'. Thus in our example the Sales Manager set himself the task of increasing sales and he set his Sales Force Manager the task of taking on more salesmen – these are the manager's task and the subordinate's task respectively. It will be noticed that, in this example, the subordinate's task is intended to do one thing only – to help the manager carry out his task. Thus the only reason that the Sales Force Manager has been asked to take on more salemen is that his boss, the Sales Manager, thinks it will increase turnover, which, of course, is his task. This is a general rule: a subordinate's task is intended to help achieve the manager's task.

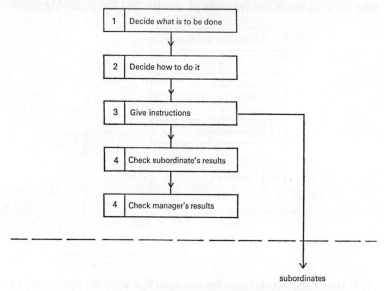

Fig 10: All managers must check two sets of results

Let us return to our example; the Sales Manager, it will be recalled, has taken his Step 3 'give instructions' and was about to take Step 4 'check results' when we discovered that there were two results to check, so the diagram ought now to be modified to show this; Fig. 10 indicates that the manager will start checking his subordinate's results before he starts checking his own because, in our example, the Sales Manager cannot expect to see turnover rising until his subordinate has taken on the new salesmen.

Now consider what might happen when the Sales Manager checks up on his subordinate's results; he might discover:

22

A. That the subordinate has taken on all the new salesmen,

or B. That he has only taken on some of them,

or C. That he has taken none on of them.

Let us consider what the Sales Manager would do in each of these cases. If he found that the subordinate had carried out his task – Case A – he would do nothing more but would sit back and wait to see if turnover started to rise – in other words he would start checking his own results. This is shown in Fig. 11 where a line marked A is drawn to represent this case.

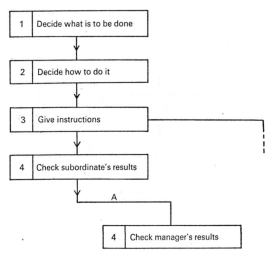

Fig 11: 'A' shows what the manager does if the subordinate's task is completed satisfactorily

Now consider Case B where the subordinate has been only partially successful. The Sales Manager's reaction would surely be to say, 'It looks as though my subordinate's partial failure will jeopardise carrying out my own task. If I am going to raise turnover successfully I had better do something to reinforce my original plan.' In other words, in Case B the manager will reconsider how to carry out his task, i.e., he will reconsider his original Step 2 'decide how to do it' in the light of the new situation. In this example the Sales Manager might decide to

C 23

launch an advertising campaign in which case he would proceed to Step 3 and give the necessary instructions to his Advertising Manager whose results he would also check. Fig. 12 shows Case B diagramatically.

Turning to Case C where the subordinate has completely failed in his task, the manager may have to confess that there is nothing he can do now to increase turnover. If a manager has to admit that he has failed in his task what should he do? Where should line C be drawn? It might be thought that he would merely revise his original Step 1 and simply say to

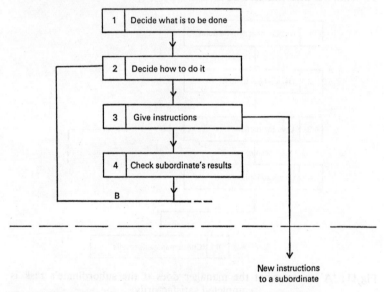

Fig 12: 'B' shows what the manager does if the subordinate fails or looks like failing to complete his task

himself 'I will now not try to increase turnover'. But it is suggested that this is not correct, for, in fact, no manager may decide his own task – his boss decides it. In other words, every one of the diagrams so far have been incorrect as far as Step 1 is concerned for we have described Step 1 of the manager's job as 'decide what is to be done' which implies that the manager decides his task himself. In fact the correct description of Step 1 is 'accept task from boss' and to represent this in a diagram

24

we should have a line coming from the next level up in the hierarchy into the manager's level as in Fig. 13.

Now we can see, for the first time, in Fig. 13, the connections between a manager, his boss above him and his subordinates below him – we said earlier that a manager was the meat in a sandwich of human relations – and Fig. 13 shows a manager

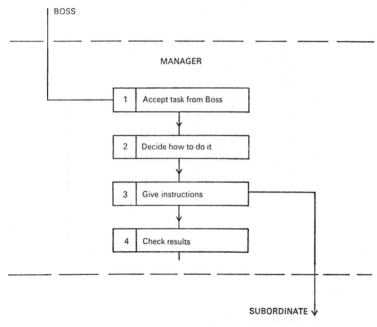

Fig 13: The *boss* decides the manager's task!

receiving a task from his boss, deciding how to carry it out and then giving instructions to his subordinates. However, Fig. 13 does not show him checking results which we left unfinished because we were not too sure what a manager should do if he had to admit that he could not now carry out his task. Now we can see what he should do – he should report to his boss since it was his boss who set the task for him in the first place; we show this in Fig. 14 by line C. Now the diagram is nearly finished; we have only to consider what happens when a manager checks the results for his own task which he will do after checking his subordinate's task. In other words we must follow up line A to 'check manager's results' and see what

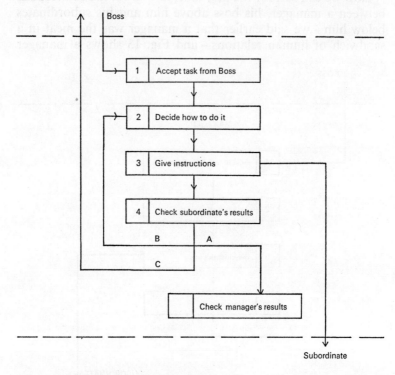

Fig 14: 'C' shows the manager reporting failure to his boss (A and B are shown as before)

happens then. Here again the manager will find one of three situations, just as when he was checking his subordinate's task:

   Either (a) he discovers that his results are satisfactory – in which case he need do nothing more apart from reporting to his boss that this task is now complete. This is shown by line 'a' in Fig. 15.

   or (b) he finds that the results are not satisfactory but there is still time to do something to improve them. In this case he will go back to Step 2 and reconsider new ways of achieving his task – see line 'b' in Fig. 15.

26

or (c) he finds that he has failed – in which case he reports to his boss as shown by line 'c'.

This diagram shows that after the Sales Manager has checked the Sales Force Manager's results he will then expect to see

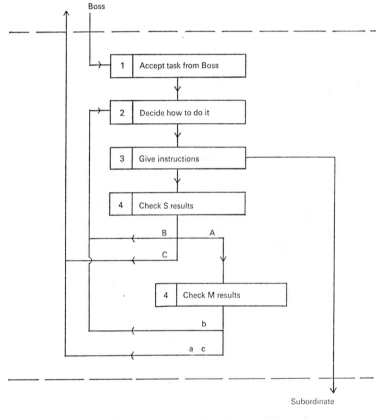

Fig 15: The manager checking his own M results

turnover rising as a consequence of taking on the extra sales-men. One of three things will happen: (a) turnover will rise – in which case he has carried out the task and need do no more except tell his boss; or (b) it will rise only slightly – in which case he will reconsider Step 2 and perhaps do something to reinforce his original decision; or (c) turnover will not rise and he has to report failure to his boss.

There is just one more line to add to complete the diagram. It will be noticed that in Fig. 15 there are two lines running upwards to the next level in the hierarchy but only one line

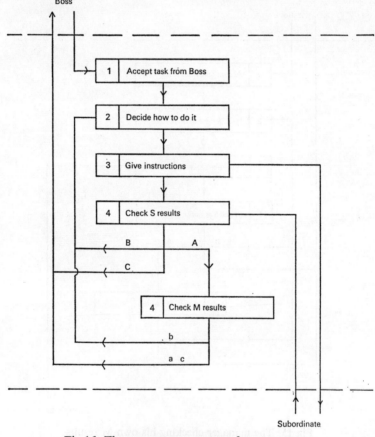

Fig 16: The management process for one manager

running down to the subordinate. There should be two in each case indicating that the relations between a manager and his boss are twofold; firstly when the boss gives his subordinate a task and the subordinate accepts it, secondly when the subordinate reports progress to the boss. The line on Fig. 15

28

which is missing is the line coming up from the subordinate to the manager and which represents the subordinate reporting results to the manager. This line will join the diagram at the point shown in Fig. 16.

Fig. 16 shows the four steps of management process, it shows how they are linked together and it shows how one manager's job fits in with those of his boss and his subordinates.

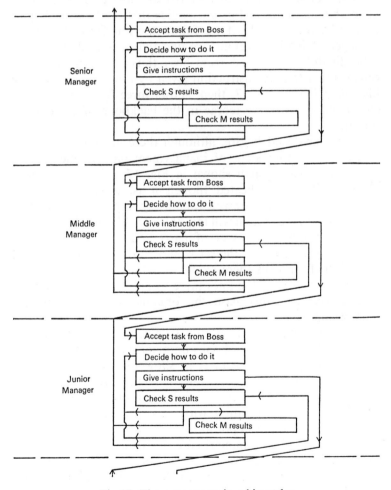

Fig 17: Three managers in a hierarchy

However, it only shows *one* manager and, to complete the picture, we ought to show at least two managers working together in a hierarchy. To demonstrate this all we have to do is to join up the pairs of loose ends; remember that Fig. 16 is valid for any manager at any level of the hierarchy so to show two managers working together in a hierarchy all we need do is to place two identical Fig. 16s one above the other and join the pairs of lines, or three Fig. 16s to show three levels in a hierarchy, as we do in Fig. 17. Notice that the loose ends join up neatly, for example, if we follow the line from the senior manager's 'give instructions' we find that it goes down to the subordinate's 'accept task from boss' thus reminding us of the obvious fact that an instruction given by a boss is received by his subordinate; Fig. 17, then, shows three links in a hierarchical chain – three vertebrae in the backbone of an organisation.

As we have said before, although there are only five basic elements – the four steps of management plus the hierarchy – the management system shown in Fig. 17 is incredibly complicated. But, complicated though it is, it is the simplest diagram that can be drawn. Take away any part, cut any of the links, and the system will fail. It is very like a radio set built with the minimum number of parts and wires – if any part fails, if any wire is cut, the set would go dead. If we removed one of the four steps there would be a failure of management and if we cut any of the lines there would be a failure in communication – in either case the organisation would be unmanageable.

The reason why our diagram is so much more complex than other similar diagrams in books on management is that ours is an attempt (possibly the first) to show the manager's job in relation to the other managers in the hierarchy; most previous descriptions of the manager's job lift him out of the hierarchy and study him in isolation with, it is suggested, disastrous results. Several quite important practical lessons emerge from this diagram and are summarised in the Conclusions at the end of this chapter; before we reach the end, however, there are a number of other points to be made and clarified before we complete MS o.

30

What we mean by 'task'

We are using the word 'task' to cover any aim, goal, objective, job, target or mission that a manager might give to one of his subordinates. There are two types of task, 'continuing' or 'project'. Continuing tasks are those for which there is no end-point in mind; for example, when a man is appointed Works Manager it means that he is to manage the works for several years and neither he nor his boss have any particular date in mind when the job will end. Projects, on the other hand, do have definite end-points, for example, a man may be asked by his boss to take on ten new salesmen; once they are taken on that particular task is ended.

Time

We have barely mentioned the fact that management takes place in time. This will be considered in detail later on but it should be noted now that it is not possible to check results unless a time scale has been given to a task. It is no good for a manager to ask his subordinate to 'take on ten new salesmen'; he *must* also say by when the task is to be completed. If he does not include time in his instructions neither he nor the subordinate know when to start checking results and certainly cannot know whether sufficient progress is being made towards the completion of the task, and therefore he will not know whether to follow line A or B or C in Fig. 16 and the management process will fail.

Managers have many concurrent tasks and several subordinates

Fig. 17 showed the wiring diagram for one task for three managers. In fact managers usually have several tasks on hand at any one time so the true picture would be better represented by several Fig. 17s superimposed on each other. Furthermore the time span will be different for each task, so Fig. 17 is an oversimplification in that sense also. And again, to make matters worse, most managers have more than one subordinate whereas Fig. 17 shows each of the three managers with only one; to put this right we could have drawn several lines coming from 'give instructions' and going to several subordinates. It is possible that one could devise a diagram like Fig. 17 to show

31

all these complications – the multiplicity of tasks, the several subordinates, the differing time spans and so on, but it would be unintelligible. For our purposes in this book Fig. 17 is an adequate diagram, but it is as well to bear in mind that the manager's job is a very complex affair, expecially in a large organisation. Most managers are very fully aware of the fact that they always have several balls in the air at any one time.

Co-ordination

We have repeatedly stated that a manager only does four things. Some writers on management add another – co-ordination. It is suggested here that managers do indeed co-ordinate but that this is not an extra activity but is the name given to a particular part of the wiring diagram of the four step management process. Co-ordination can be defined as 'the balancing and regulating of the actions of subordinates in such a way as to give the best results'. Let us use the previous example of the Sales Manager to illustrate this. Suppose in May the Sales Manager accepts the task of increasing turnover by 10 per cent before September – that is his Step 1. He decides the best way to do it (Step 2) is to take on five more salesmen and increase advertising by 10 per cent. Now he takes Step 3 and instructs his Sales Force Manager and Advertising Manager. Then he checks their results – and to his surprise he finds out on 4 July that the Sales Force Manager has not taken on a single salesman. Clearly one leg of his plan has collapsed so he sends for the Advertising Manager and asks him to increase advertising by 30 per cent to make up for it. This is a (rather simple) example of co-ordination or balancing the actions of his subordinates. But it is not a new activity, the Sales Manager has merely been following the route in heavy type in Fig. 18 (which is identical to Fig. 16), from which it will be seen that having checked the result he returns along line B to reconsider Step 2 and then reissues new instructions.

Co-ordination is not, it is suggested, a fifth step in the management process but a retaking (repeatedly, perhaps) of Steps 2, 3 and 4, with respect to several subordinates.

The people at the top of a hierarchy

If we look at Fig. 17, we will notice that there is no top and no bottom to the diagram. All it shows is three managers each at a different level in the hierarchy and there is a pair of wires left disconnected at the top and another pair at the bottom. Where do these wires go? One answer of course is that they go to yet more managers above and below the three shown, but even in a huge organisation the hierarchy must end somewhere.

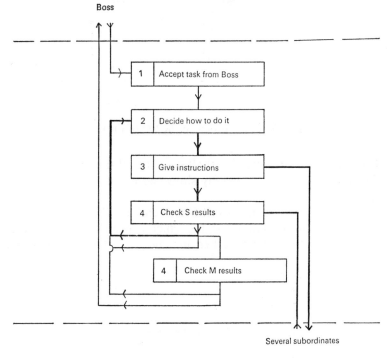

Fig 18: The 'co-ordination' loop is shown as a thick line

We have shown the vertebrae of managers, but where is the head at one end and the tail at the other? Let us recall that a manager is someone who has both a boss and a subordinate; by definition the people at the top of a hierarchy will have no boss so they cannot be managers; the people at the bottom can have no subordinates so they cannot be managers either. Let us consider the people at the top first. Their job is (1) to decide the task for the chief executive (2) to give him instructions and

33

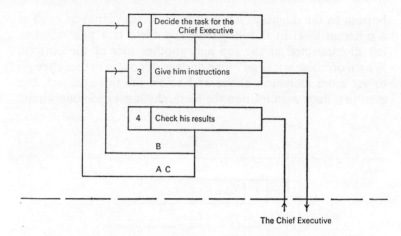

Fig 19: The job of the people at the top of the organisation

(3) to check his results. We shall describe all this in Chapter 6; for the present we will merely show these statements in a diagram (Fig. 19).

This diagram completes the top end of the hierarchy of managers; the diagram for the chief executive is of course identical to that of any other manager – a chief executive is

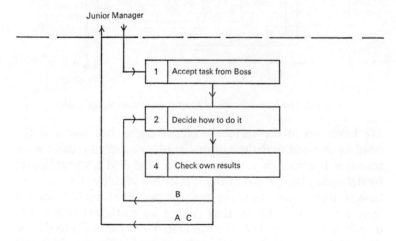

Fig 20: The job of the people at the bottom of the hierarchy (operators)

merely another name for the most senior manager in an organisation.

Operators are not managers
Turning now to the bottom end of the hierarchy we find the people who have no subordinates – we call them 'operators'. Their job is (1) to accept the task from their boss (who is a manager, of course); (2) to decide how to carry it out and (3) to check their own results. Fig. 20 shows their job in a diagram.

It will be seen that, having no subordinates, they only have to check one set of results (their own) but when they complete the task or if they look like failing to complete it, they report to their boss. This completes the bottom end of the hierarchy.

Almost anyone can be a subordinate
One of the questions that a manager must settle before he can give instructions in Step 3 is 'who is the best person to carry out my instructions?'. He will have to ask this question in Step 2 because it is part of the problem of deciding how to carry out the task his boss has given him. For example, when our Sales Manager was wondering how to increase turnover by 10 per cent by September he might have whittled down the alternatives to two: either ask the Advertising Manager to increase advertising or ask the Sales Force Manager to recruit more salesmen. It is perfectly possible that he would know that advertising would be the best of these two but would choose the other alternative because he had much more confidence in the ability of the Sales Force Manager than of the Advertising Manager. So deciding 'who' is sometimes as important as deciding 'what'. It is worth pointing out that a manager need not limit his choice of subordinates (i.e. those to whom he gives instructions) to the people who are permanently employed as his subordinates. It would have been entirely possible, for example, for the Sales Manager to ask a firm of advertising consultants to step up advertising for him; that, of course, is very obvious, but the point being made here is that if he does ask them to act for him then they instantly become his subordinates for the time being. They stand in the relationship of agreed seniority, and he must check their results, they must report progress to him, and he can punish or reward them just

35

as he can his permanent subordinates. A man can be a manager, therefore, even if he has no permanent subordinates at all; any subordinates he does have, however temporary they are, will be subject to the same rules as a permanent subordinate and will therefore take their place for the time being in the management system wiring diagram shown in Fig. 17. It should be noted that a manager can delegate (i.e. give instructions to a subordinate) the whole of his task or parts of it not only to his own permanent subordinates but to a whole range of people – almost anyone when he thinks suitable, in fact. These could include any employee in the same organisation who is not normally one of his subordinates, or someone outside the organisation (such as an outside expert, consultant, or organisation) or even the manager's own boss. Managers do quite often ask their boss to carry out a task for them, i.e. they 'give instruction' to their boss, check his results, and in all respects behave as though the boss were their subordinate for that particular task—they even punish or reward him in the sense that they can show polite and tactful pleasure or displeasure with his results.

So, returning to our example of the Sales Manager, it is perfectly possible that, having decided to recruit ten more salesmen, the Sales Manager will ask an employment agency to find nine of them and ask his boss to find one of them (because he knows that his boss happens to know a suitable candidate personally). Or he might ask his organisation's recruiting officer, or he may decide to do it all himself – but in that case he acts as an operator, not a manager.

The manager can act as an operator

If we were to eavesdrop on a Sales Manager we could see him giving instructions, checking results, deciding what to do, talking to his boss about a new task – in other words we would find him carrying out the four steps of the management process. But we would almost certainly see him doing something else as well – selling. It is true of all managers that from time to time they decide to take action themselves rather than give instructions to any subordinate. Thus, when aiming for an important order from a large customer the Sales Manager

36

might go out and meet the customer himself. A maintenance manager in a factory might himself tackle an important or difficult repair job. Most, if not all, managers decide to take action themselves rather than delegate it to a subordinate; when they do so, however, they are acting as operators (Fig. 20) and not as managers (Fig. 16). Since this book is about management we will not discuss this fifth part of a manager's job but will limit the discussion to the four steps of the management process; this should not, of course, be taken to imply that a manager is wrong to act as an operator – quite the contrary is true as long as he really is, for that particular task, the best person to carry it out.

We are now ready to summarise Chapters 2, 3 and 4; it will be recalled that the discussion in this book falls into three stages. In the first stage we wanted to design the absolutely basic minimum management system or MS o. This system would contain only those parts and interconnections that were essential to the management of an organisation and, naturally, it would be so simple that it would be almost useless as a practical management system. Then, in the second stage of the book we would try to forecast what conditions would be like for managers in the 1970s so that finally, in the third stage, we could modify MS o to turn it into a practical system specially designed for the conditions in which managers will be working over the next decade.

We have completed the design of MS o and must now summarise its main features. One feature that we hope has been rigorously excluded is any management folk-lore left over from previous decades or centuries; the system is intended to be based exclusively on logic and to contain none of the lessons of the past generations of managers; these will be added in the third stage of the book, when, after checking that it is still appropriate to the 1970s, some of the accumulated wisdom of the past will be written into the design of MS 70.

The following conclusions are intended as a summary of the last three chapters and of MS o.

Conclusion 0.1. All organisations, large or small, formal or

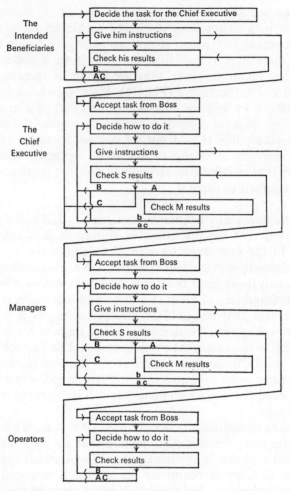

Fig 21: The complete MS o diagram for two levels of manager

informal, permanent or temporary, display the same basic management structure. This essential minimum, which we have called MSo and which is illustrated diagrammatically in Fig. 21 consists of a hierarchy of people one or more of whom are non-managers at the top of the hierarchy and one or more of whom are non-managers at the bottom; the rest are managers.

38

Conclusion 0.2. The people at the top of the hierarchy carry out their duties in three steps:
(1) they decide the task for the chief executive (i.e. the most senior of the managers);
(2) they give him instructions;
(3) they check his results and depending upon these they return to one or other of these steps.

Conclusion 0.3. Everyone in the hierarchy, except the operators, stand in the relationship of agreed seniority to one or more people at a lower level in the hierarchy.

Conclusion 0.4. The principle of agreed seniority states that there is an agreement between two or more people that one of them (the senior) shall be able to give instructions to the others, and may punish or reward them. This relationship can be formal or informal, permanent or temporary.

Conclusion 0.5. A manager is both a senior and a junior – i.e. he has a boss and a subordinate. The people at the top of a hierarchy are not managers for they have no boss. The people at the bottom (called operators) have no subordinates and are therefore not managers.

Conclusion 0.6. A manager carries out his job in four steps:
(1) he accepts a task from his boss;
(2) he decides how to do it;
(3) he gives instructions to subordinates;
(4) he checks results.

Conclusion 0.7. A task is any job, mission, goal, work or target set by a manager to his subordinate. A task can be either continuing (i.e. of indefinite or unknown duration) or a project (which has a definite beginning and end).

Conclusion 0.8. Once a manager has accepted a task from his boss he is not entitled to alter it without referring to his boss.

D   39

Conclusion 0.9. The sum of the tasks given by a manager to his subordinates (together with his own actions as an operator) should equal the task he himself has been set by his boss.

Conclusion 0.10. A manager often acts as an operator; an operator has no subordinates and carries out his job in three steps:
(1) he accepts task from boss;
(2) he decides how to do it;
(3) he checks results.
When acting as an operator a person is not at that time acting as a manager.

Conclusion 0.11. All managers have to check two sets of results; one for each task he himself has been given and one for each task he has given to any subordinate. When he checks any result he will face one of three situations: the task has or will be completed successfully; it has not or is not likely to be fully completed; or it has or will fail. The manager will return to one or other of the four steps depending upon these results.

Conclusion 0.12. Co-ordination is not a fifth management activity; it is a particular cycle of the four steps taken and retaken repeatedly with respect to more than one subordinate.

Chapter 5
Trends in the 1970s

This chapter represents the second stage of the book where we try to predict the conditions under which managers will be working over the next decade. This aim is not quite as ambitious as it sounds because most of the changes discussed here represent little more than a continuation of trends that have been evident for decades or even centuries. However, some of them seem likely to have more impact on managers in the next decade than in many previous periods and it would be wise to draw special attention to them. There are also one or two trends which appear to be mutually conflicting and the effect of these conflicts on managers must be discussed.

The rest of this chapter, then, is concerned with trends – fifteen of them – which seem likely to have an important influence on the way organisations will be managed over the next decade and therefore on the design of MS 70. When we have listed these trends we will go on to review each of the four steps of the management process and the hierarchy in the following five chapters. In each of these we will discuss what modifications are necessary to each part of MS 0 to make it appropriate to the 1970s.

Trend A. The universal nature of these trends
One of the more surprising features of the modern world is the way in which almost every nation is moving in the same general direction. Wherever one looks one sees nation after nation pursuing the same goals and passing through one stage of development after another with almost clockwork predictability. In almost every nation there is a movement away from agriculture to industry, from village life to urban life, from small organisations to larger ones, from ignorance to education

and, hopefully, from physical battle to the rational solution of disputes.

It is as though every individual person in the world had the same vision of a Utopia that lies far off, and to reach it each nation in turn must solve the same sequence of problems and pass through the same stages of development. There cannot be many nations whose government is actively planning to reduce the material standard of living of its citizens, or to cut down on facilities for education, or to reduce the efficiency of their police forces; such government policies are rare because virtually everyone in the world wants a higher standard of living, more education, less crime and so on through a long list of almost universally agreed desiderata.

There are exceptions, of course, but most nations are aligned like iron filings near a magnet. For how long they have been so is difficult to say, probably for centuries, but the chief cause and the catalyst is the improvement in communications. So long as the speed of communication was tied to the speed of a horse it was possible for quite large communities to exist without the stimulus of ideas from outside; they could continue in their own individual direction without knowing that there were any alternatives, let alone something better. In the modern world it is quite impossible for even the most isolated community to be unaware of the ways of the rest of the world, and so great is the speed and volume of communication today that no community can for long move against the mainstream.

If this is true – if communication is the cause and catalyst of conformity – then the trend towards universal conformity must surely increase in the next decade; it will become increasingly difficult for any nation to move against the general world consensus because communications are improving at a faster rate than ever before. It has been predicted that over the next decade the increase in volume of international travel will be 15 per cent per annum and that of telecommunications, 20 per cent per annum. Thus it will come about that any new idea that is considered useful by one nation will quickly be adopted by many others because so many nations face the same problems and will adopt similar solutions. But it is not only the improvements and increased volume of international communication that lies behind this trend; it appears also to be the chief aim of many international organisations, such as the United Nations Organisation and the European Ecomonic Community, to accelerate the decline of international differences in the belief, which one hopes is correct, that co-operation in economic, social, cultural and technological fields is a good substitute for war.

The effect of this trend on managers is quite simple – it means that virtually every manager in every organisation in every nation will find that in the 1970s the conditions in which he works will change in the same direction although not at the same speed, perhaps, and not from the same starting base. It means that every manager will be affected by the fourteen trends listed below. It means that a manager, wherever he works, must think twice before he claims that his organisation or his nation is immune from one or any of these trends and that he therefore need not change his ways. All of us say, 'it cannot happen here'; if it has happened anywhere, sooner or later, in one form or other, it could happen to us, so universal and relentless are these trends.

This trend, plus the fourteen listed below, will affect every manager in the world sooner or later to a greater or lesser degree.

Trend B. Communications
It is just possible that radically new methods of communication based upon new technologies will appear before the end of this decade but it is more likely that the telephone, radio and television will continue to be by far the most common forms. It is unlikely that the speed of telecommunication will increase, for it is already as fast as light. Nor is it likely that postal services will improve much over the decade. If neither the method nor the speed of communication is going to change, what trends will there be? Probably three: a vast increase in volume (possibly 20 per cent per annum in many nations); a swing to the use of personal communicators such as pocket-size walkie-talkies; a move, slow in the early part of the decade but gathering pace later, towards the visual presentation of information on TV screens, video phones, etc.

The language barrier will remain (practical translation by computer is still more than a decade away). International and inter-city travel will become slightly quicker and the volume of traffic will increase rapidly (15 per cent per annum or so) but intra-city travel will not become much quicker during the decade.

These trends will affect managers in two ways; the increase in international and inter-city implies a considerable invasion of foreign ideas, products, services and people among all nations. This implies that any manager who is now judging the performance of his organisation by local or national criteria will progressively be using the wrong standard. This is true not only of companies but of local and national charities, clubs, and governments – in other words, organisations of all types. The second effect of these trends is that managers will be able to communicate more readily with their boss and subordinates at a distance by means of walkie-talkie, car radiophones, etc. This will affect the way in which managers take Steps 2, 3 and 4 of the management process and will even begin to affect the shape of the hierarchy itself by the end of the decade. These effects will be discussed, therefore, in Chapters 7, 8, 9 and 10 respectively when we will consider the impact of these trends on the design of these parts of MS 70.

Trend C. The computer
A very large increase in the number of computers and the volume of computing is predicted, some estimates mention a fivefold rise in the decade (about 17 per cent per annum). Computers themselves will become faster and cheaper; discs, tapes, printers, etc. will become faster, cheaper and more reliable; there will be a very rapid rise in time-sharing and in the use of desk terminals which later in the decade will frequently include a visual display unit. Of more importance than these technical developments is the move toward using the computer as an aid to decision-making, as well as merely replacing accounts clerks which today is the main use to which computers are put.

The main effect of this trend will be on Steps 2 and 4, although the shape of the pyramid will also be affected later in the decade. If the estimate of a fivefold increase in computing is borne out it must mean that few managers will be able to get through the next decade without having to use a computer. This does not mean that every manager will have to learn how a computer works or how to write a programme; it does mean they will have to learn how to communicate with a computer via the keyboard of a typewriter or desk terminal. The effects of this trend on Steps 2 and 4 and on the hierarchy will be described in Chapters 7, 9 and 10.

Trend D. *Information*

Journalists have referred to the information explosion of the 1960s; information will continue to explode in the 1970s with perhaps even greater force. The volume of data on patents, social surveys, world markets, economic forecasts, research projects – indeed on every subject under the sun – will rise to new unmanageable heights. One day perhaps there will be enough computer capacity plus a fool-proof indexing system to store all this information in such a way that a manager can find out what he needs to know at the touch of a button – but this is decades away. In the meantime he will have to rely on the innumerable organisations that are growing up to search out information for him – the digests, business intelligence services, central offices of information and statistics, etc.

The effect of the information explosion will be felt mainly at Steps 2 and 4 and is therefore considered in Chapters 7 and 9.

Trend E. *Education and training*

This could turn out to be the most important trend of all, partly because many organisations have not yet changed to take account of its effects over the past two decades. When they do change, therefore, they may have to catch up on a backlog. In virtually every nation of the world facilities are provided for mass education through primary and secondary schools, and in most nations attendance is compulsory for all. Progressively more people are then going on to universities and technical colleges and more and more adults are taking advantage of facilities for adult education and training – in some nations the population seems positively greedy for new knowledge and skills. The existence of a huge mass of educated people in a society must have profound social consequences – some of which we presumably have yet to experience – and among them will be a decline in 'working-class' attitudes and behaviour, a reluctance to perform dirty, menial or repetitive tasks, a reluctance to be ordered about, an impatience with incompetence or procrastination, a desire to participate in the running of organisations, a more independent attitude of mind and a swing away from religious belief and patriotism towards a pragmatic humanism.

If all this comes to pass, and much of it is already evident in many Western societies, then the manager who ignores this trend does so at his peril, for he will fail to notice that his subordinates are not the same people as they were two decades ago. The effect of this trend is so all-pervasive that it will cause us to modify every important part of MS 70 except perhaps Step 4.

Trend F. The rate of change
During the 1970s, the rate of change is likely to continue to increase just as in the 1960s. More new things will appear than ever before and more of the things that we thought were a permanent feature of our lives will disappear. In other words more new products will be introduced in the next decade than in the last decade and goods and services will have a somewhat shorter life before being superseded; more new organisations will appear and disappear, more new technologies, more new social and moral attitudes and cults, more new fashions, more new sports, more new art forms, and so on indefinitely.

It is possible to overemphasise the rate at which changes take place in the modern world; it has been said that the rate of introduction of new technologies is no greater today than it was five decades ago. To illustrate this, people mention that Edison invented the electric lamp and had it in commercial operation in far less time than it took to develop the hovercraft or the laser. No doubt arguments could be put forward to prove it either way, but intuitively one cannot avoid the impression that changes do occur more rapidly today than ever before and that the rate of change will itself increase over the

46

next decade. There is one counter-argument to this broad prediction, namely the phenomenon that is now called 'backlash'. This states that if changes in society or in technology are pushed ahead too fast, there will be a sequence of disasters or near-disasters which will make people demand that the changes responsible should be slowed or even reversed. This implies that if, for example, a society allows a too rapid relaxation in moral attitudes (for example towards gambling or violence on the screen) a sequence of events will occur that so shocks public opinion that the trend is reversed. The same may occur in the field of technology, where a too rapid trend towards, say, supertankers or huge passenger-carrying aircraft results in a series of disasters that slows down or reverses the trend.

Again, it can only be an intuitive conclusion, but one feels that the overall rate of change in society and technology will be faster in the 1970s than in the 1960s, even if some backlash does occur in particular areas. Few managers today are unaware of this accelerating rate of change and yet organisations go on behaving as if their world was changeless. One can point to individual companies which still boast their product has stood the test of fifty years unchanged in design. One can see whole industries that have failed to move into the modern world. One can point to charities, social organisations, government departments and international organisations still providing the same goods and services that called them into existence in a previous century. While most managers know that they should move with the times, few know how to go about it or how to change their method and style of managenent to suit the needs of today.

This trend – the rate of change – will be discussed in Chapters 7, 9 and 10 since its effects will mainly be felt on Steps 2 and 4 and on the hierarchy.

Trend G. Variety
Henry Ford is quoted as saying that his customers could have their car in any colour so long as it was black. Things have changed since then; his current customers have their cars in a kaleidoscope of colour, engine size, seats, doors, headlamps, tail-lamps and everything else. This is true of all goods and

47

services – the British housewife, for example, can choose from three times as many soap powders, detergents and bleaches as she could twenty years ago. Everywhere, in every field, there is a greater range of choice than ever before, whether it is of bicycles or armaments, or outrageous ways of getting married. This trend towards increased variety will continue to accelerate through the 1970s.

The effect on managers will be mainly on Step 2, 'decide how to carry out the task' because this trend implies that there will be more alternative ways of carrying out any task and managers will be faced with making their decision from a wider range of possible actions. This point, which has not previously received much attention in management books, will be considered in detail in Chapter 7, where Step 2 of MS 70 is discussed.

Trend H. The size of organisations
There will be two trends; organisations that are already large will slowly become larger by natural growth and by amalgamation and, secondly, there will be a great increase in the number of small organisations. To put these trends another way: the total number of organisations will increase but the *number* of large organisations will not increase at anywhere near the rate of increase in the *number* of small organisations. There may even be fewer large organisations but they will be larger, due, of course, to the effect of amalgamations. It seems likely that there will be several companies each employing over a million people by the end of the decade (General Motors, the largest company in 1970, employed about 750,000). But this trend applies not only to companies but to all forms of organisation; there will be amalgamations between charities, economic federations of nations, international merging between organisations for relief of famine, natural disaster and accidents at sea or in the air, mergers of bodies devoted to research and so on.

The effect of these trends on managers will be to accentuate all the problems of management. In fact the problems of management in small organisations (up to, say, two or three hundred employees) are seldom very severe and are not likely to become much more severe in the next decade. In organisations much above this size, however, the problems are already considerable and they grow as the organisation grows – if organisations are to become even larger, and we are suggesting that they will, it follows that the management of organisations will become more difficult throughout the decade. All four steps of the management process will have to be slightly modified to meet the problems of size but the main discussion on the effect of size will be in Chapter 10 on organisation structures.

Trend J. Society's attitude to organisations
As the size and power of organisations grow society becomes increasingly apprehensive, both the state and individual people share this concern. The response of the state is normally to introduce legislation to curb the power of large organisations (such as the Anti-Trust legislation in America; the next decade may well see international agreement between governments to control the large international companies that will appear in increasing numbers). In addition to legislation, the state will certainly not discourage the press and television from exposing organisations whose behaviour is in any way anti-social. We can expect therefore to see considerable pressure exerted on organisations (especially companies and trade unions) to coerce them into paying more heed to their obligations towards society.

The main effects of these trends will be felt at Step 1 and 2. In Chapters 6 and 7, therefore, we will discuss how managers may have to respond to the increased pressure from society on organisations to be of good behaviour.

Trend K. Quantification
There has been a move towards 'scientific management' for several decades now and it will continue unabated in the 1970s. The key to 'scientific management' is quantification, or 'giving answers with numbers in them'. Just as a physicist can measure electricity in terms of amps or watts and measure light in lumens, so it is possible to measure many of the facts that are important to managers. Work can be measured, so can risk, so can information, progressively more management para-meters are being quantified. Quite recently, for example, a

new technique called cost benefit analysis began to be used to place a monetary value on such things as comfort, noise, leisure – i.e. to measure 'value judgements' in terms of money.

The effect of this trend on managers is that it will bring a further crop of management techniques*, an increased use of computers and the need to understand some of the jargon used by mathematicians. All four steps of the management process will be affected but there will be little impact on the hierarchy.

Trend L. Specialists
As a result of several trends noted in this chapter the current trend towards specialisation will continue. The number and variety of specialists available to advise managers is already bewildering, but the trend will continue unabated.

The effect on managers will be that somehow they must learn when to ask for specialist advice, where to get it, how to evaluate it and how to use it particularly at Steps 2 and 4. The increasing number of specialists may cause considerable modifications to the hierarchy.

Trend M. Conflict with central authority
As a result of several of the trends noted above (particularly the increasing size of organisations, the improvement in communications and the spread of computers) there will be a tendency towards further centralisation of power and decision-making. This trend is in direct conflict with the desire of many managers to use their own initiative (partly as a result of improved education), and in the larger organisations this conflict may become acute during the 1970s leading to strikes, more powerful trade unions, higher staff turnover and low productivity, not only on the shop floor where it is already evident, but spreading upwards to the middle and higher ranks of management.

* Unfortunately there is not space in this book to describe very many of the innumerable management techniques that will have to be used by managers in the 1970s. We do, however, show where in the management process many of them should be used and some of them are firmly embedded in the fabric of MS 70 (management by objectives, corporate planning, the principles of cybernetics and so on). Some books on techniques are recommended in the Bibliography.

This will be one of the key problems facing managers of all organisations in the 1970s and, since it will impinge chiefly on Steps 1 and 3 and on the hierarchy, it will be discussed in some detail in Chapters 6, 8 and 10.

Trend N. Wealth and leisure
The standard of living in Britain has been rising more slowly than in almost any other industrial nation, but even so it is reasonable to expect that a manager earning £3,000 per annum in 1970 will be earning £4,000 by 1980 even if he remains in the same job – in other words he can expect his standard of living to rise by 3 per cent per annum in real terms. As a general rule the further the standard of living rises above the subsistence level, the less is a man's desire for more money – he begins to prefer other non-material rewards such as leisure and a more satisfying job. We can expect that during the 1970s all wages and salaries will continue to rise at, or above, 3 per cent per annum in real terms but at the same time employees will work fewer hours. It is possible that the working day or week will be shorter or, alternatively, the annual holiday entitlement will be increased.

There will be two effects on managers: firstly, financial incentives to encourage higher ouput will become less effective, and, secondly, it will become increasingly necessary to treat employees as human. This trend will mainly affect Step 3.

Trend P. Mechanisation and automation
This well-established trend will continue through the decade, probably at a rate much higher than in the 1960s. Several of the trends mentioned above (C, E and N in particular) point strongly in this direction and one can expect that the greatest strides in mechanisation will be in those jobs (both in the factory and in the office) which are either dirty, menial or repetitive.

This trend will mainly affect Step 2 and the hierarchy and will therefore be considered in Chapters 7 and 10; the effect on managers will be that they must somehow find ways to improve productivity (in the factory and the office) by something like 7 per cent per annum. This means that if it takes a hundred men to perform some task in 1970 ways must be found by which the same job can be done by only fifty men by 1980. In Britain the rate of improvement in productivity in recent years has been around 3 per cent per annum but this will be wholly unacceptable during the 1970s.

Trend Q. Taking decisions
Almost every one of the trends listed above will have some impact on the way managers take decisions (this, in our system, is contained in Step 2 'decide how to do it'). The complexity and size of decisions will increase, the number of people who should be consulted will increase, the penalty for making the wrong decision will increase. It will take longer to make a decision so the manager will have to forecast further ahead, the further ahead he forecasts the more inaccurate the forecast will be, the more inaccurate the forecast the greater the chance that the decision will be wrong. It is a daunting prospect, one that must be discused at great length in Chapter 7, the one in which Step 2 is to be modified to bring it up to the requirements of managers in the 1970s.

This chapter completes the second stage of the book in which we have predicted the conditions in which managers will be working in the 1970s. It is clear already that to stand up to some of these conditions we shall have to make some fairly substantial changes to MS o and in the next five chapters we will examine each of its five parts with this in mind – but we must not alter the basic design of MS o or cut any of the interconnections, if we do, it will not work at all.

Chapter 6
Step 1 in the 1970s

In this chapter we will be discussing what modifications we should make to Step 1 of MS o to bring it up to the requirements of managers in the 1970s. Step 1, it will be recalled, was described as 'accept a task from the boss' and we must now consider in what ways the fifteen trends listed in Chapter 5 will cause us to modify this. In fact only four of these trends will have any really important effect on Step 1 – Trends E, J, K and M – we will examine the influence of each of these in detail as we progress through this chapter.

One of the important features of MS o was the cascade of tasks: each manager receives a task from his boss and then, having decided how to carry it out sets tasks to his subordinates who set tasks to theirs and so on down the hierarchy. We therefore have a hierarchy of tasks as well as a hierarchy of managers. This is often known as a 'hierarchy of objectives' but the word 'objective' has been used by so many authors with so many different meanings that one really despairs of knowing quite what it means. The important point is that this chain of interlocking tasks reaches right up and down the hierarchy of managers so that, for example, the plant operator in a factory can be said to be doing his job to help his boss to do his job to help his boss to do his . . . and so on, right to the top. The more closely an organisation is controlled the more true it will be that each subordinate is doing exactly those things that are required to help his manager complete his task. In real life there is always some slack in the system and subordinates do not always do exactly what their manager's task requires of them – although in an organisation faced with an emergency or one that only operates in an emergency (such as a fire service) the discipline up and down the hierarchy is so tight that the amount of slack is small.

If it is true that each man in an organisation is working to help his boss to carry out his task, then it follows that everyone in the organisation is working to help the manager at the top of the hierarchy to carry out his task. So all eyes must turn to the chief executive – if he has wrongly identified his task then there will be a lot of people at every level in the hierarchy who are taking the wrong decisions and carrying out tasks that are irrelevant. We must therefore make quite certain that we understand the nature of the chief executive's task, what exactly it is and who decides it. Does he decide it himself or is there someone above him who hands it down to him? The answer is that there is certainly someone above him, 'the people at the top of the organisation' as we described them in Chapter 4 and whose three-step job we illustrated in Fig. 19. So the chief executive is just like any other manager in the hierarchy in the sense that he does not decide his own task, he cannot alter it himself any more than any other manager and he has a boss just like any other manager. Who, then, are these people at the top of the hierarchy? They are the people for whom the organisation exists; we will call them 'the intended beneficiaries' and the task that they hand to the chief executive is *identical* to the purpose of the organisation itself. Before we can discuss the chief executive's task, therefore, we must first discuss the purpose of an organisation.

THE PURPOSE OF AN ORGANISATION

All organisations exist to benefit someone. If one traces back into the history of any organisation one would find that it was started by one or more people who believed that the formation of this organisation would best serve their purpose. Their purpose may have been largely self-centred, as it is when capitalists form a company, or golfers form a golf-club; in these cases the founders believe that they would make more money or have access to better golfing facilities than if they did not form it. Or a founder's purpose can be entirely altruistic, as when someone founds a charity to help orphan children or when a government establishes a health service. Whether the original aim is selfish or unselfish, the fact remains that all

54

those who found an organisation do so in the belief that more benefit will accrue to themselves or to others than if the organisation was not founded. All organisations exist to benefit someone, and if for any reason an organisation does not yield enough benefit to the beneficiaries it will wither and die; if it does yield enough to satisfy them, then it may grow. The purpose of any organisation can therefore only be adequately stated if both the benefit and the beneficiaries are accurately identified – only then can the beneficiaries, the management or anyone else say whether the organisation is fulfilling its purpose. The purpose of the organisation known as Shelter is to find homes (benefit) for the homeless (beneficiaries), and if it failed to find homes for the homeless or found homes for people who already had one, it would fail in its purpose; if it repeatedly failed over a period of time then Shelter would wither and die. So would the Red Cross if it repeatedly failed to bring relief (benefit) to the suffering (beneficiaries). So would a trade union if it failed to get better wages and conditions for its members. In such cases it is quite easy to see what the benefit is and who are the benficiaries, in others it is not so easy. One has only to ask, for example, what the purpose of a nation's government is in order to raise the babbling ghosts of political philosophers down the centuries. A similar controversy rages today over the purpose of a company; is it to provide goods and services to society or to make a profit for the shareholders? The same question is even more hotly debated when one asks it of companies that have been nationalised – what is the nature of the benefit they are supposed to generate and to whom is it due? It is debates of this sort that lead us to Trend J.

THE IMPACT OF TREND J

Trend J was described in Chapter 5 as the changing attitude of society towards organisations. Let us first deal with one aspect of this trend that will continue unchanged over the next decade – indefinitely in fact. This is the attitude of the state towards any organisation which, because it is successful, has grown to rival the power of the state itself. History is full of such power-struggles; the state against the Church, the state against big

E

55

business, the state versus the trade unions. The state has always acted to curb the power of the highly successful organisation and it always will. (The 1970s may witness a new battle between the state and some of the very large international companies whose size in terms of turnover already exceed the gross national product of some of the smaller nations.) This trend, then, will continue unchanged.

In recent years a new element has appeared alongside and supplementary to the attitude of the state. This is the attitude of society towards organisations. Increasingly, a better-educated population served by increasingly effective methods of mass communication are showing greater interest in the purposes and the behaviour of organisations. These topics were hitherto the subject of discussion by intelligentsia and philosophers, but today the interest is far wider and public opinion, once formed, can bring powerful pressures to bear upon any management of any organisation. While the state has always shown its displeasure by legislation, society now also shows its displeasure by agitation. The state has always acted to curb the power of large organisations, whatever their purpose, but society is less concerned with size, more with purpose and behaviour. It has become almost impossible for any organisation, large or small, to act for very long in a way that society deems anti-social or to pursue objectives which society deems undesirable. It may be strange and anomalous but it looks as though society is becoming less tolerant of irresponsible behaviour from organisations at a time when it is becoming more tolerant of irresponsible behaviour from individuals. Be that as it may, the point is that while an organisation must continue to yield a satisfactory benefit to the beneficiaries it must, in addition, forswear any means of doing so that might be considered anti-social: it must not erect ugly buildings, it must not make too much noise, it must pay higher social charges, it must give its employees longer holidays, and so on. Society imposes more of these conditions upon any organisation whose purpose is deemed to be selfish but even those organisations whose purpose is deemed to be socially desirable (e.g. a charity) will have to bear an increasing burden of social conditions and obligations.

Perhaps a diagram will clarify the effect of Trend J. Imagine a private company founded by Mr Hardcastle in 1870. He, being the owner (i.e. the intended beneficiary) and the chief executive as well, would have made certain that a large proportion of the income of the company would find its way into his pocket. He would have had to pay his suppliers enough to ensure they kept supplying (but no more), his workers enough to keep working (but no more), he would have had to lend

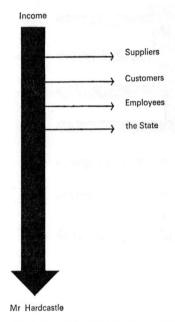

Fig 22: Hardcastle & Co Ltd—Distribution of benefit in 1870

enough quality to the product to ensure his customers kept buying, and he certainly would not have worried about polluting the environment. This is shown in Fig. 22.

The position today is shown in Fig. 23 from which it will be seen that the present owners (one of which is Hardcastle's great-granddaughter) get what is left after meeting the demands of everyone else.

As a matter of fact the intended beneficiaries of any organisation have always 'got what is left after meeting the demands of everybody else' (i.e. the intended beneficiaries have always been the 'residual legatees') – the effect of Trend J on companies is simply that 'everyone else' is now getting relatively more due to the activities of trade unions, credit collection agencies, consumer protection agencies, tax officials, factory inspectors, alkali inspectors, etc. Whether we shed a tear for Miss Hardcastle or not, we should make it plain that, although

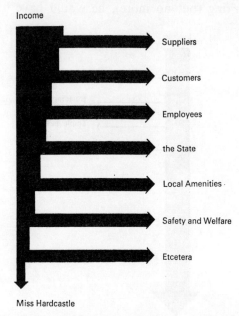

Fig 23: Hardcastle & Co Ltd—distribution of benefit in 1970

the private company has been hit more severely by Trend J than most organisations, it remains true that a similar diagram could be drawn for almost every organisation. The intended beneficiaries of a nationalised airport are the passengers, many of whom today would swear that airports are run more for the convenience of airport staff than for themselves. Similarly many students believe that their university is run more for the convenience of the teaching staff than for them.

THE BENEFICIARIES' RESPONSE TO TRENDS J AND E

Late in the 1960s there were some very violent responses to

58

Trends J and E. The students, as the intended beneficiaries of the education system, protested that the system was not yielding the benefit they expected and demanded a place on the Governing Boards to see that they got it. Workers bypassed their union officials and appointed militant unofficial leaders. Electorates protested at the decisions of their governments, especially in USA. These violent outbursts served as a sharp message from the intended beneficiaries to the management of these organisations that the nature or the volume of the benefit was not to their liking. The reason was partly because of Trend J (less benefit was filtering down to the beneficiaries) and partly the effect of Trend E – the rising standards of education which lead to impatience with inefficient management. Since both these trends will continue in the 1970s we can expect more of these violent outbursts. The disadvantage of protest is that it merely draws attention to a management failure *after* it has occurred, and beneficiaries can be expected to take two preventive measures in the 1970s that are rather more constructive in nature. They will (1) learn to state much more accurately what benefit they expect to receive from their organisation, i.e. they will more carefully brief the chief executive on his task; this will be discussed later in this chapter. They will (2) place themselves more firmly and authoritatively at the top of the organisation. To illustrate this let us return to Hardcastle & Co. and look at the organisation chart (see Fig. 24) as it might have been drawn in 1870. The box at the top of the hierarchy is Mr Hardcastle – his word is law, he is the ultimate arbiter of all things. Now look at the organisation chart for the same company in 1970 in Fig. 25 where it will be seen that Mr Smith is now the arbiter of all things – Hardcastle has long since departed this world and now a professional manager has taken over, all the other directors are also professional managers.

Now it will at once be observed that although these two organisation charts are identical, Mr Smith is not in fact in the same position as Mr Hardcastle was. Mr Hardcastle had two jobs: he was chief executive but as such was not the final arbiter of all things – he took his orders from the 'intended beneficiary' at the top of the organisation; he was, however,

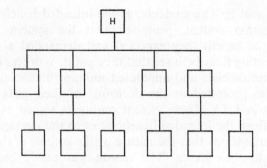

Fig 24: Hardcastle & Co Ltd—1870 organisation chart

also the intended beneficiary and as such *was* the final arbiter. Fig. 24 was incorrect, therefore, and should have shown Mr Hardcastle in both roles. But in exactly the same way Fig. 25 is wrong too – it should also have shown the 1970 intended beneficiaries or their representatives to emphasise to Mr Smith that he may have been the chief executive but he was still only a manager and took his orders from a boss just like any other manager. Organisation charts for companies never show the beneficiaries, and so the fiction grows that the chief executive of companies have no bosses. Organisation charts for many other types of organisation do show the beneficiaries and their representatives as in Fig. 26 for a school.

It will be noticed that this chart consists not of one pyramid but two. All organisation charts should be of this hourglass shape, and all beneficiaries must take as much care with the

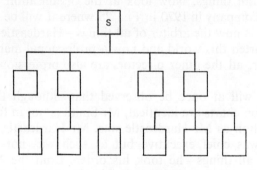

Fig 25: Hardcastle & Co Ltd—1970 organisation chart

pyramid that shows their structure as managers take with the one that shows theirs. These are the reasons why beneficiaries should place themselves firmly, formally and authoritatively at the head of their organisation:

1. The 1970s will see a further strengthening of Trend J – that is to say, everyone connected with an organisation will put pressure upon it to ensure that it meets its social obligations as they see them. Such pressures come from em-

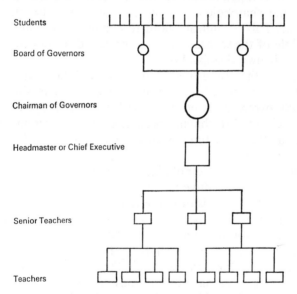

Students

Board of Governors

Chairman of Governors

Headmaster or Chief Executive

Senior Teachers

Teachers

Fig 26: Hourglass structure or double pyramid

ployees, the local community, the press and television, Government officials, protest groups, etc., and their demands are directed to the managers and especially to the chief executive. The contact between these groups and this man is often on a daily basis and he may be overwhelmed by them. If the beneficiaries do not forge equally strong links with him they must not be surprised to find themselves forgotten. There is nothing subversive or sinister about Trend J, it has existed for centuries, but the improvements in education (Trend E) and in communication (Trend B) have recently strengthened it. Its effects can be seen most vividly in the case of shareholders in companies who, by default, have lost almost all control over their companies. It could also be seen in the universities where the students' representatives failed to act on their behalf, and this has recently led to direct student participation on the governing bodies.

2. The beneficiaries of some organisations invite senior managers to act as their representatives. This is particularly common in companies where the directors are asked to represent the shareholder and at the same time to run a department. This is contrary both to common sense and to the principle of the separation of power; few directors would demand their own dismissal or the winding up of their own department in the interests of shareholders. A beneficiaries' representative cannot also be an executive – no man should be in both pyramids at once. A similar situation occurs in politics where an MP, having been elected to represent the people, is at the same time given a management job in the government machine.

3. If the beneficiaries do not place themselves authoritatively above the chief executive he may pervert the organisation to his own ends. There is evidence that some companies, for example, are run more as a vehicle for the chief executive's ambitions than for the shareholders. (It should perhaps be noted that the organisation chart in Fig. 25 showing the chief executive as the final arbiter is the organisation chart for a dictatorship, he has absolute power. The organisation chart shown in Fig. 26, on the other hand – the double pyramid or hourglass – is the organisation chart for a democracy.)

4. One of the dangers incurred by not having strong links between the beneficiaries and the chief executive, quite apart from corruption, is that managers tend to become engrossed in current problems which can assume greater importance for them than the purpose of the organisation. They become ruled by means, not ends. Thus managers in companies come to give more importance to sales turnover than to profits. Thus, governments become more concerned with schools than with education. Thus, perhaps, the British

government in the late 1960s became more concerned with the balance of payments than with economic growth.

This book is concerned with the management of organisations in the 1970s and we have now reached two important conclusions that must be woven into MS 70, the first is that the process of management begins when the chief executive accepts his task – i.e. at his Step 1. The second conclusion is that someone has got to hand this task to him and see that he does it. Those people are not managers, they are the intended beneficiaries, but their links with the chief executive are intimate – as Fig. 21 showed – and must be strongly forged.

STEP 1 FOR THE CHIEF EXECUTIVE

We suggested above (page 59) that beneficiaries would respond in two ways to Trend J. The first, examined above, was that their links with the chief executive must be strengthened and more carefully drawn. The second was that they would take more care over their instructions to the chief executive. We also said (page 54) that the task of the chief executive was identical to the purpose of the organisation itself. This last sentence means simply that when an organisation is founded the founders presumably know with considerable accuracy exactly why they are founding it. They will know what benefit it is supposed to generate and for whom; knowing this, they then appoint a chief executive and tell him to take whatever actions he thinks are best in order to carry out this purpose. So if they found a company they will say to the chief executive, 'We want you to run this organisation so that it makes a profit for us.' If they found an orphanage, they say to him, 'We want you to run this organisation to give parentless children a happy home life and education.' The point is that the chief executive's task is to ensure that the purpose of the organisation as a whole – as opposed to parts, departments or sections of it – is achieved. If he fails, the organisation fails. It is possible for an organisation that fails to have been employing a brilliantly successful departmental head; it is not possible for an organisation to fail and have a brilliantly successful chief executive – this is a logical contradiction.

It will be clear that the chief executive cannot do his job unless he knows with some precision what the organisation exists to do; he must know both who the beneficiaries are and the nature of the benefit they expect. The more accurately and unequivocally these two facts are known the more precisely and appropriately can he decide how best to carry out his task. It has always been necessary for the purpose of an organisation to be clearly stated, but never more so than today, partly because management is becoming a more precise activity, partly because of Trend J, partly because beneficiaries are better educated and know the difference between a hit and a near miss, and partly because of Trend K.

Trend K was described in Chapter 5 as the movement towards quantification in management. The relevance of this to the chief executive's task is that it will no longer be sufficient to tell him who the beneficiaries are and the nature of the benefit; he must also be given numerical targets to aim at. Now it has always been insufficient to say to a chief executive, 'Go and run this organisation' or, 'We want you to administer this organisation efficiently;' these instructions are wholly valueless since they identify neither the benefit nor the beneficiaries. In the 1970s it will also be inadequate merely to identify the benefit and the beneficiaries – one must go one step further and put a figure on the *volume* of benefit. So it will be necessary for shareholders, for example, not only to tell the chief executive to go and make a profit for them; they must also tell him *how much* profit they consider to be satisfactory. It will be necessary not only to tell a police chief to reduce crime but also to say *what* reduction in crime the citizens consider to be satisfactory. Let us illustrate this with some examples:

(a) The shareholders of a company should say something like this to their chief executive: 'We want a steady growth in profits over the years. We consider that 3 per cent per annum growth in real terms is wholly unacceptable – we will dismiss you if you can't do better than that. We will be satisfied with a growth rate of 6 per cent and 10 per cent per annum would delight us.'

(b) The citizens might say to the Police Chief: 'Crimes of

violence have been rising at about 8 per cent per annum over the past 10 years – we want you to take whatever action you can to bring this down to, say, 2 or 3 per cent rise each year – if you can't do that we will sack you. Of course, if you effect a steady *reduction* in crime each year we will reward you handsomely.'

(c) The electorate will increasingly reject politicians who say 'We will go forward shoulder to shoulder towards a new prosperity.' They will increasingly turn to those who say 'We must make our standard of living rise faster than 3 per cent per annum which is quite unacceptable in the 1970s. But don't expect us to exceed 7 per cent per annum – that is too good to be true.'

(d) Can we also imagine the Mayor of New York appointing a Director of Culture and briefing him as follows: 'This city is a Philistine jungle. We want you to raise the level of culture by 10 per cent per annum'?

We have four points to make about setting targets. The first point concerns the last example where the Mayor put a numerical target on to a task that simply cannot be quantified in this way – perhaps cannot be quantified in any way – and the result was ridiculous. This example warns us that there is a major danger in the trend towards setting numerical targets – a trend, we repeat, that will be very vigorous in the 1970s – and the danger lies in the fact that some of the really important aspects of human activity cannot be quantified; there is a natural tendency for managers to concentrate on those tasks that have been quantified at the expense of those that have not – and these could be of much greater importance. For example, it is quite possible that some nations have recently placed too much emphasis on the rising standard of living (which can be easily quantified), and not enough emphasis on what is called the quality of life (which cannot be easily measured). In a similar way some companies aim at a very high rate of growth (which can be measured) and may fail to take account of the distress (which cannot be measured) caused to employees who cannot stand up to the pressure. However, this problem of quantifying the unquantifiable has received a tremendous amount of

65

attention in recent years and, although it is highly probable that some of the most important aspects of life will always remain the province of subjective judgement, it is beginning to look as though these will be very few indeed. This takes us to the next point about setting targets.

This second point also concerns the Mayor of New York. It may not be possible to quantify 'culture' but there probably are several verifiable and quantifiable criteria by which 'culture' can be judged – or any other abstract value such as happiness, justice, tolerance, freedom. These criteria are often called Indicators today. People who think that New York is a less cultured city than London must presumably have some real-life phenomena in mind which lead them to their conclusion; the number of art galleries per million citizens, the city's expenditure on the arts, the number of statues in public parks, the architecture of the buildings, the percentage of leisure time the citizens spend on cultural activities and so on. Now it may be possible to prepare a list of indicators such as these by which the Mayor can judge whether the Director of Culture is making satisfactory progress in his task, and if this is so, the Mayor can set target figures for each of these. The point about quantification of targets is really this: when someone is given a job to do his boss presumably wants him to bring about a particular change in the real world – this being so, the boss can actually go and inspect the results in the real world and, probably, can also measure the changes in figures. So when the Mayor said, 'Go and raise the level of culture by 10 per cent' he may not have expressed himself very well but it is possible that, with due care and thought, something very precise and definitive could be made of it. Techniques such as cost benefit, preference curves and attitude surveys are proliferating in this field and we shall be giving more examples of this very important trend towards quantification of values and subjective judgement later on.

The third point to make about setting targets is that there are, as we saw earlier, two types of task, continuing and project. A continuing task is one like 'go and run our factory in Dover' which is an open-ended invitation to the factory manager to do this indefinitely – there is no known or stated point in time where this job might end. But 'go and build a factory in Dover' is a project since this task does have a known stated end. When setting targets to people it is important to know which type of task is involved. Normally one should set targets in terms of the annual rate of change to be achieved for continuing tasks. For example, 'your job is to reduce road accidents in this town by at least 5 per cent per annum' or 'your job is to improve labour productivity in this factory by 10 per cent per annum'. Of course the target figure may be changed from time to time but the point is that there will not, in the foreseeable future, ever come a time when the boss says to the managers 'O.K., that's enough – now I want you to stop trying to reduce accidents'. Project tasks are different in principle: 'build that ship by July 1975' or 'complete your report before lunch' do have definite end points. The key target with project tasks is the completion date, of course, and it is essential that this is always included in the instruction. So, with continuing tasks the crucial factor is rate of achievement, while with project tasks it is the completion date, and we will draw attention to this aspect of target-setting by referring to it as 'Rates and Dates'. Failure to recognise this distinction frequently results in chief executives, whose jobs are almost always continuing, being set targets that are only suitable for project-type tasks. Companies, for example, set profit targets for only one or two years ahead which forces the chief executive to concentrate on short-term results only. Governments set their Minister of Housing a house-building target for the following year only – an absurdly short-time horizon. The point is that to treat a continuing task as if it were a project is a sure and certain route to myopic management.

The fourth comment on target-setting is this: when a target figure is given, it must be made clear what level of achievement it represents. A target can be set at many different levels: at a minimum level that represents something just better than failure, and which must be exceeded at all costs: at a level that represents a satisfactory outcome; at a level that is considered a success; at a level that is a bold and imaginative challenge; at a level that if achieved, is success beyond words; at a level that is considered too high and must not be exceeded. In view

67

of this there is obviously great scope for misunderstanding between managers and it is essential for those who give and receive instructions to make clear what level of achievement any target represents. In fact we propose to go further than this and suggest that all tasks should have two and even three figures attached to them as in the examples above. In one of these we had the shareholders setting a profit target at three levels – 3 per cent growth was unacceptable, 6 per cent was satisfactory and 10 per cent would be a resounding success. It is usual today for managers to set targets that stretch and challenge their subordinates, and it is right to do this. But these must always be accompanied, it is suggested, by a figure that represents the failure level below which the manager is entitled to take severe or emergency action. Thus, the shareholders were perfectly entitled to say to the chief executive, 'We will sack you if you can't do better than 3 per cent per annum growth.' It is interesting that of all these levels the one representing failure is the one that is always most readily identifiable and quantifiable in advance – it is much easier to say what is unacceptably bad than what is extremely good. For this reason we will refer to this important principle as 'Failure Plus' to remind us that if we have any difficulty in quantifying any task we may find it easier to do it by thinking not what we would like to achieve, but what we must avoid achieving at all costs. It is the level below which the manager must not fall – if he does he may be dismissed or the organisation itself be closed down. Needless to say, having identified the failure plus level one also sets another target figure well above it so as to stretch the subordinate.

How does all this affect the chief executive taking his step? Well, if he is wise he will insist on knowing the following things about his job:

(a) who the intended beneficiaries are;

(b) the nature of the benefit they expect;

(c) how much of it they expect at two or three levels. Certainly he must know what they consider to be the amount that represents failure plus, and preferably the satisfactory and success levels as well.

If he is wise the chief executive will only accept a task from the beneficiaries in his Step 1 if it contains target figures. Words like 'maximum', 'as much as possible', etc., do not help at all in delineating his task. If he does not know exactly what his task is he cannot decide the best way of doing it. It is just the same for all other managers in the hierarchy, in fact more so because the further down the hierarchy we go the fewer are the tasks that cannot be quantified.

Most of the remarks made about the chief executive's Step 1, therefore, also apply to Step 1 for all other managers. During the 1970s we can expect more and more managers to be given targets in terms of annual change for continuing jobs and completion dates for project jobs. We can expect more and more hitherto unquantifiable tasks to be quantified. And, we hope there will be fewer managers who are left in doubt whether the target figure they have been given is the one that represents success or the one representing abysmal failure to be exceeded at all costs.

At the beginning of this chapter we noticed that in most organisations there was bound to be some slack in the hierarchy of tasks – the people at one level *ought* to be doing exactly those things that were called for to complete their boss's job at the higher level, but in practice this was seldom true. To illustrate this, consider the Managing Director of a company who says to himself, 'I don't like the look of things – we really must improve our profits as soon as possible.' He then tells his Production Manager to 'cut costs at once' and his Sales Manager to 'get turnover up as fast as you can'. This may sound tough and dynamic but as it stands it is useless, for neither manager knows *by how much* he needs to cut costs and raise turnover, *nor by when*. Each will make his own guess and so the slack or looseness is introduced. (One might protest that no managing director would issue such vague intructions. Even in companies such instructions are not rare and in 'non-quantifiable' organisations they are at present the rule – consider the Director of Culture in New York who has to give instructions to his subordinates to raise the standards of the

69

city's culture. What scope for misinterpretation there must be all the way down this hierarchy!)

Of course the Managing Director in the above example should have used figures. He should have compared the profit the company expected to make with the profit he had been told to make, and then set new targets to his subordinates to make up the difference. He could then have said to the Production Manager 'Cut costs by £5,000 before September' and to the Sales Manager 'Increase turnover by £25,000 before October'. There would then have been no slack at all for if both subordinates had succeeded it would have resulted in exactly the extra profit the company needed. The point is this: quantification holds out the promise of cutting down the slack in the hierarchy of tasks; it almost eliminates misunderstandings between managers; it allows a far greater precision when giving or receiving instructions. Clearly it must become an important feature of MS 70.

We have not been suggesting that all tasks can be quantified. We have been saying that more can be quantified than most people now imagine, and that progressively during the 1970s more will be. Tasks which cannot be quantified can often be stated in terms that can be verified by inspection, and an opinion given as to whether the result is the desired one or not. The key question that managers must ask themselves when they accept a task in Step 1 is, 'Have I been given this task in such terms that my results can be verified?' If there are numbers and figures attached to the task then he can be fairly sure that results can be verified. We will deal with the verification of results, especially those with long-term horizons, in Chapter 9. For the moment let us end this section with two or three examples to show how even the most abstract-sounding tasks can be quantified, or at the very least can be verified indirectly. A chief executive might ask a senior manager to improve morale in the organisation. Now, on the face of it, this is an unusual request – managers are often asked to improve sales or cut costs but not to raise morale; however there is nothing surprising about this request and the chief executive may have very good reasons for making it. What sort of reasons? He may, of course, merely have 'a feeling in his bones' that morale is low. More probably he has noticed that the sickness and

absentee rates are high, there are perpetual complaints about
the food in the employee's canteen, trade union membership
is growing, the rate of accidents at work is increasing, staff
turnover is up, productivity and punctuality are down. Now
here is a list of no less than eight indicators each of which on
its own might not be significant, but taken together must
mean something. Surely this recital of woe can only mean that
morale is low – so low, perhaps, that the next symptom is
likely to be a strike. No one has yet codified these indicators
into a Morale Index but doubtless this will come. So 'improve
morale by 10 per cent' is not yet so concrete an instruction
as 'improve sales by 10 per cent', but it is moving in that
direction.

An example similar to morale in a company is morale in
any other community – a city, for example, or a nation. Again,
no systematic attempt has been made to devise a morale index
but this seems to be the way some sociologists are moving:
the Sick Society is a phrase coined to describe one in which
there is a high rate of crime, anti-social behaviour, suicide,
materialism, and other symptoms of social stress – all of which
can be quantified with some degree of accuracy. It is just
possible, then, that we could set a target for the town planner (or
even for a national government) in terms of some sort of
morale index – a new town designed by one town planner
might be a 'happier' place to live in than one designed by
another – the first would thus be more successful at his job
than the second.*

The point being made here is this: at Step 1 the manager
agrees to try to achieve a certain result that his boss asks of
him. It is incumbent upon all managers to make sure that his
boss has correctly instructed him, and his boss will not have
done so if he has failed to attach meaningful verifiable figures
to the task. This is a general rule to which there are still (and
perhaps always will be) some exceptions, but the number of
types of task to which no figures can be attached are dwindling
as the techniques of quantification are developed. The average
manager is entitled to be sceptical if his boss says he cannot

---

* Whether a town is a happy place to live in (e.g. low suicide rates, etc.)
is surely a more valid criterion for success than its architecture!

give figures – even such abstract sounding tasks as 'improve morale' or 'improve culture' may be quantifiable so surely most management tasks must be. At Step 1, therefore, the manager is entitled to ask his boss, 'What exactly is it you want me to do?'

THE CONFLICT BETWEEN TRENDS K AND M

The movement towards the more precise statement of tasks, aided and accelerated by the trend towards quantification, appears to run directly counter to Trend M – the growing desire of better educated managers to use their own initiative and their mounting hostility towards centralised authority. The precise point at which conflict takes place is where a manager receives a task from his boss that is minutely specified by innumerable figures so that the subordinate feels bound from head to foot in coils of constraining chains. He feels there is little scope for initiative when every detail of his task has already been quantified. Managers will have to take this conflict very seriously for if no reconciliation is found they will have some very frustrated subordinates on their hands in the 1970s. At first sight no reconciliation can be found; we want to specify a task that is both precise (to reduce slack in the hierarchy) and at the same time vague (to give more scope for initiative). We want to state our subordinate's task in a way that is both narrow and broad.

The way out of the problem may be provided by the distinction we have made between telling a man what to do and telling him how to do it. We have been careful to distinguish these two by showing them as two quite separate steps in the management process; Step 1 'accept the task' refers to what is to be achieved; Step 2 is deciding how. The suggestion we are making is that managers should tell their subordinates what to do but not how to do it. This advice is as old as the hills, of course, but we are going to sharpen it up and take it further, because although many managers know of this principle they frequently flout it without knowing they are doing so. To illustrate this we will discuss several examples, the first of which is the real life case of George Beckworth, a salesman working for a publishing company. Here is his target-sheet for one year:

Annual Sales Targets
Salesman – George Beckworth

Retail value of books to be sold	£32,000
Number of calls per week	30
Average length of call	20 minutes
Number of successful calls	30 per cent
Hotel expenses allowed	£1,200
Number of successful calls	30 per cent
Car expenses allowed	£500
Maximum mileage allowed	24,000
Maximum other expenses	£300

There is nothing dreadfully wrong with a sheet of paper showing eight target figures, but in fact only one of these figures really tells George Beckworth what his task is; all the others tell him how to do it. The only figure his employers really care about is £32,000 of sales – this is the figure he is employed to achieve and none of the others (except one) add or subtract anything to or from the description of the task, all they do is to constrain the number of ways in which he can tackle it. Suppose, for example, that George Beckworth discovered that by spending 30 minutes on each call and only making 20 calls a week he could boost sales to £35,000, would his employers be angry because he had failed to hit the target for calls? Suppose he discovered that by not making any calls at all he could sell £40,000 on the telephone! Suppose he could sell £35,000 by spending £1,000 on travelling by car but only £100 on hotels. The point is that every extra target figure that George Beckworth is given cuts down the number of alternative ways in which he can tackle his job, which is simply to sell books. The only figure they need give him is the turnover; if they did so then he would be free to decide how to achieve that figure and even if he found that the best way was to make 30 calls each of 20 minutes – just as in the target sheet – at least it would have been *his* decision, arrived at by using his own initiative. (We must, of course, qualify all this by noting that his employers are certainly entitled to state what resources he

73

will be allowed – in this case, for example, he may not spend more than £2,000 to achieve his target. They must also be sure that he does not use selling techniques that would bring the company into disrepute. Both these caveats are discussed later.) Targets which unnecessarily restrict and constrain the use of initiative, such as those given to George Beckworth, will be called Constrictive Targets. Those which allow a full use of enterprise in tackling the task we will call Expansive Targets (i.e. ones that positively *invite* the subordinate to think more widely). It has always been important to encourage enterprise and initiative in managers but it will be more so in the 1970s; the full relevance of this statement will emerge in the next chapter.

The setting of an unnecessarily large number of targets is only one route to a constrictive type of target. Another is to specify the resouces to be used in unnecessary detail. It is sometimes not necessary to specify or to limit the resources at all, for example, when the job includes finding the resources to do the task as well as doing the task itself as in the case of chief executives of some charities whose jobs include raising funds as well as running the charity. Where resources do have to be stated it should be done as widely as possible. There was no point, for example, in splitting George Beckworth's expense allowance into three separate parts (car, hotel and others). It would have been perfectly sufficient to limit him to £2,000 and leave him to decide how best to spend it.

In exactly the same way the manager of the Newtown Branch of the Southminster Bank is given an 'establishment level' which is management jargon for the maximum number of people he may employ. This is a constrictive target; his employers need only specify the total expenditure that they will allow him to do his job. If they did this then the manager could spend it how he liked – more employees and less of something else or vice versa.

The examples of constrictive targets we have so far discussed were fairly glaring and obvious. We must now consider a common but rather subtle type: imagine that the Minister of Education tells all local education authorities to reduce the pupil/teacher ratio in schools from forty to thirty-five within the next five years. At first sight this is an exemplary target – one simple statement containing just the right figures. It is in fact a constricting target as can be seen when we ask how many ways there are of carrying it out. The local authority can only (1) increase the number of teachers or (2) reduce the number of pupils. There are only two alternatives, the second of which is plainly unacceptable. This instruction does not leave much room for initiative, then. Furthermore, it does not even reflect what the Minister really wants which presumably is to improve the efficiency of education; if he had said what he meant it might have resulted in an expansive target. If he had said, 'You must improve the efficiency of education by 15 per cent within the next five years,' what scope for imaginative enterprise that would have provoked – teaching machines, part-time assistants, closed-circuit television, tape recorders and so on.

Similar errors are often made in companies: imagine a director visiting one of his company factories saying to the factory manager, 'Your canteen facilities are terribly antiquated and you must build a new canteen by next winter.' What he really wanted the factory manager to do was to ensure that up-to-date canteen facilities were available and surely he could have left it to the initiative of the manager to decide whether to build a new canteen, modernise the old one, share the canteen at the factory next door, provide transport to the nearest cafe, etc. Notice that the manager's task (Step 1) was 'to provide better facilities' and one way to do this (Step 2) was 'to build a new canteen'. The boss gave his subordinate instructions that covered both these steps; he need only have covered Step 1. This was the same error made by the Minister of Education when he told the local authorities 'to improve the efficiency of education by reducing the pupil/teacher ratio' (Step 1 and Step 2 as well).

Managers at every level in the hierarchy will have to be much more careful when accepting tasks from their bosses in the 1970s. This is true right down from the chief executive who must ensure that the beneficiaries have properly briefed him, to the junior foremen or supervisor who needs to be told clearly what results he is to achieve but does not want to be told how to achieve them. As we can see from the examples above it is all too easy for a boss unwittingly to frustrate the initiative of his subordinates by setting constricting targets.

We have reached a number of conclusions concerning how managers should take Step 1 of the management process in the 1970s. We must make sure that MS 70 contains these.

Conclusion 1.1. There will be two fundamental changes to the way in which Step 1 will have to be taken in the 1970s: the first is the necessity for greater precision in specifying a task; the second, and more important, is a move away from telling a manager what he is to do towards telling him what results he is to achieve.

Conclusion 1.2. The definition of Step 1 in MS 70 should therefore now be 'agree to achieve a well-defined verifiable result'.

Conclusion 1.3. The task of the chief executive is identical to the purpose of the organisation. He must know, therefore, (1) the identity of the intended beneficiaries, (2) the nature of the benefit the organisation exists to generate for them, (3) target levels for this benefit.

Conclusion 1.4. The intended beneficiaries must clearly instruct the chief executive as to his task. They must maintain a strong formal and authoritative link with him either direct or through a carefully devised system of representatives.

Conclusion 1.5. No person should at the same time be both a representative and a manager of the same organisation.

Conclusion 1.6. All organisation charts should show the organisation structure of the intended beneficiaries and their representatives as well as showing the organisation structure of the managers. This normally will appear as a double pyramid or hour-glass.

Conclusion 1.7. It will become increasingly necessary and practical to state managers' tasks in terms of numerical or quantified targets. They can be set at three levels: (1) the result which represents failure and *must* be exceeded ('failure plus') (2) the result that the beneficiaries regard as satisfactory (3) the result which represents success.

Conclusion 1.8. A manager's task can be continuing or project. Targets for continuing tasks should be set in terms of rate of change or rate of growth, where possible. Targets for project tasks must include a target completion date (Rates and Dates). To set a target for a continuing task as if it was a project usually leads to excessive concentration on short-term issues to the neglect of the longer term.

Conclusion 1.9. Greater precision in specifying tasks will lead to less slack between the levels in the hierarchy of tasks.

Conclusion 1.10. Great care must be taken when specifying a task, especially when setting quantified targets, to avoid constricting targets, which limit the subordinate's scope for initiative. Expansive targets are more likely to be chosen (a) if the manager avoids telling his subordinate how to do the task, (b) if as few figures as possible are used, (c) if the resources are stated in wide terms and not in detail.

Conclusion 1.11. There will be an increase in the number of management techniques by which a widening range of tasks can be quantified.

Conclusion 1.12. It will be necessary for managers to guard against giving excessive attention to tasks that have been quantified at the expense of those that have not. Some of the tasks (especially those set to senior managers) which cannot yet be quantified are of much greater importance than those that can.

Conclusion 1.13. Managers must be sure that they are not being asked to do anything unethical or anti-social.

Chapter 7

Step 2 in the 1970s

We got off rather lightly in the previous chapter because only four of the fifteen trends listed in Chapter 5 caused us to modify Step 1. In this chapter we shall find that virtually all fifteen will have their impact on Step 2; something approaching a revolution is taking place in management decision-making and this chapter will therefore be a long and possibly difficult one. (It will be appreciated, of course, that what we have called Step 2 'decide how to carry out the task' is nearly identical to what is often known as 'management decision-making'.) Let us remind ourselves where Step 2 fits into the manager's job. The first step occurs when the manager agrees to carry out some specific task for his boss. The third step is when the manager tells his subordinates what actions they must take to help him carry out this task. Obviously before he can instruct them he has got to make up his mind what he wants them to do; in other words, between receiving instructions and giving them the manager has to do some thinking. He has to decide how to tackle his job and what part in it he wants each subordinate to play, and only then can he give them instructions. So the sequence has to be: receive instructions – make decisions – give instructions; Step 1 – Step 2 – Step 3.

In the good old days when life was simple, the length of time that it took to complete these three steps was quite different from today. We can imagine the scene on a field of battle in 1470 where an officer has just received the instruction, 'Charge!', and, with only a moment's thought he gallops off to his men and shouts, 'Charge!' In this case the time it took to receive the message from the commander (by horse of course) and to give instructions to his men were both far longer than the time it took him to decide what to do. In similar circum-

78

stances today the instructions would go in a flash by radio but the interval between receiving and giving instructions might now be hours or days while the field commander and his staff considered whether to use artillery or rockets or helicopters or bombers to soften up the enemy, whether to use tanks, or infantry, flamethrowers bazookas, defoliants, tear gas or napalm in the attack. This pattern is universal – giving and receiving orders now takes less time than before because of improved communications while the time taken to think out what to do has increased (see Fig. 27).

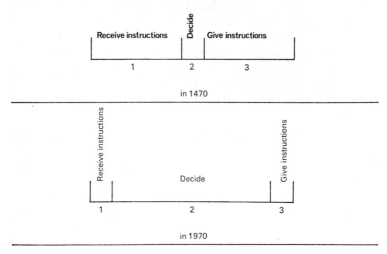

Fig 27: Changes in the time and importance of steps 1, 2 and 3

The causes behind this massive expansion of Step 2 are contained in the fifteen trends of Chapter 5. Rather than discuss them all now we will draw attention to each of them in the appropriate places in this chapter, but there is one which we must introduce at this point – Trend G. This is the one which concerns the rapidly widening range of choice that exists in the modern world. In every field of human activity there is a greater variety on offer: if one wants to buy a car there are dozens of types to choose from; if one wants to invest money there are dozens of types of investment; there are dozens of brands of cigarette, of butter, of garden chemicals – in short, a bewildering variety of everything. The word 'bewildering' was intentional; it indicates that one needs time to sort out which choice to make and this, then, is one of the reasons why it now takes longer for managers to decide how to carry out their tasks. Just as for the housewife, so for the manager the range of possible actions has increased. We must remember that the word 'decide' means that a choice of alternatives exists and that a selection has to be made; if there is no choice, there is no decision. The manager today has a far wider variety of alternative actions than ever before, and as this will become wider still during the next decade it will take even longer and be still more difficult to select the best alternative. We have so far described Step 2 as 'decide how to carry out the task' but this does not sufficiently emphasise that the crux of decision-making lies in the act of choosing between alternatives. We will therefore reword Step 2 to read 'select the best way of carrying out the task'. This explicitly indicates choice between alternatives.

How does one select the best way of doing something? First one needs to know what it is one wants to do, and we have discussed the importance of this in the previous chapter on Step 1 where we emphasised that managers must not accept a task unless it has been clearly defined. Next one would list the alternative ways of carrying it out. Then one can fairly quickly eliminate most of these, leaving one or two of the more promising ones which one would need to study in some detail before finally choosing the best; and having done that one would need to draw up some sort of action plan to put it into effect. To illustrate this procedure, take a simple task we have all experienced: that of buying a car. One first lists all makes within one's chosen range, one can quickly eliminate most of them for reasons that are fairly clear-cut, then one is left with only two or three, and to select one from these one often has to go into considerable detail. Finally, one plans how to make the purchase itself. There are three steps here: list the alternatives, select and plan. But there is a fourth step which we have not noticed – one also has to decide how much effort it is worth putting into these three steps. Obviously, if the decision is important (and to most people buying a car is) one will spend many hours with brochures and price lists; if it is not important one would not devote much time to it. Now one of the basic tenets of MS 70 is that every manager will, as the decade progresses, be faced with bigger and more difficult and more important decisions (Trend Q), and so the preliminary question 'how much time and trouble do I take over this decision' must be asked. It may sound ridiculous but the first step in the decision-making process will have to be 'decide how to decide'. So the four sub-steps of the decision-making process which we must now discuss in this chapter are:

Step 2a Decide how to decide
Step 2b List alternatives
Step 2c Select
Step 2d Action plan

STEP 2A. DECIDE HOW TO TAKE STEP 2

We have mentioned that Step 2 has been stretched over the years to become a major activity in the management process. So great is this distension that it now absorbs a significant proportion of the total resources of many organisations; in other words there are now a significant number of people in any organisation who spend all or most of their time discussing how to carry out tasks and preparing plans, furthermore most of these people are either senior managers or highly-skilled advisers, and therefore highly paid. The volume of planning, the number of interacting decisions to be taken, the number of people to be consulted – all have increased. The complexity of the calculations required to site a new airport for London, for example, must be many hundred times as great in the 1970s as it was in the 1930s. Indeed it is quite possible that the cost of making this 1970s decision is alone as great as the cost of building an entire airport would have been in 1930! We now seem to be in the position of having to take longer to decide to do something than it actually takes to do it – it can certainly take five years to decide where to build a new factory or a motorway while it only takes three years to build. By 1980 the contrast between deciding and doing will become even more marked, even more resources will have to be poured into Step 2.

The purpose of Step 2a is to remind managers that some thought should be given to how much of their resources should be spent on any given decision.

The question to be asked in Step 2a is then: what resources is it sensible to allocate to Step 2? The point is that one could devote more resources on looking for a better way of carrying out a task than is justified. Equally, one could fail to search for a better way by not appreciating how much better a job could be done. Clearly, it would be sensible to spend £1,000 to find a better alternative if that alternative was better by £1,000 or more compared with how the task is done now. In theory, then, Step 2a is simple. In practice it is exceedingly difficult because (a) it is difficult to estimate how much it will cost to investigate all the alternatives, (b) it is difficult to estimate what improvement any of these alternatives may represent, and (c) until one starts the search one does not know what the chances are of finding a better alternative at all. Unfortunately the question posed by Step 2a has one further complicating factor – time. The manager not only has to decide how much money to spend searching for alternatives, he must also know how much time he has before he must make up his mind. So there are now four interlinked questions to be answered in Step 2a: (1) how much will it cost to make the necessary enquiries – because this must not exceed (2) the extra savings in money that a better method might show over the present method – bearing in mind (3) the chances of finding a better method – not forgetting that (4) there may be a penalty if the enquiries take too long. Let us illustrate Step 2a with an imaginary example.

The manager of a road transport business is told by his engineer that one of his lorries is now so old that it will not pass the statutory safety tests which are to held in eight weeks' time. He knows that to have one lorry out of action costs his company £50 a week in lost profits. He also knows, because he keeps his technical knowledge pretty well up to date, that there are five types of lorry that he could buy to replace the old one and that any of these could be delivered within seven weeks of the order. So he has one week in which to make his choice. Unfortunately he only has detailed figures of cost and performance for three of these five lorries, but he has calculated that the best of these three would be £5 a week cheaper to run than the most expensive. Should he spend some time and money to investigate the other two? The first thing to strike the manager is that there is a very big difference in the running costs between the three lorries for which he has details – £5 a week! Taking the life of a lorry at five years this is a difference of well over £1,000 between buying the best or the worst of the three. So big is this difference that he is bound to wonder whether one of the two unknown lorries might show an even greater saving. The manager makes a guess that one of them might show a saving of, say, £200 over its whole life compared with the best of the three, but of course he cannot know this until he has made the investigation, at which time he might discover that neither of them save anything or that one of them saves £400; he can only guess at this stage. He is really saying, 'It might be worth spending £200 to find out what I can save.' The next question for him is how much it might cost to investigate these two lorries; he has to study performance data, make calculations, arrange a test drive, etc. Let us estimate these costs at £100 in travelling, salaries, etc. Now it is clear that he *should* make the investigation: it will only cost £100 to make a saving that might be at least £200. Unfortunately he only has a week in which to do this and his diary is already nearly full. Would it still be worthwhile if the decision was postponed beyond one week? The answer is that it would. The company loses £50 each week that a lorry is off the road, so it would even be worth taking three weeks over this decision. So the final calculation is as follows:

Possible cost: £100 to make investigations   £100
           £50 a week for two weeks' loss
            of business   £100

                   Total   £200

Possible savings: Anything from nil to perhaps
             as much as £400 but guessed
             at approximately   £200
Conclusion: It is worth taking up to three
             weeks over this decision.

83

This, then, is Step 2a. It will become increasingly necessary for managers to ask themselves what resources they should devote to making their decisions. This is because as organisations grow larger in the 1970s (Trend H) decisions become larger and the cost of making the wrong decision becomes greater; it is because the number of alternatives to investigate will increase (Trend G). It is because the process of decision-making will absorb a growing proportion of resources (Trend Q). The larger the organisation, the more essential will Step 2a become. The more senior the manager the more will he have to consider Step 2a because, of course, the higher up the hierarchy a manager is the more far-reaching are his decisions.

It will be appreciated that it is seldom possible to make accurate calculations in Step 2a. It was not possible in the example of the transport manager, where he could not place an accurate figure on any of the factors involved, neither on the cost of the investigation, nor on the savings, nor on the probability of even finding any savings at all, nor on the time the investigation would take. But at least he *tried* to attach some figures, he tried to quantify (Trend K) instead of giving vague answers such as 'the savings might be large' or 'it will take a long time'. Only when one quantifies can one make sense out of Step 2a; even if the figures are only of the right order of magnitude it is better than no figures at all. It is sufficient to know, for example, that an enquiry will cost pounds and that the savings might only be pennies. Or that there is a potential saving of millions of pounds while the cost of the enquiry is in thousands. If a manager does not *try* to quantify these things, difficult though it may be in many cases and impossible in others he will fail to meet the standard required of a manager in the 1970s.

The necessity for a manager to take Step 2a has an important effect on the rest of Step 2. We described Step 2 as 'select the best way of carriyng out the task' but we now see that we should modify this to 'select the best way of carrying out the task – within the limit of the resources allocated to Step 2'. The implication is this: that we should not search for *the* best way, but only for the way that is good enough to convince us that *it is not worth searching for a better one*. There is strong evidence to suggest that some organisations are spending far too much time and money on taking comparatively trivial decisions, i.e. where the difference between the best possible method and their present method cannot possibly justify the cost of the investigation, as when a Board of Directors spend the whole morning discussing what should be the price of a cup of tea in the works canteen. But the converse is also common – organisations spend far too little of their resources in searching for a better alternative to some of their major tasks. The penalty for making either of these errors will grow as the decade progresses; the managers who continue to fail to take Step 2a will increasingly be open to valid criticism.

STEP 2B. LIST ALTERNATIVES

Although we describe Step 2b as 'List alternaives' we now know from the discussion above, that what we really mean is 'List all the alternatives that one can within the limits set by Step 2a'. There will certainly be occasions when it is simply not worth spending any time or money on looking for alternative methods of carrying out a task, and when it is right to carry on with the existing method *however* old-fashioned it may be. There will be a growing number of occasions, however, when it will make sense to search for alternatives. This is partly because of the increased variety in the modern world (Trend G again) which offers managers a wider choice of methods, and partly because most beneficiaries are demanding more from their organisations at the same time as society is also demanding more (Trend J) which leads to the growing necessity to improve management efficiencies.

There is plenty of evidence that managers have not yet appreciated how important it is in the modern world to search for alternatives – we will give some examples below – and this may be due to two causes. One is that the cost of investigating alternatives has, as we have repeatedly said, risen markedly over the past decade or so but managers still find it difficult to believe that all these investigations, research teams, committees of enquiry, project appraisals, planning specialists, and so on, are really worthwhile. They long for the good old days when life was simple and one did not have to think so carefully before issuing orders. They cannot, for example, accept that it need take five years to decide where to build a motorway. The attitude adopted in this book is that decisions are taking longer to make, it is a fact of life and it is going to get progressively worse as the decade goes by. It has just got to be faced. The second reason is another management misconception: it is the widespread failure to think far enough ahead. We can say this – if one leaves a decision until the last moment, there *will* only be one alternative and time will make the decision for you. This implies that if a manager says that he has only one alternative, namely to take action *x*, then there is a *prima facie* case for suspecting that there were many alternatives but he has failed to allow enough time to investigate. This is a failure of management, one that is already serious but which will become more unforgivable as the 1970s proceed.

Let us draw attention to these two themes which recur throughout this book. One is that all managers must look further ahead, must forecast further and plan further into the future. The second is that managers must examine more alternative solutions to problems; increasingly during the 1970s a manager who says, 'I have a good idea, what do you think of it?' will be eclipsed and deposed by managers who say, 'I have five good ideas, which do you think is best?' These two themes are intimately entwined, for if a manager fails to look ahead all his problems will be upon him so quickly that he will have no time to consider alternative solutions; he will have to take whatever emergency action he can, regardless of its efficiency. And, of course, the opposite is true – the more alternatives he wishes to consider the longer it will take to select the best and, if the final decision is not to be intolerably delayed, he must start the decision-making process earlier. The theme of the longer time-span of decisions will be considered again later; meanwhile let us turn to the necessity of considering a multiplicity of alternatives.

CREATING A LIST OF ALTERNATIVES

We have repeatedly said that managers will be under increasing pressure to improve the performance of their organisations in the next decade. They will be able to harness several important developments to achieve this, such as: the computer, an increasing number of management techniques, new scientific discoveries, faster communications. It may be that more powerful than all these will be the harnessing of creative thought and inventive flair to generate alternative methods. It will not be sufficient for a manager faced with a task merely to jot down a few alternative ways of tackling it; he will have to treat this as the most important part of the whole decision-making process. It will not be sufficient to have one idea that is good enough, he will have to have several good ideas and select the best. Consider the following example:

In 1970 Hypothetics Limited were producing 1,000 tons of Hypon a week. The Sales Manager forecast that by 1972 demand would rise to 1,100 tons a week. Since the total capacity of all their factories in 1970 was just under 1,100 tons a week, the Board immediately sanctioned the expenditure of £100,000 to build a new factory by 1972 – the urgency was clear since it takes at least two years to build a factory of this sort.

The above example is typical – a major decision taken in some haste (because they had not been looking far enough into the future and had only two years left in which to do something that would take two years to do) and only one alternative was considered (to build a new factory). What other alternatives might they have thought of? How about modifying the plant at the existing factories to boost output? How about buying Hypon from a competitor? Or raising the price of Hypon which might have yielded a higher profit even if demand was restricted to the level of their 1970 production capacity? The point being made is not that these alternatives would have been better; it is that because they were not considered by the Board, we were not given a chance to test them. But these are by no means the only alternatives, let us list some more that widen the horizon even further. How about taking over a competitor who has spare plant capacity? Or cutting the price of Hypon to increase demand and build *two* new factories? Or develop an entirely new product? Or launch Hypon in a

G   87 foreign market and build a factory there? Or, instead of saying, 'We will build a factory. It will cost £100,000', suppose they said, 'We have £100,000. What is the best way of investing it?' That would widen the area of search for alternatives almost to infinity. (Notice the similarity between this and the suggestion above: one idea = new factory. How shall we invest £100,000? = several ideas.) It is not sufficient merely to jot down all the alternatives that happen to come to mind – in the 1970s managers will have to use techniques specifically designed to generate lists of alternatives.

CREATIVE TECHNIQUES

During the 1960s managers were beginning to use many of the management techniques that had been making their appearance over the past few decades. Most of these techniques were tools of analysis to be used to examine management problems. There was network analysis, interfirm comparison, risk analysis, work measurement, value analysis and so on – mostly concerned with analysis and mostly concerned with problems. During the 1970s managers will begin to master many of these techniques. However, problem analysis is essentially a rather negative mode of management; it rather implies that managers are always on the defensive, fighting a rearguard action against problems and obstacles which keep preventing them from carrying out their tasks. There will be no diminution of problems in the 1970s and managers will have to use more of these techniques of systematic analysis, but it is suggested that as they begin to master these techniques an entirely new and immensely powerful *positive* mode of management will begin to emerge. This is where the manager of the 1970s will go over to the attack, where he will make an aggressive and positive search for new ideas and new ways of harnessing old ones. There are already a number of techniques which can be used to stimulate the manager into creativity and invention, and more will be developed in the 1970s. Because these positive management techniques are less well known than the problem analysis techniques, we will briefly describe some of them below. We will pause only to recall where Step 2b fits into the management process; the manager, having been given a task by his boss is now looking for alternative methods of carrying it out. He knows, from Step 2a, that he can only devote a limited amount of time to this decision and he knows that his subordinates are waiting for their instructions and his boss is waiting for results. He needs to make a list quickly of all the ways in which he might tackle the job and, although his native wit and experience will enable him to list some alternatives, the list will be enhanced in quantity and quality if he uses some of the following methods of generating alternatives:

Logical methods
Mathematical methods
Non-systematic methods
Surveys
Predictive methods
Combined methods

Logical methods
Imagine that the manager of a city's public health department has been asked to cut the cost of garbage disposal by 50 per cent within six years. (Notice that this is an Expansive target since it provokes this manager to use his initiative because it does not tell him how to achieve the target.) Having realised that the difference between achieving this 50 per cent saving and the present method is hundreds of thousands of pounds a year the manager decides to spend a full six months on this problem. At present all domestic refuse is collected and dumped. A logical alternative is not to collect it. So now we have two alternatives. But there is a third possibility besides these two, namely to collect only some refuse. This thought leads to three more:

1. Collect all.   2. Collect none
        3. collect some – i.e.
        3a. collect all from some houses
        3b. collect some from all houses
        3c. collect some from some houses.

It is obvious why this approach is called logical – all we are doing is to perform the various operations of logic on the

89

original statement. Let us continue: take the alternative of collecting refuse (as opposed to not collecting it) and see how this might be done; underground, overhead, by lorry, by boat, by aircraft and so on. It is immediately obvious that by blindly following logic we may reach several quite absurd alternatives which need not be pursued any further so long as we are sure that they really are absurd and not just surprising or unconventional. If we think that collecting garbage by air is absurd let us pursue

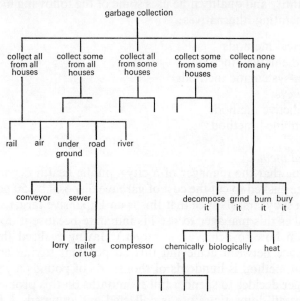

Fig 28: A logical tree

that line no further – there are plenty more possibilities left. For example, consider lorries: one can use big ones, small ones, cheap simple ones, costly complex ones. Or consider the frequency of collection: daily, weekly, monthly. Or return to the first level of alternatives and consider how 'collect none from any house' might be achieved: grind it, burn it, decompose it; by chemical means, physical means, biological means, etc.

It will be observed that this method yields a 'logical tree diagram' where each alternative can be split into several sub-alternatives, as in Fig. 28.

A useful trick with logical methods is negation. For example, 'build new airport' can be turned into a provocative negation: 'do not build new airport' – provocative because it forces one to consider other alternatives such as expanding an existing airport, using vertical take-off, etc. In the same way 'build airport near London' can be negated to 'build airport not near London' and this provokes one to consider the various methods of getting air passengers to London other than by air. A further illustration of negation is provided by the suggestion that a company should 'do some research into a new product'. This sentence contains two ideas (1) 'do research', and (2) 'new product'. Both of these can be negated so the suggestion could become either 'do research into an *existing* product' or 'do *not* do some research into a new product', which could branch into the alternatives of having the research done by someone else or licensing a product that has already been researched, etc.

Logical methods, then, consist of taking one method of carrying out the task and performing logical operations on it such as negation or opposition, then branching into sub-alternatives, negating again, then branching again. One can then combine and permutate any one alternative with any other (for example in Fig. 28 one could permutate 'large, medium, small lorry' with 'daily, weekly, monthly collection', or perhaps combine methods of collection with methods of not collecting, leading, for example, to collecting rubbish that has been partially treated in the home). Nor are these the only logical operations one can perform. Imagine that a company wishes to introduce a new product that is not too dissimilar to its existing product. A host of possibilities open up if one looks at the product and imagines it longer, shorter, thinner, fatter, doubled or twin, trebled, halved, combined, divided, backwards, upside down, and so on.

If this was a textbook we would have to consider logical methods in more detail and quote references to such methods as morphological analysis*; all we need to do here, however, is to point out that logical methods such as these will play an increas-

---

* A description of morphological analysis will be found in books on technological forecasting.

ing part in management in the 1970s, and therefore we must ensure that MS 70 is designed so as to demand their use.*

Mathematical methods
Logical methods can be used to manipulate qualities such as large, small, near London, by rail, by road, etc. Mathematical methods can be used to generate alternatives where quantities are concerned. For example, a production manager could schedule the flow of products through a process as follows:

Monday: 500 units of product A though machines P & Q
Tuesday: 1,100 units of product C through machines R & Q
Wednesday: 12 units of product A through machines R & S
      and 480 units of product B through machines P & S, etc.

Now the number of alternative schedules that could have been devised for such a production process must number millions – why did he choose 500 units of product A on Monday, for example? Why not 327 units of product C? or 492 units of B?

Take another similar problem: a company sells 8,372 different products through 782 retail shops served by 41 warehouses and 605 lorries and vans of various sizes. Would it be cheaper if they sent product number 8,076 to shop number 92 through warehouse number 28 or should it go via warehouse number 29? We must remember, by the way, that if it does go through warehouse 29, then product number 485 cannot also go through warehouse 29 and would have to be diverted either to warehouse 14 or . . . and so on to an infinity of alternative permutations and combinations.

In the 1950s anyone who suggested that the managers should consider all possible alternatives in this sort of situation would have been thought a lunatic. By the early 1960s it was just possible to visualise how it could be done using a computer; by the late 1960s many companies were doing it. In the 1970s it will be just routine.

It is possible, using techniques such as simulation or mathe-

---

* For many years experts have been looking for a use for symbolic logic in management. This, it is suggested, is where its tremendous potential could be realised – here at Step 2b.

matical programming (i.e. by building a mathematical model), to investigate an incredible number of alternatives. Before the advent of the computer it would have been possible to make by hand the thousands of calculations required to investigate complex situations like the examples above, but of course it would have been entirely uneconomic and such an idea would have been sharply rejected at Step 2a. The appearance of cheaper, more powerful computers (Trend C) has transformed the situation.

There is another category of management problem which calls for the study of a large number of alternatives. These are the problems created by the need to forecast further into the future, an activity which will grow as the time span of decisions grows in the 1970s. The difficulty arises because the error inherent in all forecasts increases as one tries to forecast further ahead. All forecasts are wrong; long-range forecasts can be very wrong. Since all plans are based on forecasts, when one plans one has to recognise that the forecast will be wrong – not to do so is plain bad management.

To illustrate: suppose the Sales Director forecasts that demand for his company's products will exceed production capacity by 10,000 units per annum in three years' time. Most companies would jump to the conclusion that they must build an extension to the factory to cope with 10,000 extra units. The wise company, however, will realise that '10,000' is only a forecast and it could be wrong by as much as, say, 3,000 units either way. This knowledge provokes the thought that perhaps the factory extension should be only 7,000 units – or should it be 13,000? The fact is that they should really calculate the economic viability of a whole range of factory sizes from 7,000 to 13,000 units to find the best alternative. Before the computer appeared it would have been ridiculous to suggest such a thing but during the 1970s most large organisations will find themselves having to consider many alternative versions of many alternative projects and having to use a computer and techniques such as decision theory, replacement theory and decision trees to study them.

Non-systematic methods
By 'non-systematic methods' of generating alternatives we mean

93

flair, inspiration, invention, creativity, intuition. In short, having bright ideas. This is certainly the most venerable method of listing alternatives; it is probably by far the most important, it is the least understood (although there is now a growing body of literature) and it is probably the method that is most neglected by managers. It is quite possible that the 1970s will witness a wider appreciation of the value of creative thinking in management. It could be argued that one brilliant and unexpected idea is worth more than a whole list of alternatives generated by logical or mathematical methods, and we may see more organisations employing 'wild men' as they are called, whose job will be to brighten the manager's prosaic thoughts with flashes of inspiration.

Surveys

The word 'survey' here is used widely to include collecting ideas or opinions from other people whether formally or informally. There are several groups of people to whom the manager may turn to widen and lengthen his list of alternatives: his subordinates, his boss, specialists and advisers inside and outside his organisation. He may also search the relevant literature or ask specialist organisations to search for him. He may invite the help of people in a 'think tank' or 'thought farm'.

As the decade proceeds it will become progressively more difficult for one man on his own to draw up a list of alternatives likely to contain one that is better than existing methods. He will have to call for help from others and survey methods will become more important; several of the trends mentioned in Chapter 5 will also increase the importance and value of survey methods. One of these is Trend E, the rising standards of education, which will provide managers at every level with more knowledgeable subordinates; it would seem sensible for a manger to tap this pool of knowledge by asking his subordinates to contribute their ideas on how to carry out his task. Quite apart from any intrinsic value their ideas may have, the fact that they have been invited to contribute to their manager's list of alternatives will greatly increase their co-operation with him, an important consideration when one remembers the tendency towards conflict between managers and managed (Trend M).

Another trend that will reinforce the importance of survey methods is the improvement in communications (Trend B) which suggests that a manager will be able to consult other people (especially his subordinates) without either him or them moving from their desks (or even their cars). Yet another reinforcing trend is the increase in specialists (Trend L) whom the manager can consult; yet another is the information explosion (Trend D) which will provide the manager with a vast reservoir of alternatives that other people have suggested or found useful for similar tasks. In this connection we must not forget Trend A which implies that managers must increasingly judge the performance of their organisations, and therefore their lists of alternatives, by international standards.

Predictive methods
One trend of enormous importance to managers is the increasing rate of change in almost every field of human activity (Trend F) which implies that the methods a manager has found satisfactory in the past may be no longer satisfactory – someone has found a better alternative. It is this trend, of course, together with the parallel Trend G of increased variety, which is the root cause behind the need to search for alternatives; Step 2b would not be necessary at all if current methods of carrying out tasks remained satisfactory for ever.

Where a manager is searching for better methods of tackling a task that is to be carried out in the near future he is entitled to be satisfied with a method that is good by current standards. Where he has been given a task with a long-time span, however, methods that are currently satisfactory will be out of date by the time the task is completed or even before it starts. In such cases he must therefore search for alternatives that will be relevant in the future, perhaps many years into the future.

To illustrate: a manager has been given the task of identifying what new products his company might introduce four years ahead; clearly his list is no use if it contains only products that are currently in demand. He must try to predict what products will be in demand in four years' time (more in fact; if the products have a life of five years then he must predict nine years ahead). As has been repeatedly stated already, the time span of

95

decisions will increase over the next decade, and more and more managers will be given tasks with horizons of several years. It follows that more managers will have to use predictive methods.

There is a considerable body of literature on social and technological forecasting techniques (such as Delphi, scenario, parameter analysis, etc.) and several institutions exist which are devoted to the study of the future. It must be said, categorically, that any manager who is given a task with a completion date some years ahead will fail in his duty if he only lists alternatives that are appropriate to the present. This is certainly true for time spans measured in decades but it is also true of time spans measured only in years, for the rate of change in the 1970s will be such that the best way of doing something today will be third rate in only a few years' time.

Combined methods
It is possible, indeed desirable, to combine two or more of the above methods; one well-known combination is 'brainstorming' which consists of an amalgam of a survey and a non-systematic method. In a 'brainstorming session' several people get together to answer a question such as 'In how many ways could we improve our product design', or 'In how many ways could we improve the state pension scheme'. One person on his own could make a list of several bright ideas but where several people come together in a brainstorming session such a list can be enormously lengthened if they each think aloud; after a matter of minutes two people's ideas may be linked by a third participant to another idea thus producing another idea and so on. Sometimes several really new and startling thoughts are produced in this way. Another combined method is known as Delphi; this is a method of forecasting change and represents a combination of a survey method with predictive methods. A 'think tank' or 'thought farm' is a combination of predictive methods, surveys and non-systematic methods.

In discussing the various methods of listing alternatives we have made a rather substantial detour away from the main purpose of this book – in which we are less concerned with describing management techniques than with developing the structure of a system of management into the relevant parts of which the various techniques can readily be slotted. However, so neglected is the whole field of listing alternatives, of creativity, of finding new ways to do things, of finding new things to do, that we have had to go deeper into these areas than was really desirable. Perhaps the detour will have served to underline the fact that managers have rather neglected to break away from their existing methods to search for new ones, possibly because they have not appreciated that so many techniques to stimulate their creativity exist. We can say this; if a manager does not positively search for new ways he will fail as a manager and his organisation will be left like a fish on the beach when the tide has ebbed. In the next decade the tides will change more swiftly than before.

STEP 2C. SELECT

In Step 2b the manager makes as long and imaginative a list of alternatives as possible within the limits imposed by Step 2a. Now he is faced with the job of eliminating all alternatives but one. If Step 2b must become more important as the decade goes by, so also must Step 2c; if we use more effective methods to lengthen the list of alternatives we must use more effective methods to select the best one. And just as Step 2b has been neglected in the 1960s, so has Step 2c; we must therefore spend some time on it.*

We now have to design a systematic procedure for eliminating alternatives which we can build into this Step 2c of MS 70. It consists of six questions which we have to ask of each alternative in turn – most alternatives will be eliminated easily and swiftly at the first pass through this sieve but a few will have to be put through it several times and in ever-increasing detail – just as we

*Parenthetically, one piece of evidence that methods of elimination and selection were neglected in the 1960s is provided by the fact that DCF was more widely used than NPV. Without going into the technicalities of these terms, experts will recognise that DCF is of greater value for testing the viability of *one* project; NPV, on the other hand, is of greater value for choosing between *alternative* projects. DCF will answer the 1960s question, 'I have a good idea, what do you think of it?' while NPV will answer the 1970s question, 'I have several good ideas, which do you think is best?'

illustrated in the example of buying a car. As a matter of fact these six questions are exactly those that one asks oneself when taking any important decision in any field of human activity. In view of this universal application – and in view of its importance to managers we will give this group of six questions a name – we call it *the Sieve*.

These are the six questions that form the Sieve:
1. Might it achieve the target?
2. Does it require resources beyond those allocated?
3. Is it in line with the organisation's ethics?
4. Is the organisation especially well equipped to use it?
5. What trends or events might help or hinder its success?
6. What might go wrong and what would happen then?

We must now briefly describe each of these questions in action.

Test 1. Might it achieve the target?
To illustrate this test, let us imagine that a manager has been asked by his boss to increase sales turnover. The alternative ways of achieving this are innumerable:

Recruit more salesmen
Improve the performance of the existing sales force
Increase advertising
Improve the efficiency of existing advertising
Improve delivery from factory
Improve product quality
Reduce selling price of product
Increase selling price to some customers, etc.

Now let us take the first alternative, 'Recruit more salesmen' and ask the first test question, 'Might it achieve the target?' i.e. 'Might we increase sales turnover if we recruited more salesmen?' And of course the answer is 'Yes'. Now try the same question for the second alternative; 'Might we increase sales turnover if we improved the performance of the existing sales force?' And the answer is 'Yes' – in fact *all* the alternatives listed above would pass through Test 1 with ease. The reason for this fiasco (fiasco it certainly is; these tests are intended to eliminate most of the alternatives and this has simply not happened) is that the task we were set was 'Increase sales turnover' – no figures, no dates – a useless instruction because it broke all the rules laid down for Step 1 in Chapter 6. If a manager does not know precisely what his task is he cannot select the best way of tackling it: 'If you don't know where you are going, any road will do', which is exactly the situation above – any alternative would do. Now let us insist on a properly stated task and try again.

Our redefined task is 'Increase sales turnover by 10 per cent within the next two months'. Now put the first alternative, 'Recruit more salesmen' through the first test again: 'Might we increase sales turnover by 10 per cent in two months if we recruited more salesmen?' Now the answer is 'No' because it would take at least two months to take on the salesmen and train them. So that alternative is out. Then the next alternative is tried and so on. Some will be ruled out entirely and without hesitation, some will pass without hesitation and later be put through the second test question. We must not forget, however, that some of the alternatives might fail on their own but pass in combination with another, for example 'Increase advertising' might fail on its own, 'Increase selling price to some customers' might fail on its own, but taking both these actions together might be so powerfully synergetic that they would pass.

Test 2. Does it require resources beyond those allocated?
When a manager is given a task he should be told, as an integral part of the instruction (see Chapers 6 and 8), what resources he may use. Test 2 simply asks if each alternative is within this resource allocation.

Test 2 also presents another opportunity for the manager to consider combining two alternatives which together might achieve the target and be within the resource allocation. For example, companies can achieve a very rapid rate of growth either by buying other companies or by launching new products. The first alternative might achieve a particular company's growth target but call for too much capital, while the second might fail to reach the target but require less than the capital allocated; a carefully proportioned mixture of both strategies might pass both tests, i.e. achieve the growth target while not exceeding the allocation of capital.

There is one special instance of Test 2 to which attention should be drawn. Most companies use what is known as a 'cut-off rate' for capital expenditure, that is to say, these companies make it a rule not to approve the expenditure of capital on any project unless the 'return on capital' is more than a certain figure (usually between 10 and 20 per cent). It will be appreciated that a 'cut-off rate' is a version of Test 2 in which a company with, say, a 15 per cent cut-off rate is saying 'If a project yields £15 we will not allocate more than £100 to it.' A cut-off rate is a statement of results and resources expressed as a ratio. In the same way 'productivity' is a statement of results and resources expressed as a ratio, as is 'efficiency'. These are all ratios of results (which we investigate in Test 1) compared with resources (which we investigate in Test 2). It is at this stage in the management process, Test 2, that managers will increasingly use the methods of project appraisal such as NPV, cost effectiveness, management ratios, etc.

Any alternatives that pass these two tests go on to Test 3.

Test 3. Is it in line with the organisation's ethics?
Having examined Trend J in considerable detail earlier and having emphasised the increasing importance that society attaches to an organisation's behaviour, it will come as no surprise to find here a test designed to eliminate any alternative that runs counter to an organisation's code of conduct towards its employees, the local community, customers, foreigners, the state, suppliers and so on. It is in Test 3, therefore, that such ideas as industrial espionage – which is undoubtedly one way for a company to boost profits – is questioned (and, one hopes, rejected). Or whether it is morally right for a government to sell armaments or whether the Church should raise funds by running lotteries, and so on. Organisations will omit Test 3 at some peril in the coming decade.

Test 4. Is the organisation especially well equipped to use it?
This test is designed to eliminate any alternative which calls for a skill that the organisation lacks. For example, suppose one

alternative is 'take on ten salesmen in the next two months'; this might have passed all the previous tests but in this test we ask whether the organisation is capable of taking on such a large number of new men, has it ever done so on such a scale before? Has it the facilities and skilled manpower to conduct all the interviews, select suitable candidates, etc.? Or another example, a government may set itself the task of reducing drug addiction and some of the alternative ways of doing this might be: conducting a massive propaganda campaign in schools; increasing the number of police drug squads; tightening up Customs searches; introducing more legislation, etc. When these alternatives reach Test 4, the decision-maker will want to consider how effective the school propaganda machine would be in carrying this message, how effective the police are in similar fields, how efficient the Customs officials are at this sort of search, and so on; the best method is likely to be the one that makes use of existing skills, knowledge and equipment.

History is full of examples of organisations choosing to tackle a task by a method that others have found enormously successful but which has failed in their hands because they lacked the skill to use it. One of the strengths of an organisation is an awareness of its own strengths and weaknesses.

Test 5. What trends or events might help or hinder its success?
This test is designed to make quite sure that the manager looks sufficiently far ahead – we have repeated *ad nauseam* that the time span of decisions will lengthen, and that forecasting the future is increasingly part of a manager's job.

If a manger has been given a task which must be completed by the end of the week he must look ahead to the end of the week to try to visualise what relevant events might occur within that time span. If the task refers to a period of ten years then the manager must look ahead ten years. Imagine, for example, that a manager has whittled down the alternatives to two: either to build one big factory in the middle of the country or to build two smaller factories, one in the south, one in the north. Now the question in Test 4 is, 'What might happen over the next, say, twenty years [the expected life of the factories] which would help or hinder these two alternatives?' One relevant trend, perhaps, is transport costs; if the manager forecasts that transport costs are going to rise faster than other costs then it would be better to build two factories. Another trend might be labour relations; if labour is going to be more difficult to control then, since labour relations are normally worse in a large factory than a small one, this trend would also favour having two smaller factories.

Where possible the manager should try to quantify his answer to all these test questions; needless to say it will not always be possible – if it was always possible managers could leave magagement entirely to the computer. It will seldom be possible to quantify the answers to Test 3, where we are concerned with ethics. Nor will it be easy to give figures in answer to this one, Test 5. However, there are a large number of techniques for forecasting the future which can be used to give figures with greater or lesser accuracy – market research, technological forecasting, mathematical models and various statistical methods.

We must not give the impression here or anywhere else that decisions must always be based on facts. Of course if one can get facts that is fine, but most important decisions have to be taken with at least one major fact unknown. (It is sometimes said that the amount of reliable information available is in inverse proportion to the importance of the decision.) When one does not have facts one has only opinions. Today even these can be quantified; imagine that one alternative open to a company is to increase the selling price of its product but, of course, the company would very much like to know by how much its sales volume would be affected. Few companies know the precise elasticity of demand for any product, so the decision to raise the price would have to be based on someone's hunch. A simple way to quantify this hunch is to ask several people, 'By how much would sales fall if we increased the price by £1?' But their replies would represent only one plot on a graph of price versus volume. If we now asked several more questions such as, 'By how much would sales decrease if we lowered the price by £1, £2, £3?' then we could get several points on the graph. Now we know, approximately, what shape an elasticity graph should have and if we also now have several points on it we may be able to draw quite an accurate line showing what these knowledgeable people think the elasticity of demand is (illustrated in Fig. 29). They may be quite wrong but it is on their opinion that this decision is going to be taken in any case whether we quantify it or not. The value of quantifying is, firstly, that it might improve the accuracy of their hunch, secondly it brings their otherwise hidden hunches into the open for discussion and thirdly we can insert their opinions into a

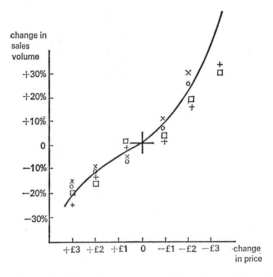

Fig 29: Graph of elasticity of demand resulting from asking four people their opinion about the effect of price changes on demand for a product

computer programme – an incredibly useful thing to be able to do, for it virtually means that we can get a computer to think like these experts. To be able to quantify opinions in this way opens up the possibility of actually using such advanced techniques at utility theory; it may also mean that one could quantify the political views of a statesman – if he would let us.

To return to Test 5; what we are doing here, of course, is to make sure that the manager does not adopt an alternative that is good enough in the current circumstances but which will be enfeebled by adverse trends during its lifetime. To give another example from the business world; a firm of mechanical

H   103 engineers, M. & Co., are looking for a company with which to merge and, let us imagine, there are two alternatives on their short list – one is a rival mechanical engineering firm and the other is an electronic engineering firm which, as it happens, supplies M. & Co. with the electronic gadgets that are an important part of their product. This test ensures that in choosing between these two, the management of M. & Co. take into account and give due weight to any trends over the next, say, twenty years, that might favour one or other alternative. One such trend, in this example, is the tendency for mechanical machines to contain progressively more electronic parts and progressively fewer moving parts (i.e. mechanical parts) and this would be a factor, perhaps an important one, in M. & Co.'s choice.

Test 6. What might go wrong and what would happen then?
This is another future-orientated question. It sometimes happens that one alternative passes all the previous tests with full honours but has the disadvantage that it is extremely risky. Test 6 is concerned therefore with the riskiness of each alternative and it is here that management techniques such as sensitivity tests, risk analysis, utility theory, pay-off tables, etc. are used.

Let us imagine that there are two alternative ways of providing a continental link, a bridge across the Channel or a tunnel under it. Let us further imagine that the tunnel passes all the other test questions better than the bridge. Now we come to Test 6: What might go wrong? The worst possible event in both cases would be a catastrophic structural failure and in the case of the tunnel this could result in a disaster of some magnitude, far worse than the bridge, and while it may not rule out the tunnel it does alter the balance between the two alternatives.

Let us illustrate Test 6 again. A company makes a profit of £10,000 a year but is searching for ways to improve this. They have eliminated all alternatives except two, one is to build a small factory and launch a new product into their local market, the other is to build a bigger factory and launch it nation-wide. The second alternative shows up the best in the first five tests but in Test 6 they calculate that they would lose £10,000 if the local launch failed and £100,000 if the bigger scheme failed.

Now it will be very clear that they must not, under any circumstances, adopt the bigger scheme – if it did fail, however unlikely this is, *if* it did, it would cripple or destroy the company – a similar example is illustrated in Fig. 30 which also demonstrates the Pay Off Table.

Test 6 then, is designed to ensure that managers think twice before they adopt an alternative which, however attractive in

Possible Events / Alternatives	Demand for the product reaches the forecast figure	Demand fails to materialise and the project is abandoned	Another competitor launches a similar product and we have to cut our selling price
Licence a product from a competitor and sell through our own retailers	£20,000	£10,000 loss	£20,000 loss
Build a new factory to make the product ourselves	£120,000	£190,000 loss	£80,000
Make the new product in our existing rather inefficient factory	£60,000	£30,000 loss	£20,000

Fig 30: A 'pay-off table' or 'outcome matrix'. In this example a company is examining various alternative ways (only three are shown) of adding a new product to its existing range. The figures (in net present values) show what effect various possible events (only three shown) might have on each alternative

other ways, nevertheless contains the seeds of disaster. But this test is intended not only as a disaster detector, although it can often be dramatically useful in this role, it is also intended to test the effect of errors in the forecasts made in Test 5 or anywhere else in the decision-making process. We have stated before that management is a future-orientated task, that it requires managers to make forecasts of what they think will happen over the time span of their decision, that nearly all forecasts are wrong, especially long-range ones, that managers must take account of these possible errors when they plan. This test is where he considers how sensitive an alternative is to errors in the forecast. For example, a company is considering whether to go ahead with a new factory costing £1 million. The calculations show that the return on capital* is 20 per cent (i.e. the profits will be £200,000 per annum). But this return is based on many forecasts: sales of the product being, say, 10,000 units, selling price £100 per unit, cost per unit £40, overheads £400,000, etc. Test 6 invites the managers to calculate how sensitive this 20 per cent return is to an error in any of these forecasts; what would the return be, for example, if they only sold 8,000 units, or 7,000 units at a selling price of £90? These are the sort of questions which the various techniques such as sensitivity tests, risk analysis are designed to answer, and which, especially in conjunction with the computer, will come into increasing use in the seventies.

Another very important by-product of Test 6 is the contingency plan. The ideal alternative is one that passes all the previous five tests and then, in Test 6, is shown to be 'robust', i.e. that one cannot think of anything that might happen in the future which would seriously affect the success of the alternative. Such things do exist; it is possible to devise a way of carrying out a task that is so cunningly contrived that whatever happens the plan will not be upset. But where this is not possible the plan obviously contains a flaw, as most of them do. Now Test 6 is designed to identify this flaw in advance and if, in spite of it, a certain alternative is still the best one to adopt then one should prepare a contingency plan to protect oneself against this flaw. For example, of all the known designs for car wheels the best is the pneumatic tyre. There is one event, however, which can happen and in that contingency it becomes a significantly worse alternative to, say, foam plastic. To guard against this flaw we carry a spare. It is our contingency plan – we plan a response to a predictable event that would turn our best alternative into second best.

* To keep the example simple we are not using DCF.

106

THE VALUE OF THE SIEVE

These tests play two crucial parts in the management process. The first, already described, is to act as a highly selective and efficient screen or sieve by which defective alternatives are rejected swiftly, leaving only a short list of useful alternatives which can then be further thinned down by successive passes through the Sieve. It may have been noticed that at each successive pass more and more detail would have to be added to each of the remaining alternatives. Where several alternatives are almost equally effective one can only select the best by inspecting them in increasing detail, so that by the time one has made the final selection it will already have become a fairly detailed plan. Planning is, in fact, the second function that these tests play. The act of planning *is* the act of eliminating alternatives: in describing these six tests we were describing the process known as 'planning'. So now we can go smoothly to Step 2d.*

STEP 2D. PREPARE ACTION PLAN

The words 'plan' and 'planning' have become so extensively used that we tend to forget their meaning and purpose. A 'plan' is a set of carefully considered directions for action. Thus an engineer's blueprint is his set of directions to the manufacturer to use rivets here not bolts, and to fix the cross-member here, not there. A plan of campaign is a set of instructions from a general to his officers that at 18.00 hours they will attack across the river here, not there. A manager's plan is a set of instructions

* Most of the books on planning seem to cover the steps that we call Step 2c and 2d; that is to say the planning literature seems to deal adequately with the way that a manager eliminates alternatives (2c) and with the methods of adding details and presenting the plan in convenient ways for subordinates to understand (2d). Some of the literature also deals with what we call Step 2a – deciding what resources to put into the planning effort. But one seldom sees any mention of Step 2b – making a list of alternatives. Where this is mentioned it is seldom discussed in detail and one searches in vain to find a description of how to generate, to force out, to extrude or extract by artificial means a long imaginative list of alternatives. Step 2b on which we place such emphasis could well turn out to have been the 'missing link' in management planning in the 1960s.

to a salesman, for example, showing when he should call on which customers and what he is to say to them. Notice two things about a plan, firstly it is a set of instructions to people, usually subordinates. In other words it is the vehicle which allows a manager to move from Step 1 to Step 3 in the management process; in Step 1 he receives his task, then in Step 2 he decides how to carry it out and when he has decided he draws up a plan, i.e. a formal or informal set of instructions to his subordinates.

Secondly a plan is a set of decisions that are made *before* actions have to be taken. In other words a plan is a statement of intention about future actions, it is the result of making up one's mind before one has to. Thus the engineer in his blueprint says to the manufacturer, 'Don't keep coming to me when you have completed one thing to ask what to do next. I will tell you in advance, by means of this blueprint, everything you need to know'. In the same way a manager says to his salesmen, 'Don't keep ringing me up to ask which customers to visit next. I will tell you now, by means of this plan'.

A plan, then, is 'a set of carefully considered directions for future action'. It is one way of giving instructions to subordinates; another way is to wait until the last moment, when the subordinate is just about to take action, and then decide what instruction to give. Both methods are legitimate but the 1970s will see a further decline in the number of managers adopting the second method.

'Planning' is the process one goes through in order to draw up a plan. We said above that a plan is a set of decisions made before action is taken; we have also said that a decision is the making of a choice between alternatives, planning is therefore the act of choosing between alternatives before action has to be taken. When an engineer is working on his blueprint, he is choosing between alternatives – rivets, not bolts or screws, for example. When the manager is planning a salesman's route he is choosing between sending him to customer A before B or B before A, etc. Thus a detailed plan is one where a manager has not only eliminated alternatives on a broad scale but has gone on to eliminate alternatives of detail; for example a manager may not only decide where to build a new factory but may also decide its layout, where the works canteen is to be sited, the layout of the rooms in the canteen, the arrangement of the tables, right down to the design of the teaspoons.

It is not proposed to discuss the methodology of planning here; much of it was well known to managers in the 1960s and will certainly be known to them in the 1970s when such techniques as corporate planning, decision trees, network analysis, resource allocation, programme budgets, mathematical programming and so on will come into widespread use. All it is necessary to do here is to note that an action-plan is the end-product of Step 2, and to remember that a plan is a set of instructions to subordinates. In Step 2c the manager selects the best way to carry out his task and in Step 2d he adds what detail he thinks is necessary to ensure that his subordinates do not misunderstand what he wants each of them to do.

THE CHANGING NATURE OF STEP 2

We have already drawn attention to the centuries-old trend of the expansion of Step 2. If we could go back in time we would see that managers did not give much time to planning and decision-making; instead they barked out some orders to obedient subordinates. If we could go forward in time we would see the other end of the same trend – managers thinking over each instruction in great depth before giving orders. The time to decide on an action will grow, the time to take action may shrink.

Not only is Step 2 expanding *in toto*, however, but the length of each sub-stage is changing in such a way as to alter the whole character of Step 2 (with, as we will see in later chapters, extraordinary consequential changes in the character of organisations and even in the personality requirements of managers themselves). Perhaps the best way to describe this transformation of Step 2 is to present a series of diagrams with a running commentary. Let us start with a reproduction of Fig. 27 which illustrates the way in which Step 2 as a whole has expanded.

Now let us concentrate on Step 2 itself and draw a diagram to show its internal structure as it would have appeared at any time over the past few centuries up to a decade or two ago.

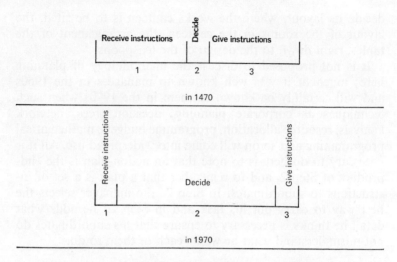

Fig 27: Changes in the time and importance of Steps 1, 2 and 3

This shows the composition of Step 2 as three sub-steps in, say, 1750 with exactly the same three sub-steps in 1950; the only difference being that all three sub-steps took longer to do in 1950 than in 1750; the proportion of the total time into which the three sub-steps were divided did not change. But about two

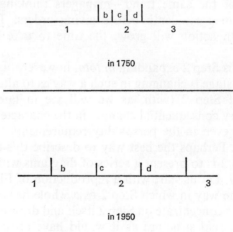

Fig 31: Expansion of Step 2

decades ago, during the 1950s and 1960s, managers realised that the great expansion of Step 2 was absorbing so much of their resources that it would be necessary to add a small sub-step, which we call Step 2a, in which to consider what resources they were justified in allocating to each decision. Fig. 32 shows the position in say, 1960.

Fig 32: Step 2 in 1960 showing some further expansion of b,c,d – and the appearance of a

Towards the end of the 1960s managers began to realise that it was no longer sufficient to take great care in detailing a plan if the plan itself was a selection from only two or three alternatives; it was, in other words, not sensible to spend a lot of time and resources in planning the layout of a new factory unless one was quite sure that a new factory was what was needed rather than another alternative which may not have been considered. It was in the 1960s that techniques for generating a longer list of alternatives first emerged – brainstorming, simulation, think tanks, wild men, and so on. Step 2b had started its explosion. Concurrently so did Step 2c for it was also in the 1960s that methods of alternative project appraisal began to be used. By 1970, therefore, Step 2 as a whole continued to expand as a result of the expansion of Steps 2b and 2c. Fig. 33 shows this –

Fig 33: Continued expansion with b and c growing rapidly

note that neither Step 2a nor 2d had expanded, only 2b and 2c.

The prediction being made now is that during the 1970s Step 2a will expand slightly, i.e. slightly more time will have to be spent deciding what resources to put into planning and decision-making. Step 2b will expand enormously as managers come to realise the importance of a more creative and positive approach to their tasks (we said we could call it the Positive Mode of Management). Step 2c will have to expand to provide the time

111

necessary to evaluate the greater number of alternatives. But Step 2d may contract – that is to say, managers may spend *less* time preparing detailed action plans (i.e. detailed sets of instructions to subordinates) in accordance with the principle of setting expansive targets to subordinates which we discussed in Chapter 6 and will return to in Chapters 8 and 10. So by 1980 Step 2 will look more like Fig. 34.

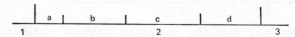

Fig 34: Step 2 in 1980 showing continued expansion with rapid increase of b and, to a lesser extent, a and c; *reduction* in d

It is interesting to note, incidentally, that had we been designing a management system for the 1950s (or MS 50) it would, while still retaining the basic essentials of MS 0 of course, have looked very different to a system for the 1970s especially at Step 2 (and, as we see in Chapter 10 especially in the hierarchy, too).

We must now summarise this chapter by recording the major conclusions which we must build into MS 70;

Conclusion 2.1. Nearly all the changes that will take place in the manager's environment over the next decade suggest and confirm that Step 2 will take longer and be more difficult and demand more resources.

Conclusion 2.2. It will no longer be possible to describe Step 2 as 'decide how to carry out a task' because this implies that a manager will still be able to make a decision in one simple mental jump, as he used to decades ago. In the 1970s he will have to follow a rigorous decision-making procedure which can be described in four distinct sub-steps, which we call Step 2, a,b,c,d.

Conclusion 2.3. In Step 2a the manager must consider what resources he is justified in committing to each decision and how long he may take before making up his mind. In effect Step 2a implies that he should not try to select the best alternative but only the one that convinces him that it is not worth searching for a better one.

Conclusion 2.4. In Step 2b the manager will conduct a positive and imaginative search for alternative ways of carrying out his task. Several techniques already exist to supplement and stimulate creativity – a quality that will be highly prized in managers during the 1970s when Step 2b will dominate decision taking.

Conclusion 2.5. There is a prima facie case for accusing a manager of bad management if he has only considered one or two alternatives for an important task. If lack of time precluded the examination he could then be accused of lack of foresight.

Conclusion 2.6. In Step 2b managers will gather ideas from an increasing range of people, especially their subordinates, with whom they will be able to communicate more readily. Senior managers in larger organisations will also increasingly seek ideas from experts, specialists, specialist publications and data banks, often on an international scale.

Conclusion 2.7. In Step 2c managers will use an increasing number of management techniques to select the best alternative. Systematic procedures for evaluation, such as the Sieve, will come into widespread use and there will be a marked increase in the use of computers.

Conclusion 2.8. Ethical considerations will become important criteria in the selection of alternatives.

Conclusion 2.9. There will be a marked increase in the use of methods of forecasting at Step 2b and 2c, accompanied by an increased use of techniques for evaluating risk in Step 2c in recognition of the error inherent in all forecasts.

Conclusion 2.10. There may be a decline in the volume of detailed planning that each manager will do at Step 2d but there will be an extension of the time horizon of most plans.

Conclusion 2.11. 'Planning' is the process of eliminating alternatives before action becomes necessary.

Conclusion 2.12. A 'Plan' is a set of instructions for future action by subordinates.

Conclusion 2.13. Step 2d consists of continuing to eliminate alternatives in progressively greater detail until the plan so defines and delineates the future actions of subordinates that they are unlikely to misunderstand their instructions.

Chapter 8

Step 3 in the 1970s

This chapter is concerned with that step in the management process by which a manager gives instructions to his subordinates – Step 3, 'give instructions'. It is obvious that the act of giving instructions is complementary to Step 1 where a manager receives instructions from his boss; anything said in Chapter 6 about receiving instructions could be said here in Chapter 8 about giving them – and vice versa – for we are discussing two sides of the same coin. In a very real sense, therefore, this chapter is a continuation of Chaper 6. However, it will be recalled that the management process has to take place in sequence and some of the remarks to be made now about Step 3 could not have been made until we had considered Step 2 which in its turn could not have been considered until certain aspects of Step 1 had been discussed in Chapter 6.

Let us first ask what exactly is the role of an instruction in management? It will be recalled that organisations achieve their purpose by getting a group of people to work together; each man is doing something to help his boss to carry out his task who is doing this to help his boss carry out his task – and so on in what we called a hierarchy of tasks, linked to each other by the principle of agreed seniority. We also introduced the very important idea of 'slack' in an organisation, by which we meant that there was always someone in any organisation who was not doing exactly what was required by his boss. In very slack organisations there will be many such people carrying out tasks that are to some extent irrelevant to the purpose of that organisation; in a highly disciplined organisation (such as those facing an emergency) there will be very few. The role of an instruction is to ensure that subordinates do what is required of them by their boss. Instructions are the nuts and bolts which hold the members of an organisation together; if these joints are loose the organisation will rattle. Let us imagine an organisation in which there is no slack at all, where everyone is doing exactly and precisely what his boss demands; what features would instructions have to have to achieve this? Firstly each boss would have to define his subordinate's task in great detail to ensure that there were no misunderstandings between them. But each boss would also have to tell his subordinates exactly what resources they could use and exactly how to use them. He would also have to keep his eye on them at frequent intervals or even continuously. Finally, he would have to warn them that if he caught them doing something that was not in exact accordance with their instructions he would punish them severely. In this way a boss could reasonably expect his subordinates to do exactly what he wanted them to do. It is interesting to note that 'give instructions' is really quite a complex act which far exceeds merely stating the task – there are four other constituents as well. In addition to 'defining the task' there are: state the resources, describe how the resources are to be used, say when a check on progress is to be made and state rewards or punishments. To be truly definitive, then, an instruction must contain no less than five parts, the omission of any of which could result in slack being introduced into the organisation. Most of the rest of this chapter is concerned with how managers will handle these five parts of an instruction in the 1970s. One thing is certain about management in the 1970s, and that is that few managers will be able to give instructions in the disciplined form we illustrated above – too many of the trends discussed in Chapter 5 point away from this dictatorial style of management – and in that case we must expect an increase in the amount of slack in organisations unless we can find some other way of avoiding it.

The layout of this chapter is as follows: firstly we will briefly restate how an instruction and its five consitutent parts fits in to the whole management system, then we will discuss which of the trends will affect Step 3 in the 1970s, finally we will discuss how each of the five parts of an instruction must be modified so as to fit the conditions of the next decade – remembering all the time that the further we depart from the highly disciplined

116

form of instruction above the more slack we may introduce into an organisation's management.

THE ROLE OF STEP 3 IN MANAGEMENT

Let us start at the beginning again: an organisation consists of 'a group of people working together towards a common purpose'. That purpose is to generate some specific benefit for a specific body of people which we have called the intended beneficiaries and only they, or their representatives, can say what benefit they expect from the organisation and what amount of it they would accept as being satisfactory. We gave some examples in Chapter 6: shareholders in a company expect a satisfactory return on their capital; the members of a golf club expect satisfactory golfing facilities; the suffering expect satisfactory aid from the Red Cross, etc. Furthermore, all these beneficiaries, or their representatives, can say what 'satisfactory' means, or, more probably, can say what 'unsatisfactory' means. Shareholders in British companies would consider a return of less than 10 per cent on their money rather unsatisfactory; victims of a flood disaster in Britain would consider it highly unsatisfactory if relief was not at hand within twenty-four hours. And so on. Having made up their minds about this fundamental purpose of their organisation the intended beneficiaries then appoint a suitable chief executive (managing director, headmaster, prime minister, etc.) and hand to him the task (usually a continuing task rather than a project task) of achieving this purpose. Sometimes they will give him a completely free hand to decide for himself how to achieve it, sometimes they will lay down broad policies for him to follow; once he accepts this task from them the management process begins. It starts when he, the chief executive, or most senior manager, takes his Step 1, 'agree to achieve a well-defined verifiable result' and then the management process continues down the hierarchy in a cascade of decisions handed from one level to another branching and rebranching as it goes, in progressively greater detail, down to the operators. We have seen how each manager, including the chief executive, having taken Step 1 must pause to think how to carry out the task he has accepted, must consider as many

117

alternatives as is sensible, evaluate them, select the best and then, in Step 2d, add sufficient detail to his decision to enable him to give unequivocal instructions to his subordinates. Now, unless these instructions contain all five elements they will not be unequivocal, they will be ambiguous, open to misinterpretation and slack will enter the system; if that happens there is a danger that the 'group of people' that make up the organisation will no longer be 'working together towards a common purpose' and the organisation may fail.

The five elements of an instruction are:

Step 3a: Define the task. i.e. the boss must clearly describe, preferably with figures, exactly what result he wishes his subordinate to achieve and by when.

Step 3b: Allocate resources. i.e. the boss must tell his subordinate what resources he can use in achieving the above results.

Step 3c: Describe the method. The boss must explain how the resources are to be used and how they are not to be used.

Step 3d: State checkpoints. i.e. the boss must tell the subordinate when he, the boss, intends to check the subordinate's result or progress towards it.

Step 3e: Rewards and penalties. i.e. the boss will tell the subordinate what will happen to him if he fails and if he succeeds.

These, then, are the five essential elements of any instruction, but, in the 1970s, some will become pre-eminent, others will atrophy almost to vanishing point. These changes of emphasis in the 'give instructions' step will result in a slow fundamental change in the whole atmosphere of the human relationship between managers and managed during the 1970s, a change that will be forced upon us by five of the fifteen trends that we described in Chapter 5.

118

Let us start with Trend B which suggests that there will be a further and rapid expansion in the existing methods of communication (telephone, walkie-talkie, television, etc.); obviously this will enable managers to transmit detailed instructions to their subordinates as to the task, the resources and the method to be used, and will also allow them to make frequent or even continuous checks on their subordinate's progress. If this were the only trend affecting Step 3 it is clear that it could be harnessed to reduce the amount of slack – for a manager to be in constant touch with his subordinates wherever they may be, perhaps even watching them at work by television, would indeed provide a powerful tool for closer supervision and tighter control. Any manager who uses communication in this way in the 1970s will, however, be heading for trouble; for he must not ignore Trend M, the growing revolt against authority, especially against the needless or inept or officious use of authority. This trend is evident everywhere at every level of every organisation – it is not limited to students, dissident minorities, hippies or Maoist revolutionaries. It has its roots in Trend E, the rising standard of education, for if education is intended to do anything it is to instil a spirit of enquiry and a sense of self-sufficiency in the student – qualities which are the opposite of those required of an obedient subordinate. As suggested in an earlier chapter this is where we meet one of the crucial conflicts of management; the need to issue strict and detailed instructions to reduce slack to a minimum to improve the efficiency of an organisation on the one hand, and on the other, to issue wide and imaginative instructions to encourage a subordinate's initiative. This is the key dilemma which must be tackled in this chapter.

Two other trends are relevant. The first is quantification (Trend K); we discussed in Chapter 6 how this was affecting the giving and receiving of instructions. Briefly, what we suggested was that quantification would help managers to specify tasks and resources in more detail and with less ambiguity. The other is Trend N, the rising standard of living all over the world which has the effect of eroding the efficacy of penalties and rewards which managers used to use as a powerful means of reducing slack. In other words, it reduces their value as instruments of motivation and so motivation becomes another constituent of the problem for the manager in the 1970s, and certainly one that the designers of MS 70 must tackle.

We said earlier that a manager was the meat in a sandwich of human relationships. When he gives or receives an instruction he makes contact with the people above and below him, and this is where most human conflicts arise – but just consider the position outlined above; two of the five trends are working powerfully towards the setting of more detailed targets and tighter control while three trends are pushing in the opposite direction. On the one hand improved communications and quantification are placing the power of almost continuous detailed supervision of subordinates into the hands of the manager; on the other, the insistent desire of subordinates to use their initiative and their growing freedom from the effects of either penalty or reward. If one side wins this battle the result will be a highly efficient organisation run by Big Brother. If the other side wins the result will be an unmanageable organisation which would collapse into anarchy. In the rest of this chapter we will be searching for a third solution which we can incorporate into MS 70.

Briefly, the solution offered is this: the whole of Step 3 will be downgraded to little more than a formal tailpiece of the all-important Step 2. But within Step 3 each of the five parts of an instruction will themselves undergo considerable change, and in such a way that, while the scope for initiative will be greatly widened, the amount of slack may increase only imperceptibly. How this will be achieved is described below where we discuss what changes are necessary to each of the five parts in the 1970s.

STEP 3A. 'DEFINING THE TASK' IN THE 1970s

Most of what could be said in this section on Step 3a has already been said in Chapter 6 so let us merely briefly repeat the main points. Firstly, any task that is simple and quickly carried out can be given to a subordinate by his manager with little previous thought or planning as when, for example a surgeon says 'scalpel' and all his assistant need do is hand him a scalpel, or when a foreman says to a workman 'take this box to the stores'. However, one of the trends we have mentioned (Trend E) suggests that jobs that are simple or repetitive are likely to be fewer as educational standards rise and this suggests that fewer occasions will occur when this sort of instant decision-making will be taken well before action is required. In other words, there will be more and more planning. Planning, it will be recalled, is the process of eliminating alternatives prior to action, and a plan is a set of instructions to subordinates showing them the part they are to play in carrying out their boss' task. What will happen, then, is that an instruction to subordinates will tend to become the tailpiece of a decision. Whereas the boss used to bark out an order to a subordinate – who knew nothing of the reasoning that lay behind this order – in the 1970s the trend will be towards bringing the subordinate into decision-making and planning, and then giving the instruction in the form; 'O.K. then. That's the plan on which we all agree. Will you now go and carry out your part of it'. So Step 3a, 'defining the task' will virtually merge with Step 2d, 'prepare action plan' rather than be rigorously separate and distinct as it was in the past. It is interesting to note that this merger comes about not only because modern subordinates like to know why they are being given a particular task to do but also because tasks are becoming more complex and, to avoid errors, they just *have* to know the logic that lies behind them.

Another conclusion we reached in Chapter 6 was that managers would have to try to quantify the tasks they handed down to their subordinates – 'Rates and Dates' was the slogan we coined for this powerful tool in the fight against organisational slack. We emphasised also that a task should be described by reference to the *results* the subordinate was to achieve, not by telling him what to do. We mentioned the different types of task, continuing and project, and suggested that a different approach should be used to set targets for each. We emphasised the difference between expansive and constricting targets. We also emphasised that the need to pay more attention to defining the task was nowhere more important and nowhere more neglected than at the level of the chief executive; if we get that task wrong, many of the tasks set to the other managers in the organisation will be wrong too. Unfortunately, it is patently true that only a very few organisations have properly briefed their chief executive, mainly because of the widespread misconception that the chief executive is the boss of any organisation and decides his own task. He is not; the beneficiaries are and this fact should be clearly demonstrated by always showing the organisation structure as an hourglass, not as a pyramid. Nor is it sufficiently realised that the task of the chief executive is identical to the very purpose for which the organisation exists.

One further point; when discussing expansive targets in Chapter 6 we examined the book salesman George Beckworth's target sheet and discovered that many of the target figures he was given were superfluous. There was only one figure that really mattered – sales turnover – all the others merely constricted his approach to the main task. Now this error is common; there is a danger that it will become more common as communications become better, for this will enable bosses to give more detail more often to their subordinates. This is a misuse of communications – their true value lies elsewhere in the management process as we will see later.

Now let us end this section by making a statement of profound importance. It is this: provided that these rules, summarised below, are followed it is almost impossible for a misunderstanding to occur between boss and subordinate over the task being handed down; it is also therefore inexcusable for slack to occur in an organisation due to subordinates not understanding what results they are expected to achieve. The rules are as follows:

(a) It is *essential* that the chief executive knows who the intended beneficiaries are, what is the nature of the benefit they expect and in what volume.

(b) It is *essential* to state all tasks (including the chief executive's) in terms of results to be achieved.

(c) It is *essential* to distinguish between continuing and project tasks. Continuing tasks (e.g. reducing the crime rate, improving productivity, achieving economic growth)

122

must have targets set in terms of rates per annum or per month, etc. Project tasks (build a ship, finish that report, recruit ten salesmen) must have target dates by which the project is to be completed.

(d) It is *essential* that the results to be achieved are verifiable (even if they cannot be verified for many years ahead) and it is *desirable* to quantify them – and this can be done in the great proportion of managerial tasks.

(e) It is *essential* to make clear whether the level of achievement being set as a target is intended as a minimum result that must be exceeded, a satisfactory one or as a challenge. It is therefore *desirable* to set three target levels for all tasks. The level that is often most easily identifiable is the minimum level, the one that represents failure ('Failure Plus').

(f) It is *desirable* to set an expansive target. This usually means that very few figures need to be used to identify the task – often just one figure will do. It is undesirable to use communication systems to overspecify a task.

(g) As simple repetitive tasks decline it will become more essential to decide a subordinate's task only after careful thought. Their instructions will emerge from plans rather than from decisions made off-the-cuff.

STEP 3B. 'ALLOCATING RESOURCES' IN THE 1970S

It is obvious that it is inadequate merely to tell a subordinate to achieve a certain result. One must also tell him what resources he may employ or consume in achieving the result; the word 'efficiency' means simply the ratio of resources used compared with the result achieved, and efficiency is likely to be no less important in the 1970s than at any other time. No, there will be no changes there; where there will be a change over the next decade is in the way in which resources are stated because, as we mentioned in Chapter 6, subordinates will increasingly resent being told how to do their jobs. The implication is that the boss will have to clarify his own mind more carefully before telling a subordinate what resources he may use, and he will be guilty of stultifying a subordinate's initiative if he needlessly overspecifies these resources. A manager is always entitled to state the *total* resources available for a task but he is not always entitled to set them out in detail – if he does he may constrict the number of alternative ways in which the subordinate may tackle the task. Let us again remind ourselves of the case of George Beckworth who was told not to spend more than £1,200 on hotels, £500 on his car, £300 on miscellaneous items when, in fact, his employers really only required that he should not spend more than £2,000 in total. As a general rule, and it is valid for nearly every task ever likely to be set to a subordinate in any organisation, one can say that resources can be allocated by simply giving one figure in terms of money. There is one major exception to this rule, namely when any resource cannot be stated in terms of money as when, for example, an officer is told to capture an enemy position but to abandon the attack if he loses more than five men. Apart from such occasions the rule is sufficiently general for one to be justified in looking closely at senior managers who do not obey it, for it may mean that they are not yet attuned to this new atmosphere in management. However, as one moves down the hierarchy in any organisation one will find progressively more managers stating the resources in terms other than money simply because their subordinates lack the knowledge and skill to cost resources in money terms. Nevertheless, during the 1970s more managers at all levels will learn to make these calculations; it is well that they should for the only way that they can evaluate alternative methods of tackling their tasks is by stating each alternative in terms of a common denominator – money – and this is true of all organisations, not just companies.*

Once again we see that managers must take more thought before giving instructions to subordinates; it is not going to be good enough in the 1970s for a manager to allocate resources to his subordinates until he has sorted out in his mind what it is he really wants them to do and what limits on what resources really matter. Are 'establishment levels' ever necessary? Is it ever necessary to allocate a certain number of paper-clips to each typist as is still done in some offices? Is it necessary for the national government to tell every parish and village how many

* One has to state resources in terms of money if one is to use the very useful 'cost/effective' technique for example.

street lamps they must have? What really matters, surely, is the total *overall* cost of achieving a given result; if this is so, then it makes sense to allocate an overall sum only and leave it to the subordinates to decide how they should spend it. As the 1970s proceed, more subordinates will learn how to make their own resource allocation decisions; more will resent it if they are not given the opportunity to do so.

We must now draw attention to an apparent anomaly. In this chapter we have repeatedly said that managers must do more planning before giving instructions to subordinates and yet in Chapter 7 we said 'There may be a decline in the detailed planning that each manager will do' (Conclusion 2.10, page 113). How can these two statements be reconciled? Well, like this; imagine a manager in 1970 who spends five hours a week planning (remember, planning means selecting the best way of carrying out a job), the rest of his time is spent receiving instructions from his boss, checking results, acting as an operator and giving instructions to his subordinates. Let us imagine that he gives 100 instructions of which 30 are the result of his planning and 70 are simple off-the-cuff decisions. By 1980 he may spend fifteen hours a week planning but he will now give, say, 60 instructions of which 40 are the result of planning and only 20 off-the-cuff.* Notice these points: he will give fewer instructions overall; far fewer simple off-the-cuff decisions; rather more planned decisions; each of these planned decisions takes more planning time on average. Why? Because each instruction he gives in 1980 will be for tasks that are more complex and have longer time spans than in 1970 and so require more thought. That explains why there will be more planning, but what about that 'decline in detailed planning?' The key word is 'detailed' of course. Managers will do more planning because they will consider more alternatives, use more care in evaluating them, consult more people, etc., but they will do less *detailed* planning because they will leave the details to their subordinates. They will do enough planning to allow them to state clearly what results they want subordinates to achieve and what overall resources can be allocated to each task, and they will

* Of course, these figures are chosen quite arbitrarily merely to illustrate the trends.

125

take a great deal of time and trouble over this; but that is where they will stop, they will leave the detailed allocation of resources and how they are to be used to be decided by their subordinates.

STEP 3C: 'DESCRIBING THE METHOD' IN THE 1970S

The preceding paragraph will have set the tone for this section; there will be a trend in the 1970s for Step 3c to decline in importance just as Step 3b will. In other words, as far as possible, managers in the 1970s will refrain from telling a subordinate how to carry out his task and how to use the resources allocated to it. It is true that improved communications will allow the manager to supervise his subordinates more closely – even continuously – and to be able constantly to correct him as he goes about his task. To do so is to misuse communications, and it will infuriate his subordinates.

Unfortunately it is beginning to look as though we are reaching some very dangerous conclusions in this chapter. Step 3a was all right because there we suggested that managers would have to go to great lengths to tighten up the way they defined the tasks for their subordinates and this would certainly reduce slack in the organisation. But now we are saying that Step 3b and 3c will almost disappear, that subordinates will be left to tackle their tasks any way they like – goodness knows what they might get up to and what a mess they might make; the amount of slack in the hierarchy will rise to the point of anarchy, surely? Let us be quite honest: yes, there is that danger! It is not unknown for managers to put too much trust in the ability of a subordinate; it has happened before and it will again. Part of the skill of managing lies in judging how far to trust each subordinate, and therefore how far to accept the proposals being made in this chapter. But, during the 1970s subordinates will demand more and more insistently that they are given more rein to their own initiative. How, then, are we to guard against the undoubted dangers that this will create? Let us mention six powerful safeguards.

Firstly, remember that although we are suggesting that managers should refrain from telling subordinates how to tackle a task, we also suggest that managers should take enormous pains to define the task in clear unequivocal, verifiable terms. That in itself is a new and potent measure. Secondly we are going to suggest (below and in Chapter 9) that more care must be taken in checking a subordinate's progress – so here is a second fence we can erect to contain a subordinate within reasonable bounds. Thirdly, we can train our subordinates, surely? Not only to do his present job better today but also to undertake tasks which his manager may wish to delegate to him in future. Nor is that the limit to training (most organisations already train their employees in this way), it should also cover the whole decision-making process; if managers are going to have to delegate more decisions to subordinates – and they are going to – then subordinates must be taught how to take decisions. This includes the consideration of alternatives, evaluation of risk, costing alternatives, allocating resources and so on. Fourthly, managers can take more care not to appoint subordinates who are not suitable for the job – there are many techniques available today for selection (aptitude tests, intelligence tests, even personality tests, etc.) Fifthly, we must not forget that managers are fully entitled to ask a subordinate how he intends to carry out his task and the manager can always tell the subordinate to think again. In other words, managers in the past would tell a subordinate what to do and how to do it whereas in the 1970s the trend will be to tell the subordinate what to do and ask *him* how he intends to do it. Given all these constraints surely it should be possible for a boss to prevent any subordinate from making too big a mess of things? There is one other approach to the problem; it is called Venture Management. Here the boss gives the subordinate a task and some resources and leaves the rest to the subordinate – he makes no attempt at all to control him and the subordinate sinks or swims – and in many cases it is abundantly clear which has happened! The most extreme form of venture management is when a company selects one of its senior and trusted executives, hands him a cheque and says, 'Go and form a company in any field of business you like – all we want is a dividend each year and, eventually, our money back. Let us know how you are getting on.' This is taking the advice in this chapter to its logical conclusion!

127

We can conclude, then, that Step 3c – 'describe the method' – will decline, perhaps vanish, in the 1970s. There is, however, one aspect of Step 3c that will increase. We have said that managers must refrain from telling subordinates how to carry out their tasks but, in contrast, they must not refrain from telling them how not to. Let us recall Trend J from Chapter 5 in which we suggested that society is becoming increasingly resentful of anti-social or unethical behaviour on the part of any organisation. Managers must ensure, therefore, that their subordinates do not adopt unethical or anti-social methods in carrying out their tasks. We have criticised the targets given to George Beckworth on the grounds that he was given too many figures, his task and the resources were seriously over-specified and constricting. But we must also criticise that document because it omitted to tell him not to use unethical methods of selling – of which there are many – some of which Mr Beckworth might be sorely tempted to use.* Managers just cannot afford to omit ethical constraints when giving instructions and Step 3c is the place for them.

STEP 3D. 'STATING CHECKPOINTS' IN THE 1970s

We will devote the whole of the next chapter to 'checking results' and will not therefore say very much here. Let us remind ourselves, however, that when a boss 'gives instructions' to a subordinate he does not tell him only one thing but five: (a) the task itself, (b) the resources, (c) the method, (d) when the boss intends to check the subordinate's progress, and (e) penalties and rewards. Step 3d – check – is one of the few steps that will demand more attention in the 1970s just as Step 3a will (but unlike Steps 3b, c, and e). All we need say here is that the manager who fails to establish the earliest sensible moment at which to check his subordinate's progress is guilty of mismanagement – as we shall see in the next chapter, however, this is not as simple as it sounds.

---

* In fact, of course, George Beckworth works for a highly respectable firm; he is fully aware of this and does not really need reminding about it. Not every employee is quite so sure!

One of the trends mentioned in Chapter 5 was Trend N which drew attention to the erosion of the efficacy of material rewards and penalties (as a result of rising standards of living, full employment, etc.). In this chapter, where we are concerned mainly with the problem of slack, this trend is clearly of some importance – rewards and penalties have for centuries been powerful methods of making subordinates do what they are told. While it is certainly true that these have been eroded we have not reached the stage yet when managers can ignore them – it is doubtful if they will ever completely disappear as a means of motivation. It would indeed be a strange and far-off society where a salesman was not encouraged by the chance of winning a £1,000 competition for increasing sales, or where a factory manager failed to try to improve costs even though he knew it meant the sack if he does not. Let us now make some predictions for the 1970s on the topic of material rewards and penalties: (1) Penalties will decline much more quickly than rewards as a means of motivation. (2) Minor penalties will disappear rapidly leaving only a few major penalties such as dismissal, demotion and, for example, suspension without pay for several weeks. (3) Minor rewards will decline (e.g. a weekly bonus or reward equal to a few percent of a week's pay or an annual bonus of a few percent of a year's pay). (4) There will be a marked increase in the size of bonuses and rewards (e.g. £1,000, a holiday abroad, double promotion, etc.). In other words, taking (3) and (4) together, managers will not try to motivate their subordinates with petty rewards; when they are given a bonus at all it will be a big one. (5) The rewards for real excellence in management will be enormous, just as it is already in sport, entertainment, etc. (6) The swing away from petty rewards will be accelerated by two other trends: firstly, the cost of making the calculations to arrive at the bonus figure will begin to exceed the value of the award itself; secondly the increasing time-span of tasks will delay the payment of a bonus on it, and the further away an incentive is from the recipient the larger it has to be. Finally (7), rewards and penalties however large, will decline in importance relative to other forms

129

of motivation or, to put it another way, the 1970s will see rewards and penalties supplemented by many other forms of motivation.

Some of these new forms of motivation began to appear in the 1950s, methods of joint consultation became firmly established in the form of Works Councils, Joint Industrial Councils, Canteen Committees and so on. Then, in the 1960s we heard the cry for participation and, a little later, the phrase 'job enrichment'. Each of these concepts – joint consultation, participation, job enrichment – is a valuable motivator and all of them point in roughly the same direction; however, each represents only a part of the movement towards new forms of motivation that will come into use over the next few decades. Underlying this movement is the idea that employees should be treated as thinking, sensible adults, capable of contributing more to the organisation than they have so far been asked to contribute, leading freer and fuller lives at work, enjoying what they do, being treated more as equals than menials. It is difficult to coin a phrase that adequately reflects all these ideals but perhaps 'wider discretion' is as close as we can get. We give below more than a dozen ways in which the principle of wider discretion can be used to motivate employees.

We must utter one word of warning: in Chapter 5 we drew attention to Trend A which suggests that all the trends that underlie the design of MS 70 are taking place all over the world and, therefore, that no manager would be immune from them. But we were careful to point out that not every nation was starting from the same baseline nor following these trends all at the same rate; it follows that not all managers will be able to adopt the principles embodied in MS 70 at the same rate. This is particularly so with the principle of wider discretion where, no doubt, the management of a think tank in California (where all the employees are very highly educated) will already have adopted every one of the ideas listed below; but on the other hand the manager of a copper mine in an undeveloped region of Africa will have adopted none of them – and will need to think twice before he does. Here, then, is a list of changes that managers can make in the way they manage people; each is intended to represent one step towards the conditions of work in which

130

employees can contribute more to the organisation for which they work and, equally important, towards conditions in which the manager can help his subordinates to lead a more satisfying working life. Most organisations will already have adopted a few of these ideas; by the end of the decade many organisations will have adopted most of them.

THE MOVEMENT TOWARDS WIDER DISCRETION FOR EMPLOYEES

Simple, repetitive tasks

During the 1970s there will continue to be a rapid decline in the number of people willing to carry out simple repetitive tasks such as packing eggs or spot welding on a production line. This means that the cost of getting human beings to do this work will rise, so that this type of job will either have to be automated or will be eliminated by process redesign; many of these jobs can readily be done by a machine just because they are simple and repetitive. This is such an obvious and widespread trend throughout the world that one would have thought that all managers would already have accepted it as a fact; some of them still believe, however, that it does not apply to women who, the story goes, are much happier performing mindless tasks so long as conditions of work allow them to chat about their domestic affairs at the same time. While this is probably quite correct for the older generation, a much higher proportion in each succeeding generation will follow the trend. (If they do not it presumably means the money spent on their education has been wasted!) Managers who do accept the trend will have to decide how rapidly it will be necessary for these simple jobs to be eliminated; it is hard to believe that the trend is anywhere running at less than 10 per cent per annum so a manager who is responsible for ten people doing repetitive jobs will have to plan to cut this to less than four within a decade.

This trend away from simple jobs is interesting because it reverses the widely practised aim of simplifying jobs that started with the introduction of method study well before World War II. Method study is still valid, of course, but the

131

economies that were to be found by allocating each human operator a single repetitive task are no longer available.

Where a repetitive job cannot yet be automated or eliminated there are other solutions – see Job Enrichment, Group Work and Increased Variety below.

Menial tasks

By 'menial' we mean those performing minor services for other people such as lavatory attendant, porter, domestic cleaners. Such jobs are not necessarily dirty or repetitive but owe their growing unpopularity to social attitudes only – people who perform these tasks are looked upon as being rather low down the social scale. It is generally predicted that this type of job will also rapidly be eliminated, mechanised or automated and this is probable However, another view is tentatively suggested here. It will be noted that these jobs are not necessarily dirty or repetitive – their main stigma is society's low estimation of them; now it is conceivable that society will become more tolerant towards them over the next decade, and if society no longer treats such people as menials the unpopularity of these jobs may be reversed. Such a trend is fairly evident in domestic service, for example. While employers who treat their servants as menials find it hard to retain their services, those who treat them with some respect enjoy an easy and effective relationship. This remark leads to an important point.

Respect and concern

One of the most extraordinary aspects of the modern world is the difference in the way people behave in an organisation compared with when they are at home or at leisure. It is not merely that they become more ruthless and aggressive at work; it is that they so often cease to treat people with the respect and concern that they otherwise show when not in the work situation. This is not intended as a moral judgement (such would be out of place in this book) but as a general statement of fact. Nor is this phenomenon new, for membership of an organisation has probably always caused human beings to behave in this way, but in Western-style democracies the contrast between behaviour at work and behaviour elsewhere seems to be growing. Many managers believe that an organisation can only be efficient if those in authority (1) make tough, prompt, dynamic decisions, and (2) demand obedience from their subordinates, which means, therefore, that managers have to be tough, dynamic people. ('Tough' in this context often means 'ruthless'.) Now there is no doubt that this was generally true until a few decades ago and it is still certainly true of organisations facing emergencies. But society seems now to be saying that the pursuit of efficiency must no longer be allowed to take priority over the well-being and rights of people both inside and outside organisations (this is Trend J again). In its extreme form this view leads to the Hippy philosophy which is that they would rather see standards of living collapse than be treated as 'slaves' in an efficient organisation.

Now the point being made in this book is that efficiency and humanity can be compatible partners and not mutually exclusive opposites. If there is no dilemma between efficiency and humanity we do not need to choose between them and do not have to decide between being a miserable, ruthless manager or a happy Hippy. It is fairly generally recognised that an organisation can achieve its objectives efficiently in one of two ways: either by taking prompt ruthless decisions and demanding total obedience, or by taking great care over important decisions and leaving less important ones to groups of self-disciplined subordinates. The first system is incompatible with, or at least discourages, respect and concern for subordinates; the second type of system (of which MS 70 is one example) demands that respect and concern be shown, and can only work if they are present.

One minor but not completely trivial way in which one can show respect to others is in the tone of voice and the words used when giving instructions to subordinates. Those who receive their instructions through computers (a growing practice) are often justified in taking offence at the pre-emptory style often built into their missives by those responsible for programming the print out. (This is odd because computer programmers are not normally impolite; perhaps they are just trying to be 'dynamic'.)

Dirty jobs
Dirty jobs, such as those connected with human or animal wastes or products, those done in conditions of great heat or cold, dust or smell, etc., are also increasingly unpopular. Such jobs are not always simple or repetitive – indeed farming, relining a furnace, etc., are interesting and skilful – so the jobs themselves will probably not be quickly eliminated. A great deal of money and ingenuity will have to be spent on improving working conditions, however, and managers who persist in believing that 'there's nothing more we can do' will soon run into trouble. These trends away from repetitive and dirty jobs are remorseless, and sooner or later employees will refuse to do them at any price.

Semi-skilled, skilled, highly-skilled jobs
This is the type of work where job enrichment will become increasingly appropriate – jobs such as telephonist, mechanic, junior managers, chef, instrument maker, clerk, lathe operator, computer programmer, plant operator, lorry driver, nurse, secretary, draughtsman, etc. The term job enrichment is used so widely that it is sensible to describe it under separate headings of which 'Increased Variety', 'Group Work' and 'Greater Complexity' are the three discussed below. In general, job enrichment implies a conscious effort on the part of the management gradually and steadily to give greater discretion to employees by making their jobs more interesting, more rewarding and more demanding.

Increased variety
One obvious way in which an employee's work can be made more interesting, and where he can use his discretion more widely, is to add activities that are normally performed by other people. Telephonists could repair their own switchboard, lorry drivers maintain their own vehicles, a motor mechanic could road-test his own repair job, etc. This approach often involves breaking down traditional lines of demarcation between skilled or semi-skilled trades or professions. (It has been said that the most beautiful pottery, furniture, stonemasonry was made when craftsmen designed their own products and that the

134

quality of design declined during the nineteenth century as the design function was taken from the craftsmen and given to specialist designers. Perhaps it is time we gave it back.)

Group work
Another way of increasing the content of any job is to amalgamate it with other adjacent jobs and share out the total with the original group of employees; for example, in a group of seven clerks each man completes one section of a complicated government form before passing it to his neighbour – each clerk performs one specialist task on one section of the form. But an alternative is for the manager of the group to leave it entirely to the clerks themselves as to who should do what – so long as the form is completed correctly and output and accuracy do not fall it would be immaterial to him how the job was distributed among them. Where this has been tried it has been found that error rates go down and output goes up, especially where each clerk completes the whole form himself, including checking his own errors. Similarly with engineering assembly work, for example, where each man adds one item to the product and passes it on to his neighbour to add the next item; if each man is allowed to assemble the whole product, however, output may rise, scrap may fall, pride in the job returns. This is really another example of 'increased variety' described above or 'increased complexity' below, but the point is that if left to themselves to organise their own group work people can adopt new methods of work that are actually better than those thrust upon them by their boss.

Increased complexity
Another way in which a job can be enriched is by upgrading it in terms of skill. This can be done, for example, by setting higher standards of quality requiring more care or thought on the part of the operator or by installing more sophisticated equipment, etc. A modern boiler, for example, demands much higher skill to operate than an older one. A hospital nurse today has to work with much more complex equipment than ten years ago.

These three items above – 'increased variety', 'group work'

K   135 and 'increased complexity' – represent three ways in which jobs that cannot be automated or eliminated can be expanded and extended so as to allow the employee more scope for the use of his own initiative and discretion.

Expansive targets
We have probably said enough about the difference between expansive and constricting targets to demonstrate the value of the former as an instrument in achieving wider discretion. The keys to an expansive target are (a) use as few figures as possible to define the task; (b) state resources as generally as possible and with no unnecessary detail (c) refrain as far as one dare from telling the subordinate how to tackle the job. The examination we made in Chapter 6 on how to avoid constricting targets must be considered an important part of the rule-book for managers who take seriously the effect that the trends of the 1970s will have on how he handles people.

Venture management
This represents the logical end-point of the expansive target technique. As explained above, in venture management a boss simply tells a subordinate to achieve a result, gives him a sum of money (money, as we said, was the most general and least constricting form in which to state resources) and asks him to report progress from time to time – usually rather a long time. Where this is adopted by companies they often do not even tell him what line of business to pursue; they give him some money, say they want a certain dividend each year and that is all. One can imagine other organisations doing the same thing – a church organisation might send a medical missionary to Northern Tibet with £50,000 and instructions to set up a hospital. Nowadays few subordinates are entrusted with this sort of task – those who are sent to perform such feats are usually bound from head to foot in detailed instructions, frequent messages from Head Office, miles of red tape – but a few generations ago 'venture management' was commonplace; poor communications precluded any other way of carrying out tasks at a distance. Today managers use communications to watch and to regulate their subordinate's every move and this, as we

mentioned above, is a misuse of communications. There is nothing like good communications for killing initative.

(One interesting consequence of the increasing trend towards venture management in companies is the possible appearance of Disintegrated Companies, as they might be called. A disintegrated company will consist of a small head office whose sole function is to identify managers who can be trusted, decide how much money to give them and check that each venture is yielding the required dividend. These companies would be like the conglomerates of the 1960s (i.e. no planned relationship between the subsidiaries) but contain far more subsidiaries each of which would be smaller than those of the typical 1960 conglomerate. They might therefore avoid most of the problems of managing large units.

Time span of instructions

One way in which a manager can widen the field in which a subordinate may use his own discretion is to give instructions less often but so organize it that each instruction covers a correspondingly greater period of time. For example, a sales manager can tell a salesman to sell 1,000 units next week, check his performance at the end of the week and then set him a target for the following week – a cycle time of one week. Or he can set him a target of 4,000 units and check and reset on a four-week cycle – or ten weeks or a year. The same considerations apply to setting research projects, production planning, nursing patients, to all tasks.

Incidentally, it should be noted that this method of widening discretion links up with and is consistent with the trend towards taking more care before giving instructions (i.e. spending more time on Step 2). Thus the Sales Manager will think more carefully before giving a monthly target to a salesman than he would before giving him a weekly target, but he will give only a quarter of the number of instructions. Fewer decisions and instructions, then, but each of a better quality.

Rules and Regulations

Some organisations, especially those employing large numbers of people, give each employee a book of rules and regulations.

137

Where these describe rules designed to improve safety there can be no possible objection. Where, however, they regulate the day-to-day behaviour of employees it may be necessary to consider the need for simplification or elimination. An increasing number of companies, for example, are eliminating the practice of clocking-in and are leaving it to the employees' own sense of justice to turn up at the right time. Some companies have gone further and told their employees that, providing a day's work is completed, they can come to work and leave when they like. Some have told their shift-workers that, providing the plant is fully manned at all times, each man can agree his hours of work with his mates. Other organisations have abolished set times for tea breaks – employees take the break when they like.

In general, then, any organisation issuing a revised rule-book in the 1970s that contains more rules than the previous edition is likely to be facing the wrong way; this does not of course apply to such rules as 'No smoking in the explosives stores'. Perhaps this is the place to remind ourselves that these remarks, this chapter, and indeed MS 70 itself are all intended to be relevant to all organisations, and not just to companies. In this context it could be said that any Government which passed more laws in the 1970s regulating private behaviour than it passed in the 1960s is also facing the wrong way – we could go further and suggest that the 1970s will see many such laws repealed, including restrictions on opening hours for shops and pubs, a further reduction in censorship and laws of libel, etc. (We shall see in Chapter 12 that the principles that make up MS 70 apply no less to national governments than to any other organisation – perhaps they apply above all to governments.)

Democracy
It was noted many years ago that parallel with the official management structure of many organisations there were often powerful unofficial ones. Thus an organisation may have appointed Mr Jones as Office Manager and may look upon him as the boss of the office, while everyone in the office in fact takes their lead from Mr Smith who is, perhaps, less of an old fuddy-duddy than Jones or has a more powerful personality or

because the office girls think he is better-looking. The same unofficial 'ghost' organisation appears, often in a very fleshy manifestation, in trade unions and many other organisations. One obvious way round this problem is to allow subordinates to elect their own manager – and to demote him. An alternative is not to have a manager at all but to give a task to a group of employees (see Group Work above) and if a leader is necessary one will emerge temporarily for that particular task (we noticed in Chapter 3 that agreed seniority could be a temporary phenomenon). There is no doubt whatever that such practices will grow during the 1970s.

One consequence of this trend is interesting: when large organisations select managers they usually place considerable weight on the formal qualifications held by the candidates and, when other things are equal, tend to promote the man with the highest formal qualification. It is possible that the democratic election of leaders will tend to place less weight on this and more on that somewhat unquantifiable aspect of human personality known as leadership.

THE SLIDE TOWARDS CHAOS AND ANARCHY

We have so far listed about a dozen ways in which managers may allow their subordinates wider discretion; there are five more to come, but we must pause here for it may be objected that we have already had enough. Surely, it will be said, what is being proposed is that managers should virtually abdicate all power and decisions to their subordinates and leave them to do as they please without control? In fact this is not being suggested although it must be admitted that, judging solely by the last few pages, we are in danger of not merely allowing slack to enter the system but of opening the doors to chaos and even anarchy. This problem is real and we must deal with it.

This problem is basically due to the rising standards of mass education; one of the intended by-products of higher education is a heightened desire to use one's own initiative. Managers can approach this new breed of more independent-minded subordinates in two ways – he can give him his head but keep an eye on him or he can keep him on a short lead. If the latter, the educated subordinate will fret, become irritable and eventually rebel unless the lead is strengthened and shortened and the whip is used. Fewer managers will adopt this solution in the 1970s. The former solution is obviously more appropriate but an important caveat is contained in the words 'but keep an eye on him' – and so far our list only contains measures designed to lengthen the lead but no measures for control, no safeguards.* The five safeguards listed below are all designed to limit the slack, the chaos and the anarchy that *would* threaten to overwhelm any organisation if it only adopted the measures listed above.

Training

If we are going to allow subordinates more latitude, and if we are going to give them tasks that are more complex and have much longer time horizons, we must be certain that they know how to carry out their task to the same standard as they would achieve if their boss was constantly guiding them. This means that they must be *trained* in two skills. Firstly, they must understand how to tackle the sort of jobs that their boss will ask them to do – if a man is appointed Works Manager then he must know all the skills relevant to managing the type of works he is being asked to manage – the technology of the product, production planning, statistical control, industrial law, and so on through a staggering range of topics. Secondly, they must be trained in management – skills relevant to taking decisions,† giving instructions, checking results. These are the two areas in

* All this assumes that organisations will continue to retain the ultimate sanctions such as dismissal. As suggested earlier, managers will apply penalties far less often in the 1970s but when they do they will be severe.

† Incidentally, there was a trend in the late 1960s, which looks like continuing, towards the use of 'business games' as an instrument of training in decision-making for managers. Such games are usually played at speed – often with a computer acting as data-bank and referee – and the participants are given very little time in which to make their decisions. Whatever else these games teach (and whatever it is may well be of value) they certainly do not encourage managers to adopt the MS 70 approach which relies heavily on managers in the 1970s taking great care over each major decision even if it takes a long time (subject only to step 2a). MS 70 suggests: take far fewer decisions but get them right. Business games seem to encourage 'instant management'. This *must* be wrong.

140

which every subordinate must be trained before he can be given
the wider discretion that he will increasingly demand during the
1970s. The manager who gives wider discretion to a subordinate
who does not know how to tackle the job and does not know the
skills and techniques of management is inviting chaos. But it
can be said with equal force that the subordinate who demands
wider discretion without making the effort to train himself, or at
the least to be trained, is asking too much and must be refused.
Training in these two areas will, during the 1970s, be of prime
importance.

Participation
We heard much of participation towards the end of the 1960s –
so much that its meaning became somewhat blurred. It can have
several meanings of which two are really important.

The first form of participation is when the employees of an
organisation gain representation on the highest levels of the
hierarchy, workers on the Board, for example. Where this has
been attempted (the Glacier Project, the German Co-determination Schemes, etc.) it appears not to be too successful, possibly
for two reasons: firstly, great skill and knowledge is required to
take the top-level strategic decisions that are, or should be, the
main function of the Board and workers normally lack these
skills; secondly there is a danger that the purpose of the organisation will be perverted. It will be recalled that society is making
increasing demands on organisations (Trend J) and most organisations are so burdened by these demands that they have great
difficulty in fulfilling their duties to the intended beneficiaries.
(Again, no moral judgements are being made here; it may or
may not be desirable for society to make demands on organisations – that is not at issue here – all that is being said is that
these demands exist, are considerable and will grow throughout
the 1970s.) So, organisations already have to bow to demands
such as those made by society, employees, suppliers and the
state, if some of these groups of people are also actually present
on the Boards of organisations then the pressures could become
so great as to divert and even pervert the energies of the organisation from its intended purpose.

The second form of participation is not only more valid but is

141

a useful partner to job enrichment and an essential part of wider discretion. In this form participation means that subordinates participate in their boss's decision-making, i.e. the manager invites his subordinates to help him with the whole of his Step 2 and Step 3. He therefore says to them, 'Look, I have been given this task by *my* boss. We can't argue with his decisions but I do want you to help me sort out what alternative ways there are for me to carry out my task, to help me evaluate the alternatives, to select the best one, to plan it out, help me decide what part each of you can play, when I can expect results from each of you, and so on.' This approach represents the most astonishing change in management over the span of only one generation.* Before the war most managers took Step 2 themselves and would not have considered even explaining their decisions or plans to their subordinates, nor would they have discussed their orders with their subordinates before giving them. As a result they achieved instant obedience and a minimum of slack – but they failed to obtain any bright ideas that their subordinates might have had to contribute if they had been invited to do so. Today many managers recognise that this form of participation can reveal a rich pool of ideas lying hitherto unused in the lower depths of the hierarchy. Nor, in practice, is there ever much increase in slack because, having themselves contributed to their boss's plan, subordinates are more inclined to accept his instructions to them. Often they themselves have suggested their own part in his plan and have even suggested to him details of the instructions that he is to give to them, including the target level of achievement at which they should aim.

Checking results

We must postpone this subject until the next chapter. It is sufficient to say that checking results is the only sure way to control the actions and progress of a subordinate, the only way to ensure that slack is kept to acceptable levels. In the next chapter we will examine more efficient ways of checking results.

* In the 1950s it would have been entirely sufficient if MS 50 had only contained the well-known advice, 'tell people in advance of changes that will affect them'. This does not go nearly far enough for MS 70.

Cascade Planning
During the 1960s a great increase in all forms of planning took place. These had two major defects. Firstly, as we mentioned before (page 107) the professional planners gave far too little thought to methods of generating and evaluating a sufficiently wide range of alternatives before getting down to the detailed planning (we called this 'the missing link of planning in the 1960s'). Secondly, plans were often made by planners with scant regard for, or consultation with, the people who were going to carry them out. This was particularly evident in the case of large complex projects where huge wall-sized charts of unbelievably complex detail suggest that consultation had not even been attempted. There are probably two ways of planning a major project; one is to do all the planning, even the details, on one central plan and programme a computer to co-ordinate and control the project, allocate resources, issue progress warnings, etc. Where this is necessary – and it sometimes is – this is how it should be done. But where it is not necessary – and it often is not – it is possible to have a central but simple overall plan split down into a cascade of simple sub-plans in ever progressing detail, each plan being drawn up by the man responsible for carrying out that part of the project. Thus one can have either a massively complex diagram or a cascade of plans in which the general outline of the project appears on the master plan (supervised by the man in charge of the whole project) but each major part of this plan is detailed on a sub plan on which each major part is detailed on a sub-sub-plan, and so on, each sub-plan being drawn up by the man responsible for carrying it out.

Unfortunately the professional planners of the 1960s were so intent on developing bigger and bolder plans – a trend manifestly against many of the trends in the 1960s (and certainly contrary to the principles of MS 70) – that they have not yet turned their attention to the technology of cascade planning. It is predicted here that they will have to do this in the 1970s; the trend towards consultation and participation will demand it, even if the ever-growing unintelligibility of those ever more massive plans does not.

Selection of Employees

It seems likely that during the 1970s managers will be more selective in their choice of subordinates and that this will apply, it is suggested, throughout every level of any hierarchy of managers. They will no longer merely be looking for people who do what they are told, however well, but for people who will contribute to discussions, are creative, understand specialist advice and work well with their colleagues. In general, personality and character will begin to be more important relative to skill, knowledge and paper qualifications – not less important as is often supposed. Among specialists and advisers, knowledge and paper qualifications will, of course, continue to grow in importance.

STEP 3. GIVING INSTRUCTIONS IN THE 1970S

Let us now stand back from the detail of this chapter and try to visualise the salient facts as an integrated whole. We can start by looking at Fig. 35 which shows Step 3 as it might have been

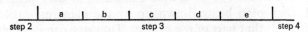

Fig 35: Step 3 and its sub-steps in, say, 1910

at any time up to the past few decades – as in all our previous diagrams of this sort, the size of the various sub-steps is meant to indicate the importance that managers attached to each and the care with which they would have carried them out.

Notice that each of the sub-steps are of roughly equal importance, implying that a manager would take as much care to define the task that he wanted his subordinate to do (Step 3a) as he would take to tell him what resources he could use (Step 3b). He would have equally carefully explained how the job was to be done (Step 3c) and equally carefully told the subordinate when he, the manager, would be coming back to check up (Step 3d) and finally the manager would have made it clear what he would do if the task was not done satisfactorily (Step 3e) – in fact he would probably have put more stress on these rewards and penalties than on any of the other sub-steps.

Now the role of an instruction in a system of management is to act rather like screws that hold two pieces of wood together; an instruction links the tasks that a subordinate is doing to the task the manager is doing. A subordinate will only be instructed to do x if the doing of x contributes to the completion of his boss's task; if the subordinate accurately carries out his task (and if all the other subordinates do likewise) the boss's task will also be carried out accurately. If a subordinate does not accurately complete x (i.e. if there is 'slack' in the organisation) then the boss's task is in jeopardy. We can imagine this hierarchy of tasks as a tall wooden structure where each piece of wood is held to the other with screws – if any of the joints are loose the whole structure will wobble, so we must be careful about those screws. The old-style manager used five screws of roughly equal size, which we have called a, b, c, d, and e. In the past few decades subordinates have been protesting at the rigidity of this union,

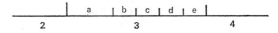

Fig 36: Step 3 and its sub-steps in 1970

and managers have been forced to reduce the size of most of the screws, thus introducing the danger of slack, chaos and even anarchy. However, subordinates do not object to being told what to do as much as they object to being told how to do it or having the boss breathing down their necks or dealing out penalties to them as if they were naughty children. This means that managers must make sure that the screw we call Step 3a (defining the job) must be longer and stronger because the other four are so much smaller and weaker. Step 3 is therefore beginning to look as in Fig. 36.

If we left it like this we would be courting disaster: however large we make Step 3a, however much time and effort a manager spends on defining the task, we are still denied a guarantee that the subordinate will carry out the task willingly or conscientiously. If the manager checks results he is 'breathing down their necks'. If he uses penalties or rewards he is 'treating them like children'. Increased slack is inevitable unless we can obtain willing co-operation and self-discipline from our subordinates.

145

This is what wider discretion, job enrichment, participation are all about. So we are going to add another element to Step 3 and call it Step 3x – see Fig. 37.

It will be seen at once that Step 3x is quite unlike any of the other steps we have seen in MS 70. This is because it describes a relationship between a manager and his subordinates. Step 3x represents that continuous participative co-operation between them that should start right back at the point when the manager has accepted a task from his boss, and when he calls in his subordinates to discuss how to tackle it, to get their ideas, hear their evaluations, discuss his plans and how their sub-plans mesh in with his, agree who does what, agree targets, discuss resources, check-points and rewards or penalties. Step 3x is

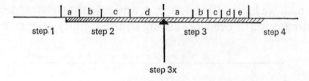

Fig 37: Step 3x

not a single screw – it is the glue that binds a manager to his subordinates and it is spread right through Step 2 as well as Step 3. So instead of five large screws to hold a subordinate's task to his manager's without slack we now have one larger screw (Step 3a), four small ones (Steps 3, b, c, d, e) and some glue!

Now, in spite of all our efforts to keep slack to an old-fashioned minimum it must be admitted that if subordinates are going to be better educated then the chances are that, whatever we do, they are going to use their new-found initiative, and consequently there will be more slack than in the old days when a sharp tongue and the threat of the sack kept them toeing the line. So there will be more slack. But against that we have opened a new door – perhaps to Aladdin's cave – for each manager can gain access to the skill, knowledge, creativity, flair and common sense of his subordinates. And, if he can get his relationship with them right, he may find that he need spend far less time supervising them. Now we can see, incidentally,

146

how modern communication systems (Trend B) should be used – not for continuously regulating a subordinate as he goes about his task but for frequent participative discussion and consultation on creating alternatives, using the Sieve, altering plans or targets and so on.

Conclusion 3.1. A manager's instruction to a subordinate is incomplete unless it contains five essential parts: the task must be clearly stated; the resources must be stated; the method to be used must be stated; the check-up points must be known; the rewards or penalities must be known.

Conclusion 3.2. During the 1970s managers will have to make important alterations to each of these five sub-steps and must add another element (Step 3x). These changes will be necessary because of Trend E (improved mass education), Trend M (the revolt against excessive, arbitrary or inept authority), Trend K (quantification) and Trend N (rising standards of living). Trend B (improved communications) will also play an important role.

Conclusion 3.3. Managers will spend more time in defining the tasks they set to subordinates at Step 3a. They will try to set targets in quantitative terms where possible and where not possible, will define tasks in terms of verifiable results to be achieved at a target rate or date. Targets will increasingly be set at three levels of achievement.

Conclusion 3.4. Due to the decline in simple tasks and to the increased complexity of decision-making, managers will increasingly give instructions as a result of careful planning; off-the-cuff decisions and instructions will decline.

Conclusion 3.5. Targets will become more expansive. Managers will use fewer figures to define each task in recognition of the fact that the more a task is detailed to a subordinate the less discretion he can exercise.

Conclusion 3.6. At Step 3b managers will allocate resources

147

in less detail. In the extreme case they will state the resources available simply as one figure in money terms and leave it to the subordinate's discretion how that money is spent.

Conclusion 3.7. At Step 3c managers will progressively reduce the volume of instructions as to how the subordinate should carry out the task or use the resources.

Conclusion 3.8. It will be vital, in view of the decline of Steps 3b and 3c and because subordinates will be left alone unsupervised for longer periods, for managers to ensure that their subordinates are properly trained in two fields; the skills of their job and the skills and techniques of decision-making, giving instructions and checking results, i.e. the skills and techniques of management.

Conclusion 3.9. At Step 3c there will be a growing need to instruct subordinates not to use unethical or anti-social methods of achieving results.

Conclusion 3.10. Managers will continue to say when they intend to check results at Step 3d.

Conclusion 3.11. The motivational value of minor rewards and penalties will decline; where rewards or penalties are used to motivate at Step 3e they will be substantial.

Conclusion 3.12. There will be a massive increase in the use of methods of achieving wider discretion at Step 3x. These methods are already numerous and include job enrichment, participation, joint consultation, venture management, cascade planning, democratic elections, etc. Taken together these add up to a revolution in the relationship between manager and subordinate.

Conclusion 3.13. The improved communication systems of the 1970s should not be used by managers to achieve closer supervision of subordinates but as a means of facilitating participative discussions.

Conclusion 3.14. There will be some increase in slack in organisations as a result of changes in this step. This may be more than compensated by improved human relationships between manager and managed leading to better decisions and more realistic plans.

Conclusion 3.15. Managers will give fewer instructions but each instruction they do give will be more carefully considered and will refer to tasks having longer time-spans.

Chapter 9

Step 4 in the 1970s

Management is essentially a practical activity and managers are essentially concerned with real-life practical events. So far in this book we have barely touched the real world; we have been discussing how to take decisions, how to plan, how to give instructions, but all these activities are just talking or putting things down on paper. Checking results, which is the subject of this chapter, is the step where managers inspect the real live world to see if it really has reacted in the way they wanted; has the new factory, hitherto only a plan on a piece of paper, really been built, has sales turnover really increased by 10 per cent and are the customers' cheques safely in the bank?

It is odd – in fact in view of the importance of this step, it is very odd indeed – but managers often seem to forget it altogether! It is by no means rare for a manager to give instructions to a subordinate, send him on his way and then, as soon as the office door is closed behind him, he turns his mind to other matters in the apparent belief that he has completed the management process for that particular task. The management process is not complete without Step 4 – far from it, as we saw from Fig. 16 right back in Chapter 4 where 'check results' proved to be unexpectedly complex and important. It will become more important in the 1970s because, as we saw in the last chapter managers are in danger of losing control over their subordinates and one of the few remaining safeguards that are left is to check results. What is the reason for this reticence to check results? Without doubt it is this: you cannot check a result unless you know what result you expect to see! Since many managers fail to specify their subordinates' tasks in terms of verifiable results it is a waste of time for them to try to verify them; the mistake, then, is not that they fail to check results (Step 4), it is that they fail to specify any results capable of being checked – the failure is at Step 3a, 'define the task'. Goodness knows, we have already said enough about the importance of setting tasks in terms of verifiable targets but let us look at it again from the point of view of checking the results. How, for example, can one check the progress of a subordinate to whom we have given the task 'you must cut costs as far as you can'? The point is that, left as it is, we cannot check this because we have given no indication what 'as far as you can' means in the real world, does it mean 3 per cent or 30 per cent or what? But let us try to check this result and see what happens – we find that the subordinate has, in fact, been able to cut costs by 3 per cent. Now that we have been handed a figure we can at once decide whether it is good enough and we might say, 'Oh no, that's not good enough, I meant more like 30 per cent'. In which case the subordinate could justifiably ask why we didn't say so before! (If we had also put a date on this task – all project tasks should have a date – such as 'cut by 30 per cent within the next ten weeks' then we could not only check the figure at the end of ten weeks, but check progress towards this result every week.) It is obvious that, if we had bothered to think about it before we handed down this task, we *could* have said 'Cut costs by 30 per cent' for that was really what we wanted him to do; we did *not* want him 'to do your best' or 'as much as possible' or 'to the maximum' or anything even remotely like it – we simply wanted him to cut costs by 30 per cent. This example shows that if we cannot be bothered to set a verifiable target there is no point in bothering to check results either – and we won't be a manager for very long in the 1970s!

Unfortunately this error is not only common among managers; it is even more prevalent among beneficiaries. Shareholders fail to check results because they have no clear target expectations in mind; if they had decided that their definition of failure was a company whose earnings did not grow by an average of 5 per cent per annum they would check results with this figure in mind; instead they check results with no figure in mind or do not check at all. If an electorate had decided that a nation whose economy grows by less than 4 per cent per annum is a failure, they would know what to do with their government if

L

they did not achieve this minimum. If anyone knew what role the Church was supposed to play in society we could check its results. And so on, with nationalised industries, schools, prisons, welfare schemes, etc.; if we could set targets we could check results. If we cannot check results we do not even know whether the manager or the organisation is a success or a failure. In the 1970s it will be mandatory to do so but it means that managers must take enormous care when giving instructions at Step 3a to say exactly what they want; then Step 4 also becomes meaningful. What results do we really want from a salesman, for example, do we want orders or do we want the customers' cheques in the bank? What do we really want from the man in charge of building a new factory, do we want the factory completed on the target date or do we want it to be actually producing at its designed capacity? What do we want from a welfare scheme for old people, do we want to know how many meals have been supplied to the pensioners, or do we want to know how many pensioners suffer from malnutrition? Again, do we want to know how many welfare visits per head have been made or how many old people are 'Found Dead' in their homes? Take these last two welfare examples; surely the reason we have such welfare services and the result we want from them is nothing to do with 'giving them meals', but is to do with our dismay at the idea of old people in England suffering from malnutrition, not because we think they should be visited but because we are horrified that old people can be so neglected as to die alone and uncared for. The meals are merely the *means* – the *aim* of such a welfare scheme is to reduce malnutrition.

The purpose of checking results is simply to determine whether our decisions are proving a success or a failure. The criteria by which a decision should be judged are the results; a 'good' decision by the manager of that welfare scheme is one that reduces malnutrition among the old people (or reduces the number who are Found Dead). This is why it is desirable to set a target at three levels: the result that represents failure, a satisfactory result, and one that can be considered a success. Then, when we check results we can see at once whether he had been taking good decisions and whether further action is needed or not. If the beneficiaries of an organisation do not set meaningful verifiable targets they will not know what to do with a result when it is reported to them; it is the same with a manager. If they do nothing else, beneficiaries and managers must make clear what result, in their opinion, represents failure, so that when a result that approaches failure is reported to them they know that immediate action is needed. It is the omission of this elementary precaution that leads to the painful decline and decay of so many of our well-known organisations – companies, churches, the administration of justice, great sections of national government, urban government, clubs, societies, charities, professional bodies, etc. They do not check results because they have not taken the trouble to decide what results should be checked, not even the results that represent failure or the approach of failure.

THE SIGNIFICANCE OF RESULTS

Now imagine that a manager has taken Steps 2 and 3 correctly, has specified what results he wishes to see, has correctly briefed his subordinates and they have gone off to do their several tasks. The next thing we expect to happen is that results will start coming in (of course this assumes that the manager has arranged a results reporting system which is itself sometimes difficult and costly). Let us imagine that, just as an example, a certain works manager wishes to see output from his factory rising by 10 per cent within the next ten days and his subordinates have all gone off to oil the wheels, brief the workers, order material, etc. The next day he gets the first result: 73 units have been produced! On its own this figure is useless. In fact we can state that as a general rule in management one figure is *always* useless. Targets should have three figures – failure, satisfactory and success levels; forecasts should have at least two figures – the forecast coupled with an estimate of the error (as we saw on page 106); results should have at least two figures – the result itself and another figure with which to compare it. If we assume that output from this factory normally averages 70 units a day we can see that this first result is better than average; the problem is whether this is statistically significant, for obviously

153

if normal daily output varies between 60 and 80 then 73 is pretty meaningless. It is this failure to establish the significance of figures that leads dynamic managers to take vigorous corrective action when none is called for, while at the same time encouraging lazy managers to do nothing when the results do call for corrective action. Failure to consider the significance of results was well illustrated by the comments that one of the motoring organisations used to make on the daily road casualty results that were officially announced during Bank Holidays; on one occasion the toll was announced as sixteen people killed. 'This is much better', said an official spokesman, 'it indicates that drivers are showing great care and courtesy on the roads.' Since these figures normally fluctuate between ten and thirty a day it obviously indicated nothing of the sort – which was nicely underlined when it was officially announced that an error in the figure had been made – it was not sixteen but twenty-six.

Managers have been aware of the need to establish the statistical significance of figures for generations so there is nothing new about all this as far as MS 70 is concerned, but four of the trends we discussed in Chapter 5 are new and demand that special consideration is given to them in MS 70. The first is Trend K, quantification, about which we need say no more than repeat that during the 1970s, managers will find that valid figures can be attached to an increasing range of tasks that previously they had thought could not be quantified, and this means that there will be progressively less and less excuse for not stating targets in figures, not checking results and not using the power of mathematical statistics for testing significance. The second is Trend L, the increasing number and variety of specialists attached to management, one of whom, the mathematical statistician, is clearly important at Step 4. It is he who can advise managers as to whether a given result is significant or not, and therefore whether action is needed.

The third and most important is Trend C, the rise of the computer; and this is allied to Trend B, improvements in communications. A computer linked through a telecommunications system to desk terminals – an increasingly common procedure in the 1970s – will provide an extraordinarily

154

powerful and comprehensive results service. In fact, it will be too powerful and too comprehensive; line printers linked to computers can already print out an entire book every few minutes and as these get even faster managers will be inundated by figures. This is such a real threat that we must incorporate some rules in MS 70 to prevent it happening. Just imagine what could happen later in the 1970s if we did not; take a company with 100 sales representatives selling 500 different products to 7,000 retailers. Every time a salesman makes a sale he will radio the computer from his car (so that the computer can send the invoice, adjust stocks, replan production schedules, order materials, etc.) and, even before the day is ended every manager, sub-manager, area manager, supervisor and representative has the day's results report showing sales of each product in each area to each customer expressed as a figure, a percentage of last year, of last week, of this week's target, etc. Now all this will look very impressive to visitors to the computer room but will not help the managers who must be protected from the chore of wading through a mass of figures only a few of which indicate that he should take action. The following rules are suggested:

(a) The results report given to a manager should highlight those figures relating to his task and those of his immediate subordinates only.

(b) Figures that are statistically significant, i.e. figures that suggest the results are sufficiently above or below target to be statistically significant, should be highlighted.

These two simple rules are often broken today without harmful effects, but once the over-prolific computer is harnessed to the results system of an organisation they will have to be observed. Both these rules suggest that figures indicating that action may be necessary should be 'highlighted'. What does this mean? It is suggested that no real harm will be done if a manager does get a whole book of results every day or every week from the computer so long as the ones that indicate that action from him is required are clearly differentiated from those that do not; all we want to do is to protect him from having to read through hundreds of figures which he himself has to test for relevance to his responsibilities and for statistical significance; the computer carries out both these tasks so much better than he can. Perhaps this suggests a rule for all computer printouts; no computer should be permitted to print a figure unless it has been tested for statistical significance (at one or more relevant confidence levels) and if it is significant it should be clearly differentiated from figures that are not.

So this is the growing problem: more and more management tasks will be quantified, the computer will pour out more and more numerical results, managers will be flooded with figures and many of these will be misinterpreted; managers will take action when they should not and fail to take action when the results mean that they should. The solution: make the computer highlight the figures that are statistically meaningful within the area of responsibility for each manager and his immediate subordinates.

It is impossible to over-emphasise the importance of correctly interpreting results in management. 'Check results' is the last link in the four-step chain and, depending on how he interprets a result, a manager will either do nothing, or he must admit failure, or he must do something – one of these. To illustrate, let us return to the manager who wanted to increase output by 10 per cent within ten days; current output is 70 units a day so he is now aiming for 77 and, it will be remembered, he has given instructions to his subordinates designed to remove the obstacles to hitting this target. Having done all this he is now ready to check results. Whose results? Well, surely not his yet – he cannot expect output to rise until some of his subordinates have completed or started their tasks. So, at the end of the first day, he will ask what progress they have made: has Jones been able to recruit twenty more men, did Smith alter that gear ratio, etc. If (a) all his subordinates have completed their tasks he, the manager, need do no more – he just waits for the day when he expects output will start rising. Or (b) if some of his subordinates have failed in their tasks he has to decide whether his target is now in jeopardy – if so, he may go back to Step 2 and consider what other action to take or whether he needs some other subordinate to take over from the one who let him down. Or (c) he may discover that for some reason there is no hope of achieving his target and then, of course, he has to report to his boss (who gave him the job of increasing output, of course). These three routes branching out from 'check subordinate's task' were shown in Figs. 11, 12 and 14. What happens when he starts checking his own results is shown in Fig. 15; in this example let us suppose, output on day 1 is 73, day 2 is 72, day 3 is 71. What does he do? Does he assume that he will not reach the target, or that he will, or that he must supplement his first decisions with new action? Which route in Fig. 14 should he follow? Obviously it would be enormously helpful if a statistician could say at this stage whether these three production figures are all so much above daily average as to show that output was rising when it appears to be falling. Perhaps the statistician could say, 'Don't be so impatient, you cannot expect a valid conclusion until we have five days' figures'. Even that would help!

Let us draw some conclusions from this example:

(i) A manager must check his subordinate's results first.

(ii) He must then check his own results.

(iii) When he checks results there is often some doubt about what they mean, and whether to (a) do nothing, (b) do something, (c) report impending failure to his boss.

(iv) A mathematical analysis can sometimes help to decide which of these three courses to follow. This is why all results should be given a statistical significance test.

(v) Of these three courses the middle one (b) is the one most frequently followed. This is because there is seldom enough evidence from the result to hand at any given time to be sure that the task definitely will or will not be completed. Unfortunately route (b) takes the manager back to Step 2 – the decision-making process – which is the one that will become more and more difficult in the 1970s. To return to Step 2 on the basis of a result that has not been tested for significance is to risk wasting management time.

(vi) There is obviously a best time at which to check results – too soon and the figures may not yet be significant; too late and there is no time for corrective action. This is discussed below.

(vii) When managers check results what they are really doing is testing their confidence in achieving their task. This is discussed later in this chapter.

WHEN TO CHECK RESULTS

One of the sub-steps in the five part Instructions procedure discussed in the previous chapter was Step 3d, 'agree checkpoints', on which we postponed discussion until now. We suggested then that managers, as an integral part of an instruction, should tell their subordinates when they intended to check their progress – or in view of the desirability of participation, not to tell them but to agree it with them. We also suggested that, in deference to the idea of wider discretion, managers should check up as seldom as possible because subordinates dislike their boss 'breathing down their neck'. So that is one pointer to a trend in management in the 1970s – check results as seldom as possible. We saw another pointer in the same direction above – there is no sense in checking results until there are enough figures to establish statistical significance. So it looks like an open-and-shut case; the manager and subordinate agree on the answer to the question, 'How soon should we expect to see significant results?' and that establishes the minimum time to the first checkpoint. What determines the maximum time that a manager can leave his subordinate unchecked? The answer is clear: a manager must not leave it so long that there is no time left to take corrective action to achieve his target. Remember that the subordinate's task is geared to the manager's task; if the subordinate fails the manager also fails unless there is time (and resources) to underpin the manager's task by some extra action. This extra action will take time so the manager must check his subordinate's results before this 'lead time' expires. (If it also requires resources in excess of those allocated to the task, the manager must report to his boss.) In just the same way a manager must check progress on his own task sufficiently often to ensure that corrective action can take effect before the target becomes unattainable. To give an example: that works manager has to increase output by 10 per cent within ten days. He knows that no significant results can be expected within five days of instructing his subordinates. But he also knows that if output does not rise as a result of the action they have taken, it might take three days to take further action (perhaps he will have to modify a machine, for example). Clearly, therefore, he must check results before day 7; but we saw there is no point in checking before day 5. In fact, this discussion takes us one stage further – it is clear that the manager must not only check results on day 7, this is also the day on which he must make up his mind what action he is going to take. If he leaves it any longer and if it turns out that that machine does have to be modified, he will miss the target. Indeed if no significant results are available by day 7 he could be justified in taking corrective action in spite of – or because of – not having them.

So the rules here are simple:

(a) Check results as seldom as possible.

(b) Do not check results before they are likely to be statistically significant.

(c) Always check results in time to take corrective action.

(d) It may often be wise to take corrective action if no significant results are available by this critical time.

Although these rules are valid for a large number of occasions, especially for simple, short-term tasks, the 1970s will witness an expansion of large complex, long-term tasks for which these rules are less relevant.

CHECKING LONG-RANGE RESULTS

The problem here is this: there are an increasing number of tasks for which significant results are obtainable only after a very long period of time indeed – years or decades. How does one take corrective action in such cases where it is years before one knows that one is drifting off course? Before taking a closer look at the problem let us give an example of it: someone, presumably a Minister of Education, has laid down what pattern of education our children should receive in the state schools; this decision cannot be validated until those children are grown up so it might be ten, twenty or even thirty years before we can tell whether we should alter the Minister's original decision. Does that mean that we should not alter it, or is there some way in which we can judge it before the results are known?

Let us first consider the difference between short-term simple jobs and long-term complex ones. Short-term simple jobs have these features: they are usually easily quantifiable; the results are readily identifiable, and can easily be collected and recorded; there are usually plenty of figures for statistical analysis; significant trends and movements away from target can rapidly and easily be identified; up to a point it is not disastrous if results are misinterpreted and corrective action is not taken, or taken when it should not be, partly because these jobs are minor, partly because the cycle for checking results is repeated rapidly and the error may quickly be discovered. We have stressed many times that short-term simple jobs are on the decline for a great number of reasons and as a result of many of the trends described in Chapter 5. Larger-scale tasks of more complexity and longer time spans, which are on the increase, have these characteristics: they often are more difficult to quantify; it is not easy to collect data; there are few historical records for comparisons; statistically significant trends away from target take months or years to show themselves; if corrective action is not taken, or taken when it should not be, the penalties can be enormous.

Up to the last few decades the number of large long-term tasks were comparatively few and could be looked upon as exceptional; now, and increasingly in the future, many more managers (especially chief executives and senior managers in large organisations) will be given tasks for which no verifiable or statistically significant results are expected for months, years, decades, or even for a generation. Even today, one cannot judge a managing director by the results his company achieves over less than a year or two – for large companies this could be from five to seven years. One would be rash to judge a government's economic strategy in less than three years. To confirm that a new jet engine is safe and economic in service takes years. To prove a new teaching syllabus in a university take years. We are forced to the extraordinary conclusion that, in fact, we can no longer judge by results; the proof of the pudding is not in the eating – we cannot wait that long in the case of these long-term tasks. If we do wait for the results we run the risk of wasting years of time and intolerable sums of money by continuing on an ill-conceived course, and yet, if we have no results how can we tell whether the course is right or wrong?

It is as well to admit and to recognise that, for these ever-growing long-term tasks we cannot judge by results because they come too late to be useful; we cannot 'manage by results' and this popular slogan becomes deeply suspect for the 1970s – the whole theory of management control is placed in jeopardy – we must even ask if there is any point in setting long-term targets if we are not going to be able to verify them – and this raises the whole question of what management is about if it is not about setting targets and trying to achieve them. Mercifully, there are ways of judging other than by results which we will now discuss – but we must certainly stop calling Step 4 'check results'; instead we will call it, 'monitor confidence'.

'MONITORING CONFIDENCE' – STEP 4 IN THE 1970s

We said earlier in this chapter (page 158) that what a manager was really doing when checking results was testing his confidence in the chances of achieving his target. As an example: if a manager has been told to increase output by 10 per cent within ten days and if on day 7 output has increased by 8 per cent he can look forward with considerable confidence to achieving the final goal. The question of confidence is important; if he is confident of hitting the target he will be justified in not taking any further action. If he loses this confidence he has to go back to Step 2 and reconsider his original decision with all the problems that involves – more evaluations, reallocating resources, rebriefing his subordinates and so on. Where only short-term tasks are involved it is right to place considerable reliance on results (if they are statistically significant); in other words, the level of confidence that a manager is justified in feeling can properly be very closely related to the results – good results should give confidence, poor results should undermine it. However, it must be remembered that results refer to the past, not the future and although the immediate past is quite a good

161

guide to the immediate future this becomes less and less true as the time span increases. Past success is a good pointer to continuing success for short-term tasks; but it is not for long-term tasks. This suggests that even if we could check results for long-term tasks we cannot assume that a good run of results for the early months or years is a useful guide to the eventual outcome. In long-term tasks, then, confidence does not depend solely or largely on results or past trends – a conclusion that will come as a surprise to Budgetary Control and cybernetics enthusiasts. If confidence does not depend on results, on what does it depend? The answer is twofold. First, on the progress made by subordinates. Second, and much more important, on the continuing validity of the original assumptions that lay behind the original decision.

Take the first one. A manager gives instructions to subordinates in such a way that the successful completion of his task depends on the successful completion of the tasks he gives them. It is quite obvious then, since his task cannot logically be completed before theirs, that the progress they are making provides a valuable early-warning system for him. This is why all managers should check progress on their subordinates' tasks. This being so, might he not obtain an even earlier warning if he checked the progress made by his subordinates' subordinates? There may be occasions when this is so (and these therefore break the rules we made about managers only checking two sets of results – his own and those of his immediate subordinates) but the hierarchical mechanism we have described should already have provided for failure lower down to be reported upwards. So there is this sequential early-warning system built into MS 70: its efficacy depends on managers remembering to take Step 3d – agreeing a specific time at which they will check their subordinates' results in the expectation of seeing something statistically significant – and it also depends on them warning their boss if they discover that their subordinate has so seriously failed as to jeopardise the completion of their task. Thus the message passes up and the manager gets a valuable early warning – perhaps months or years before his task is due to be completed.

Now consider the second prop on which confidence rests.

162

Bearing in mind we are discussing a manager's confidence in achieving a long-term target, let us take as an example the case of Mr Brown who was appointed General Manager of the new Thetix Division of Hypothetics, Ltd, in 1965. His task was to 'run the Thetix Division for the next ten years in such a way that the profits reach £1·7m. by 1969 and rise to £3m. by 1975, the Division being formed by a capital expenditure of £7m. in 1965–8'. The record shows that the new factory was built at a cost of £7m. in 1968 and by 1969 profits were £1·7m. – exactly on target. In 1970 Mr Brown feels fairly confident of achieving the 1975 target because profits in 1970 are expected to rise to £2·3m. Is his confidence justified? Not really – a lot can happen in five years! The fact that the first five years' results are bang on target is not much guide to the next five. But his subordinates are all turning in excellent results, even for some of the tasks they have been given which are designed to take profits to £3·0m. in 1974; surely that is a good sign? Again it helps, but is not conclusive and Mr Brown might still be wondering whether to lay any further long-term plans to underpin his 1975 target. What would convince him that further action was unnecessary would be if he was confident that the major assumptions that underlay the original Thetix project were likely to remain valid for another five years. So we should look at these and this means going right back to the original decision in 1965. The Project Proposal, put to the Hypothetics Board then included this information:

'The proposal to expand production of Thetix and form a Thetix Division was selected from a short list of several alternatives designed to increase our profits by 10 per cent per annum (to £12m. in 1975) including the formation of a subsidiary company in Venezuela, a merger with the French company ETC and the expansion of another product, Hypon. The Thetix proposal was selected because of the following long-term assumptions: (1) That interruptions to oil supplies from Middle East and African producers would grow in frequency and severity for at least another decade. (2) That standards of living would rise in Europe by 5 per cent per annum or more. (3) That our competitors, especially Bunglers of New York will continue to . . .'.

And so on for several pages of major assumptions including those relating to costs of materials, labour productivity, taxation and so on. Notice what this document is, it is a written summary of how the senior managers of Hypothetics took Step 2 in 1965, it records how in Step 2b they considered several alternative strategies (to boost their total profits to a target of £12m. by 1975), it shows how they selected one of them (the Thetix project) by putting these alternatives through the Sieve at Step 2c (presumably the Middle East oil problems, the 5 per cent rise in living standards, etc., were expected to favour the Thetix project more than the other alternatives) and then they draw up a plan of action including the building of a factory, etc. (Step 2d). This document contains, then, a recitation of assumptions about all the trends and events that would materially affect the success of the project over the next ten years (as is required by Test 5 in the Sieve). So all Mr Brown need do in 1970 is to look through those, decide whether they are likely to hold good for another five years and, to the extent that he thinks they will, then his confidence in eventual success will be strengthened. Will the standard of living in Europe rise by 5 per cent per annum over the 1970–5 period? What is the Middle East situation likely to be? What might happen in the next five years that was not foreseen in the 1965 document, but which would seriously affect his task? If any of the original assumptions is suspect then the success of the project is in doubt and Mr Brown must return to Step 2 and decide what additional action to take, what new instructions to issue, etc.

Now let us generalise: for short-term tasks a manager's confidence in eventual success is largely conditioned by his results in the past – because the immediate past is a fairly good guide to the immediate future; for long-term tasks his confidence is dependent not so much on past results (the rate of change [Trend F] is such that the past is not a good guide to the distant future) but much more on the continuing validity of assumptions. For both short- and long-term tasks confidence is partly conditioned by the results or progress towards them made by his subordinates. Confidence, then, depends on three things:

164

1. Past results obtained by the manager in the task so far.
2. Subordinate's results so far.
3. Continuing validity of assumptions into the relevant future.

Because so many managers still believe that (1) and (2) are paramount (a habit left over from the days when most tasks were short term) we attempt to show, in Fig. 38, how the value of these three factors in confidence varies with the lengthening time-span of tasks.

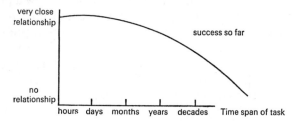

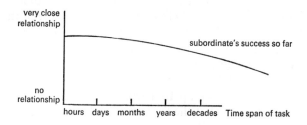

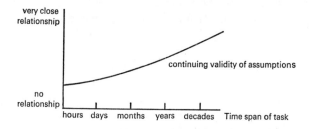

Fig 38: The level of confidence a manager feels in achieving his task is related to three factors—his success so far, his subordinate's success so far and the continuing validity of assumptions. The graphs show how this relationship varies with the time span of the task

One quite useful by-product of this discussion is that we can now see how far ahead a manager ought to plan. If we had limited our discussion to checking past results it would not have given us this valuable clue; because we are discussing confidence, however, we realise that confidence depends on the extent to which a manager has given thought to the future. To illustrate: let us imagine that the chief executive of a company has been told by the shareholders to increase profits by 10 per cent per annum for at least the next ten years; assume profits in 1970 are £100,000 so this means that by 1980 he must show a profit of around £260,000. Now imagine that the chief executive forecasts that if the company continues to carry on as it is at present the profits in 1980 might have fallen to £60,000. It is very obvious that he must do something! The gap between target and forecast even in 1972 – only two years ahead – is going to be £30,000 which is enough to scare him stiff, let alone the gap of £200,000 in 1980. (A target is what one wants to achieve, a forecast is what one expects to achieve and a plan is what one proposes to do about closing the gap between them.) This situation is shown in Fig. 39 from which it will be seen that this sort of Gap Analysis can also be applied to housing targets, productivity targets and so on over any span of time. Now turn back to our chief executive; he goes through Step 2 and selects a bold and imaginative strategy which, he calculates, will close the gap right up to 1976. This is shown in Fig. 40 where it will be seen that the forecast equals the target for some time ahead and then falls away again. Now the question we are trying to answer is; how far ahead should a manager plan? The answer is obvious from Fig. 40; we should plan far enough ahead to be confident that there is time to close the remaining gap. So if the chief executive forecasts a gap of nil in 1976, £10,000 in 1977, £30,000 in 1978, £50,000 in 1979 and £80,000 in 1980 and if he is confident that he can find some means of closing these gaps between now and 1977 then he need do no more planning today. He has planned far enough. If he thinks it will only take two years to close these gaps then he need not take any more major strategic decisions until 1975. If he thinks it might take ten years then he is already too late – he should have planned further ahead in 1970.

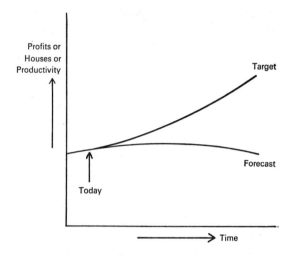

Fig 39: The forecast shows that the target will not be achieved and that action is necessary

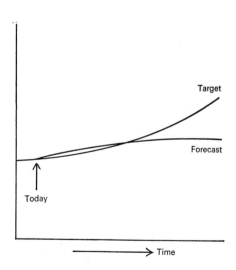

Fig 40: The manager has taken action or has plans to do so

M

So important are most long-term tasks (because they are usually large-scale jobs given to senior managers) and so important is it to monitor confidence in them that many companies have set up long-term forecasting units whose job is continually to monitor changes in society, technology, economic conditions, etc., and to warn managers when any of these changes might affect their long-term tasks. (Yes, more specialists! But we have come to expect that now, see Trend L in Chapter 5.) There are also an increasing number of organisations whose sole function is to predict the future, often for decades ahead, and a growing pool of information about their predictions and the methods they use is available; this information will become extensive during the 1970s (Trend D) and managers will have to learn where to find it and how to use it.

Conclusion 4.1. When a manager gives instructions to a subordinate he should tell him (or agree with him) when he is going to check progress on the task. In the interests of wider discretion he should check as seldom as possible.

Conclusion 4.2. A manager should not check progress on either his subordinate's task or his own until the results are likely to be statistically significant.

Conclusion 4.3. A manager must check progress in time to take any corrective action that may be necessary in order to achieve his target. He is often justified in taking corrective action if no significant results are available before this critical time.

Conclusion 4.4. When a manager checks results what he is really doing is measuring the confidence he feels in achieving his target.

Conclusion 4.5. For short-term tasks his confidence will depend mainly on his subordinate's progress with their tasks and his own progress with his task.

Conclusion 4.6. For long-term tasks, where past results are a poor guide to the long-term future, his confidence depends far more on the continuing validity of the assumptions he made at Step 2 (especially Step 2d) for that task.

Conclusion 4.7. Step 4 is called 'Monitoring Confidence' and consists of checking progress on subordinates' tasks, on the manager's task and on verifying the continuing validity of assumptions.

Conclusion 4.8. Depending upon his level of confidence in achieving his target a manager will either do nothing, or take action to increase the chances of achieving the target, or, if confidence is low, he will report impending failure to his boss.

Conclusion 4.9. The computer (coupled with telecommunications) will greatly facilitate the reporting of results; it should, however, be programmed to highlight results relating to the manager's task and those of his subordinates that are statistically significant variations from target.

Conclusion 4.10. Even though some tasks have such long-term spans that no verifiable results can be expected for years or decades, it is still sensible to set long-term targets that are clear, quantified, unambiguous and verifiable. (It is not sensible, however, to try to control the management process by checking results. The decision to take corrective action [to 'exercise control' or 'feed-back'] must be based on the level of confidence.)

Conclusion 4.11. All the conclusions relating to long-term tasks apply with greatest force to chief executives' jobs since their task necessarily has the longest time span of all the managers in any organisation. Beneficiaries should note Conclusion 4.10 in particular, therefore.

Conclusion 4.12. In management a single figure on its own is always useless. This applies to all forecasts, targets and results.

169

Conclusion 4.13. Managers do not sufficiently appreciate the value of mathematical statistics. By establishing the significance of a figure a statistician (or a computer) can sometimes save managers taking action when none is necessary and vice versa.

Chapter 10

The Hierarchy in the 1970s

In the past four chapters we have discussed how the process of management will change in the 1970s; we have seen how in Step 1 each manager (especially chief executives) will have to ensure that the task he agrees to carry out is properly specified – otherwise he cannot (and should not) attempt to carry it out. We noted the enormous extension of the problems of decision-making at Step 2. We noted the contraction of Step 3, 'give instructions', but we also saw that the contraction itself was not the main change – of much greater significance was the change in the whole flavour of the human relationship between manager and subordinate. We saw, at Step 4, how we could no longer judge by results for many of the tasks that will be set to managers in the 1970s because the results are too far away. All this adds up to a revolution. In the old days one took a decision, barked out some orders to obedient subordinates and then watched them at work checking their results almost continuously. In the 1970s managers will have to take enormous pains with each decision, discuss it at length with their subordinates but then spend a minimum of time on checking results. If we could apportion the time an old-fashioned manager spent on each step we might have found that he spent 20 per cent of his day on decisions, 20 per cent on giving instructions and 60 per cent on checking results. In the 1970s it will be more like 80 per cent on Steps 2 and 3 amalgamated together and 20 per cent on monitoring confidence. Such a revolution could not take place without substantial changes having to be made in the hierarchy. These changes are not trivial – they involve the decline of the whole hierarchical form of organisation structure itself and the appearance of quite new forms of structure alongside it – and these changes will come about quite rapidly. They will be rapid in the 1970s for several reasons: firstly, the general rate of change itself will continue to accelerate (as suggested in Chapter 5, Trend F). Secondly and more important, there is a serious backlog of change left over from the 1960s and even the 1950s; one of the most changeless features of management has always been the hierarchy, or pyramid, or family tree, structure. This particular arrangement has been the *only* form of organisation structure for thousands of years, all organisations are structured as a hierarchy of managers, virtually no organisation has ever been organised in any other way. But not only has this been the form in which to arrange managers in an organisation, in any given organisation even the details of the hierarchy have remained remarkably constant over periods of years or even decades. One could understand this inertia if an organisation was not growing or contracting, or if its activities continued unchanged and unchanging for years at a time. Where this was so one could imagine that Mr Jones the Office Manager might sit at the same desk doing the same things, giving the same orders at the same time each day to Mr Smith and Mrs Brown and Miss White year after year. But things have not been like that for decades; nowadays all organisations grow or decline with dramatic rapidity, and certainly all change the nature of their activities not only in detail but on a grand scale. Huge government departments are formed or axed overnight, in companies new subsidiaries are formed or sold off, more experts are taken on, automation causes redundancies; how can we possibly expect the hierarchy to remain unchanged, broadly or in detail, for years at a time? And yet, in some organisations, it does! Especially in those organisations concerned with local or national government where even some of the detailed management procedures are laid down by law. There are two very good reasons why both the detail and the broad outline of the hierarchy of any organisation is subject to such slow change. One is that the pyramid or family tree has been such a highly successful form of organisation structure. The other is that a hierarchy consists of managers, and managers are human. When an organisational change is made, it usually results in someone being promoted – but someone is also demoted; a new department may be formed, which gives an exciting opportunity for many employees – but departments are also eliminated. However, managers have recently begun to understand that the structure within which they work is important and that, regardless of the human problems that changes always bring, they can no longer postpone making the modifications they should have made in the past twenty years to accommodate the dramatically changing style of management of organisations, which we have been discussing in the past four chapters.

In this chapter, then, we must examine how the managers in an organisation will be fitted into the new patterns and relationships that the 1970s will demand. We shall tackle this in two parts, the new non-pyramid structures will be described first and then we will examine how the traditional pyramid will be affected. However, before we go on to these two major subjects we must first deal with another organisational problem which we have noted before but not yet considered in any detail – this is the top half of the hour-glass structure we described in Chapter 6 (Conclusion 1.6 on page 76) where it was suggested that the beneficiaries should also be arranged in a hierarchical pattern or structure.

THE HIERARCHY OF BENEFICIARIES

The problem, it will be remembered, was this: over the past few decades society has become increasingly concerned about the behaviour of some organisations (mainly, but not only, those whose purpose is to make profits), and this concern is likely to increase further in the 1970s (Trend J). The effect of it is to divert some of the resources and management energy away from the achievement of the intended purpose of the organisation towards meeting the demands imposed by society and sections of society. No moral judgement is being made here as to whether all these claims are valid or desirable – we are merely drawing attention to a fact. The fact is that some companies, for example, have been denied some of their time-honoured methods of making large profits; few companies today dare use switch-selling, high-pressure selling, inertia selling, false description of goods, meaningless guarantees, etc., because they know that there is now a high probability that any dissatisfied customer

173

has only to telephone a newspaper reporter or broadcaster to bring down a massive public attack on the company. But this pressure extends to all organisations; governments have to be more careful now about selling armaments, trade unions about the closed shop and kangaroo courts, churches and charities about money-raising methods such as lotteries, and so on. But Trend J not only causes organisations to stop doing certain things that are now considered unethical, they also have to provide better conditions for employees, better quality for customers, contribute more to the local community and so on.

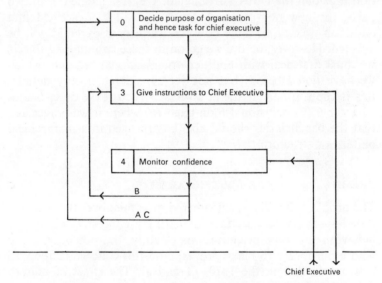

Fig 41: Three steps for the intended beneficiaries

In these circumstances it is inevitable that, given a constant standard of management ability, any given organisation will yield progressively less benefit to its intended beneficiaries; the volume of benefit can remain constant or improve only if its standard of management improves. Now only one group of people can ensure that the volume of benefit does not fall and that is the intended beneficiaries themselves, who must therefore establish a powerful supervisory liaison with their organisation. Their job is (1) to decide what they want from their organisation,

(2) to appoint and give instructions to a chief executive, and (3) to monitor confidence in the organisation's ability to yield the required benefit; their job was shown diagramatically in Fig. 19, but since then we have, as a result of our discussion in the past four chapters, had reason to modify the description of some of these tasks for managers and these changes apply also to beneficiaries. The new version of Fig. 19 is shown in Fig. 41; note also that, as we discovered in our discussions, the chief executive's job is to achieve the purpose of the organisation, that give instructions has five essential parts and that monitor confidence means the same to beneficiaries as to managers – not merely checking past results and the chief executive's present results but asking themselves what confidence they have in the organisation's continuing ability to yield a satisfactory level of benefit in the future.

This, then, is their job. How should they be organised to do it? Remember, we concluded that all organisation charts should be in the form of an hour-glass or double pyramid where the design of the upper pyramid of beneficiaries was just as important as the lower pyramid of managers. Unfortunately very little study has been given to this question, books on management deal extensively with the lower pyramid and never mention the upper one. This is a huge field and cannot be considered in detail here – certainly we can say that this is another of the missing links in management, and all we can do is to review, briefly, a few fundamental principles for inclusion in MS 70.

There is no doubt that, from the beneficiary's point of view, the best relationship he could have with the chief executive is a personal one in which he had direct access to him and can therefore make known clearly and in detail just what he, as an individual, requires from the organisation. Unfortunately, where there are more than a dozen or two beneficiaries or when the organisation is in crisis or where the beneficiaries are incapable of communicating their views (children for example) this system would break down. The next best, from the beneficiaries' point of view, would be if they had direct personal access to a representative who, having collected the views of each individual, passed them on to the chief executive – but this representative would have to add some measure of averaging or interpretation so as to present a coherent message to the chief executive. Where there are too many beneficiaries for even this system to work in practice, each representative would have to pass his amalgam of views to a further representative who in turn would pass them (perhaps through several further levels of representation) to the chief executive. The greater the number of levels of representation the greater would be the slack in the structure –

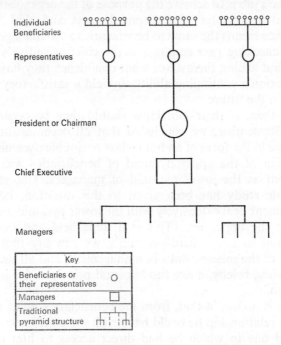

Fig 42: The personal representation of beneficiaries

this, of course, is the same problem that occurs in the management hierarchy except that in that case slack refers to actions that do not reflect a manager's wishes, while in the beneficiaries' hierarchy it refers to the accuracy with which each beneficiary's requirements are passed to the chief executive. We show this hierarchy in Fig. 42; notice that each representative is in direct contact with each individual beneficiary – we could call this

Personal Representation* to distinguish it from the other forms some of which are described below. We have called the chief representative 'Chairman' or 'President' and it is he who confronts the chief executive on the beneficiary's behalf.

An alternative which is normally used for organisations with large numbers of beneficiaries is shown in Fig. 43. Notice that each representative is no longer in direct personal contact with each individual beneficiary but represents a large group of them – we could call this Group Representation – and the amount of slack will be enormous.†

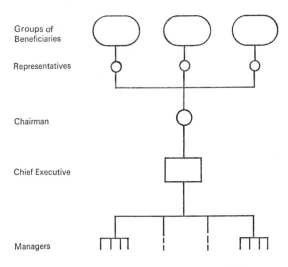

Fig 43: Group representation of beneficiaries

There is one further type of representation which we might call Indirect Representation where, as shown in Fig. 44, no attempt is made to build a hierarchy of representatives but

* This system is often found in British trade unions where the shop steward has direct contact with the men in his shop and he has direct contact with the next level up the union hierarchy.

† One of the reasons why small organisations are often more successful than large ones is that the beneficiaries, being smaller in number, can adopt the personal representation form of organisation structure which allows less slack than the group or indirect form.

instead a group or Board of people represent all the beneficiaries collectively. Of all the methods one could adopt by which the beneficiaries of an organisation could make their views known and check results this is probably the weakest for it depends upon the members of the Board exerting their influence on the chief executive on behalf of the beneficiaries but, as can be seen from Fig. 44, the Board has only a tenuous impersonal

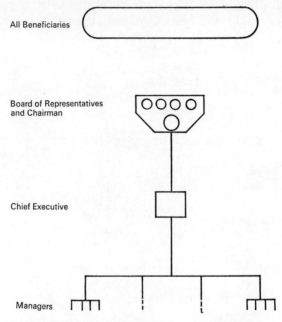

All Beneficiaries

Board of Representatives and Chairman

Chief Executive

Managers

Fig 44: Indirect representation of beneficiaries

contact with them. It may be significant that this was the pattern of many University Boards of Governers until the student revolts of the 1960s and is also the design used by shareholders in Britain. In their case the design is even further weakened by the extraordinary trick of electing people to the Board who are not primarily shareholders' representatives but senior managers! It is difficult to imagine a surer recipe for disaster. When, in addition, the man who is the chief representative of the share-holders (we have called him chairman or president) is also chief executive, then one can guarantee that the manager's

178

aims for the organisation will win a handsome victory over the beneficiaries' aims.*

Whatever the ideal arrangement is – and Fig. 45 may be as near as one can get – a great deal more thought will have to be given to the top half of the hierachy in the 1970s; if it is not beneficiaries will be unable to exercise sufficient control and, in the increasingly difficult management environment caused by

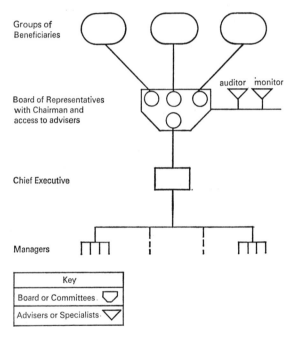

Fig 45: Group representation of beneficiaries with Board and access to advisers

Trend J and many others, the intended benefits will disappear; if profits were the only benefit to disappear that would be serious enough but profit-making organisations are certainly not the only ones at risk. It must be stressed, however, that if beneficiaries do strengthen their control over the management in some way and if they use their power to draw benefit to

* Compare the shareholders system of representation with that of the shop stewards in the footnote on page 177.

themselves at the expense of the legitimate claims on organisations of other groups of society (employees, local community,
etc.) then society will rightly react. This is not the use of
beneficiaries' power which is being suggested here; what is being
suggested is that of all the people connected with an organisation the beneficiaries are most responsible for ensuring that the
management is up to its task. If the managers of the organisation
cannot produce a satisfactory level of benefit for the beneficiaries
except by using unethical means or by neglecting the legitimate
claims of other groups, then the management should be
changed. This is the task of the beneficiaries.

One final point, in all advanced societies organisations have
to be registered and have their books of account audited. This
audit tells the beneficiaries that no improper use of funds has
occurred. The auditor is the only specialist that the beneficiaries
have to advise them. Perhaps they need another (especially if
they adopt the indirect form of representation) – a specialist
who can audit the competence of their management and who
can give them an informed opinion on the chances of their
organisation continuing to provide them with a satisfactory
level of benefit in the future. (This is the role of the press in a
democracy, after all.) Since he would essentially be helping
them to monitor their confidence in the organisation's continuing efficacy perhaps he should be called a Monitor.

THE MANAGER'S HIERARCHY – SOME RADICAL DEPAR-
TURES

We must now introduce two radical departures from the traditional hierarchy or pyramid or family tree structure – the
Cell and the Matrix. These two are not mere variations on the
pyramid – they are different in principle – and to demonstrate
that they are different we must first briefly describe the pyramid.
The pyramid has been virtually the only form of organisation
structure for thousands of years – ever since man formed his
first organisation right up to a few years ago. The principle on
which it is founded is the one we have called agreed seniority
(page 12) which states that in any group of people in an organisation there is always one man who is the boss and several

others who are the subordinates, and it is agreed between them (sometimes formally, sometimes very informally, sometimes at the point of a gun, more often voluntarily) that the subordinates will agree to carry out the boss's orders and that he may punish or reward them. The reason for the enduring success of the pyramid is its efficacy as a command structure. A general can give orders to, say, ten colonels, they each give orders to ten majors, to ten lieutenants, to ten sergeants, to ten corporals, to ten soldiers and, in a matter of minutes, the general's orders are obeyed by the astonishing total of 1,000,000 men – all this is accomplished in the time it takes for each level of the hierarchy to gallop off on his horse to the next level, a mere six or seven journey-times. Our use of this example – a military one – is simply that the pyramid structure is at its best in a battle or emergency situation because the pyramid is an ideal *command* structure. It depends for its efficacy on two conditions: (1) that each subordinate has one clearly identified boss from whom he takes orders, and (2) that these orders are obeyed without hesitation and without question. It was absolutely ideal, therefore, for the social conditions in which most managers worked until a few decades ago. We saw in the last few chapters, however, that condition (2) is crumbling rapidly due to improved mass education (Trend E) and we shall discuss how this will affect the pyramid in the 1970s later in the chapter. But now we must consider breaking down condition (1), that each subordinate must only have one clearly identified boss.

The alternatives to having one boss are (a) to have no boss and (b) to have several. The first leads to the cell, the second to the matrix. Let us first consider the cell structure – or rather, lack of it. The cell consists of a group of people having no official structure (i.e. no structure imposed on it by the management of the organisation) and no official manager although it might have a manager elected by the members of the group temporarily or even permanently. The traditional pyramid structure for an office is shown in Fig. 46; the equivalent cell-structure is shown in Fig. 47. Fig. 48 takes it one stage further where not only the sections of the office have no structure, the whole office has become a cell, but to the probable confusion of everyone, for presumably it is possible to go too fast along this

181

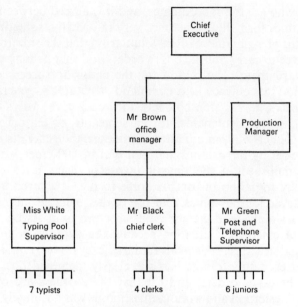

Fig 46: Part of a traditional pyramid

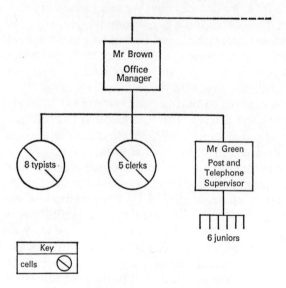

Fig 47: Mr. Brown introduces two cells

route and it is possible to have so large a group that even the members themselves are unable to organise their work and thus destroy the whole purpose of the cell structure. What is the purpose? To enable groups of people to organise and supervise their own work as described on page 135 (group work) as part of the movement towards wider discretion. Towards the end of the 1960s the idea that (small) groups of people could produce better results on their own than if they were managed by a boss was gaining currency. It was certainly being suggested that one of the reasons why small organisations were often more successful than large ones was that, having less formality and disci-

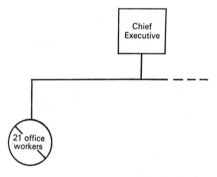

Fig 48: Mr Brown takes the cell structure to its logical conclusion. But is it not going too far in the seventies?

pline, their employees were left alone to organise and to supervise more of their own work. If this theory proves correct we can expect to see more of these cells in the 1970s, and considerable research will no doubt be done by social scientists and psychologists to determine the optimum number of people per cell and how to increase that optimum. (It should be noted incidentally that Fig. 49 probably represents a logical contradiction and that one cannot have a hierarchy of cells; they can only occur at the extremity of any hierarchical limb and so should perhaps be called Terminal Cells.) We will see an important application for these cells later in the chapter.

Now let us turn to the other alternative – the matrix form of management where each subordinate has more than one boss.

It is immediately obvious that one outstanding objection exists to having more than one boss – that confusion would arise in the mind of the subordinate especially if he received conflicting or even contradictory orders from his several bosses. This objection is partially or wholly removed if we take account of the rising standard of education, for, it is suggested, an educated subordinate would not be struck dumb by such a situation but would refer for a ruling on priority to his bosses and, if they could not agree, they could refer it to theirs. Nor is the idea of

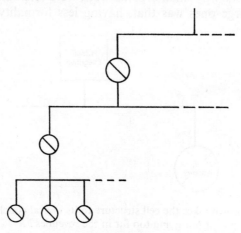

Fig 49: Impossible to have a hierarchy of cells? Or only too advanced for the seventies?

having more than one boss particularly new or remarkable. One secretary often works for half-a-dozen middle managers and, unless she is particularly sensitive, is perfectly capable of referring the problem of conflicting instructions to her bosses. Again, the clerk of works on a construction site often takes orders from the architect, the main contractors, sub-contractors, various inspectors, the local electricity engineers, etc. So there is nothing odd about this idea, the only question is why it is being put forward as an important element of a management system for the 1970s. The reasons for its growing importance are worth discussing in some detail.

One is Trend F (the increasing rate of change in the 1970s)

and the other is Trend H (the increasing size and complexity of organisations). Let us first imagine an organisation which neither expands nor contracts over a period of years, whose activities remain unchanged and where even the employees remain the same. In such an entirely static organisation there would be no need for long and careful thought over the next major decision because there would be no major decisions. Everyone would continue to do just what he had done the day before in just the same way at the same time each day. In these circumstances the overheads of the organisation would be very low – very few managers would be needed in the hierarchy because no decisions have to be taken and there would be no need for any management services such as a personnel department. One result of this discussion is to reveal how difficult it is to compare the 'efficiency' of one organisation with another; it is so easy to point to organisation A and to say that its overheads are too high compared with B when, in fact, B's overheads are too low because it has not yet realised that it lives in a changing world. So let us now recognise that the world is changing and organisations must also change; what effect would this have on the organisation we were discussing? Firstly they would need more management service departments – a personnel department, for example, to cope with the fact that employees do leave, retire, die and do have to be recruited, trained and retrained – but we will return to the effect of change on management services later in the chapter. The organisation would also need more managers since major decisions to bring about changes are needed. If the only changes envisaged were that the organisation would expand or contract in size then all that would be needed would be more managers in each department. For example, imagine a company producing 1,000 units of product a week with a staff of ten managers in the production department; now assume it decides to expand production: if ten fully occupied managers are needed to maintain a constant 1,000 units, more than ten will be needed to take the decisions necessary to increase it and to monitor confidence, etc. – and this is over and above the number of extra managers required to supervise the extra operators that the increased output will eventually demand. But it should be noted that *all* the extra managers will be required within the production department itself. Expansion or contraction of themselves require managing – it is sometimes said that the real task of a manager is 'to manage change', and while this is a mere slogan it clearly has some validity. However, we have so far assumed that the only change taking place is contraction or expansion, the organisation we have been discussing is merely doing more or less of the same things. If we now admit that the nature of its activities also change then we have a further difficulty: some of these changes will affect different parts of the organisation differently and will have to be co-ordinated across departmental boundaries. This leads us to a relatively new problem, the management of projects that affect several parts of an organisation; we could call them Transdepartmental Projects. We must discuss the rising significance of these.

In the old days, before the rate of change (Trend F) became so fast, it was possible for organisations to continue performing the same broad activities for decades – a company producing oil lamps could go on doing so for decades, making only small changes to design, or small changes in production or selling methods; a government department could go on providing the same service; a charity could continue alleviating the same social problems among the same type of people. Today and increasingly in the 1970s organisations will have to make radical changes affecting every one of their activities at an ever increasing rate, their managers will have to take major strategic decisions far more often than in previous generations. This means that there will be more transdepartmental projects and these bring their own special problem of co-ordination; a project that affects, say, seven major departments cannot be managed by seven separate departmental heads who are in any case already fully occupied with the day-to-day management of their departments. The solution is to appoint a Project Manager who is responsible for completing the project up to the point where the major changes in each department have been made when he hands over to the departmental managers for routine continued management as part of their new activities. If there are several projects in hand at any time then there will be several project managers perhaps working under a Projects

186

Director. We show such a situation in Fig. 50, where a company has three major projects on hand. Project A is the introduction of a new product which requires an extension to be built to the existing factory (so this Project Manager has the authority, shown by the circle, to give instructions to some of the employees in the Factory Director's department and they, of course, will

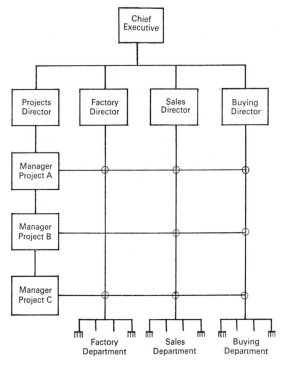

Fig 50: A matrix structure for managing projects

therefore be taking instructions from two bosses). It also requires new salesmen to be recruited and some of the existing ones to be trained with them (so the Project Manager gives instructions to some of the Sales Director's men). It also requires new components to be purchased, hence the symbol linking the Project Manager and the Buying Director's Department. Project B, on the other hand, is for a new product that involves no manufacturing facilities so Project Manager B gives no instructions to the Factory Director's men although he does to some of the sales and buying department. Finally, the third Project, C, is the introduction of a new personnel policy so its manager has authority to supervise this change in each of the departments. (A 'project' is not necessarily a physical thing like building a factory; it can be any change such as a new training scheme, an attack on costs, a programme of improved productivity and so on.) Changes do not occur of themselves, they have to be managed by someone.

Rapid change in the 1970s will mean more major projects and the successful completion of these will increasingly be made the formal responsibility of one man, the Project Manager, and the matrix form of management will become widely adopted. But the matrix form is appropriate in many other circumstances, not just when a project has to be co-ordinated across departmental boundaries.* The most powerful stimulus to its use is another of the features that will characterise management in the 1970s – the size and complexity of organisations (Trend H). In the days when an organisation carried out one simple activity in one locality the traditional functional hierarchy was appropriate. Imagine a Scottish company making one product and selling it only in Scotland; the only major departments required are one production department and one sales department. But as soon as that company starts making a second, different product or builds a second factory it needs two production staffs, either with two different skills, or in two different places. If it also starts exporting to Ireland it needs a second sales department as well. Now one of the trends in the 1970s is for large organisations to become larger, more international and more diversified – large companies are moving towards multi-

---

* A doctor is a project manager, too. Ideally he looks upon the continued good health of each patient as a project. His success can easily be verified by the number of days' illness each patient has, their longevity, and so on. The doctor also uses the matrix form of organisation when he calls upon the many medical services provided by the state and others. Many managers are, in fact, project managers although they may not have realised it; it might help them considerably if they did, for then the logic of their job within the framework of their organisation becomes clear and so does the nature of their personal relationships with other managers in a matrix.

188

national multiproduct conglomerates, large specialist charities are tending to become multinational multipurpose, trade unions are moving the same way; in general, then, organisations that are already large are becoming multicomplex. Multicomplex organisations will progressively adopt the matrix form of organisation, an example of which is shown in Fig. 51 where all the senior managers have two bosses – the manager of the company's plastics factory in India, for example, has two bosses:

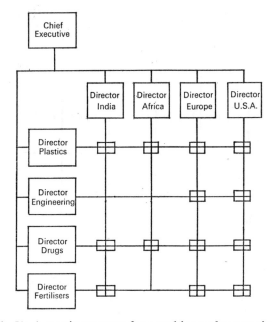

Fig 51: A matrix structure for a multi-complex organisation

the director in charge of plastics all over the world and the director in charge of all activities in India. He may have a third boss if there is a major world wide project involving his factory so we could arrive at a matrix in several dimensions, or multimatrix form of organisation.

Let us end this section of the chapter by pointing to a marked divergence of trends in management during the 1970s. In Chapter 5 we noted (page 48) that large organisations would become larger and more complex but that there would also be far more small organisations. Now the cell form of organisation is ideally suited to small organisations where the best organisation structure may well be no structure at all, especially if the employees are fairly well educated. But, as a contrast, large organisations are becoming so large and so incredibly complex that it is almost inconceivable that a one-dimensional structure could possibly be adequate; the traditional pyramid is of one

1974

Section / Project	Expenditure allocated to Manager of Chemistry Section	Expenditure allocated to Manager of Physics Section	Expenditure allocated to Manager of Biology Section	Expenditure allocated to Manager of Experimental Section	Expenditure allocated to Admin – istrative Manager	Totals
Expenditure allocated to Manager of Routine Process Development	£40,000	£60,000	£10,000	£80,000	£20,000	£210,000
Expenditure allocated to Manager of Bio-electric Cell Project	£10,000	£40,000	£180,000	£300,000	£30,000	£560,000
Expenditure allocated to Manager of Bio-thermic Materials Project	£70,000	—	£20,000	£60,000	£30,000	£180,000
Totals	£120,000	£100,000	£210,000	£44,000	£80,000	£950,000

Fig 52: A matrix budget for a research department

dimension and to try to structure a multinational multiproduct company into a pyramid is like trying to build a colour television receiver with a child's Meccano set. So it is for the government machinery of a modern nation, the International Red Cross, UNESCO, FAO, The Greater London Council, Kennedy Airport, etc. Perhaps the frightening failure of some of our large modern organisations can be traced to their continued attempt to squash an organisational quart into the pint pot of

the pyramid. Nor is it only the organisation structure that
must become multi-dimensional; all the planning and control
mechanisms must be too and this leads to the idea of two-
dimensional budgets (sometimes called Programme Budgets)
where the Departmental Manager controls his expenditure,
the Project Manager controls his and both are responsible for
the expenditure that is common to them both as shown in Fig.
52 (notice, incidentally, there is here a matrix *within* a department). It seems probable that there will be less slack in a large
organisation if it is managed, planned and controlled in two
dimensions rather than in only one. Both the cell and the
matrix are important elements in MS 70.*

THE DECLINE OF THE PYRAMID IN THE 1970s

One of the reasons why the pyramid will play a less important
role in the 1970s is that its efficacy depends to some extent on
the unhesitating obedience of each subordinate at each level and
this type of obedience is clearly in decline. Another reason is
that each decision at each level in the hierarchy is taking longer
today so the speed of response from top to bottom of the
pyramid – one of its most valuable characteristics – is also
reduced. Many other trends are running against the pyramid and
will contribute to its decline:

1. Trend P, for example, which reflects the movement
towards mechanisation in the office and factory. If we assume
that the volume of work in an organisation remains the same
but that mechanisation and automation displace human
operators at the rate of 7 per cent per annum then the number
of operators (i.e. shop-floor workers, clerks, salesmen, etc.)
will be halved in a decade. So an organisation employing
1,000 operators in 1970 will employ only 500 in 1980. Thus
the number of managers at each level will also be halved and
the whole pyramid will be halved.

* Looking further ahead, perhaps to MS 8o – we might see cells
within the matrix. In other words, two or more managers will be giving
instructions to quite large groups of people who organise the work among
themselves. But by then there will be other rather complex organisational
forms as well – the Cartwheel and the Honeycomb, perhaps!

2. The calculation above assumes that the number of subordinates that each manager can control – the span of control as it is called – will remain constant. In fact it is likely to increase very rapidly in the 1970s because (1) the principle of wider discretion implies that managers will spend far less time supervising each subordinate so they will be able to supervise more of them and (2) improved communications (Trend B) and the computer (Trend C) will both remove some of the problems of supervision, especially the chore of laboriously checking results by wading through figures (see page 155). As a rough guide it is suggested that the span of control will increase as a result of these two trends by at least 50 per cent in the decade, i.e. if the average manager now has six subordinates this may increase to nine or ten over the decade. This reduction of the intensity of supervision is of major importance in the battle against Trend M – the revolt against centralisation of power and the officious use of authority.

3. Trend L is important here. This suggests that more and more specialists and advisers will be employed by organisations, their numbers may well increase by 50 per cent in the decade even in an organisation that was not otherwise expanding. If these specialists were placed in the pyramid, that would tend to expand it, but it would be surprising if they were; it is more likely that they will be placed in a management services department for reasons described later.

Let us now consider what might happen to the pyramid in the light of all these trends. Imagine an organisation employing 400 operators in 1970, and imagine that the nature of its activities does not change nor does its output of goods or services expand or contract. Let us further assume that it employs 100 specialists and that each of its managers can control only six subordinates. (All this is very unrealistic but we are less concerned with realism here than with illustrating the principles.) So this organisation employs 500 advisers and operators; how many managers will there have to be? At the lowest level there will be 83, each supervising 6 advisers and operators, at the next level there will be 14, then at the next 3, then 1, the chief executive. A total of about 100 managers. Now move forward to 1980 when there may be only 200 operators (50 per cent down) but the number of specialists will have risen to 150 (50 per cent up), a total of 350. If the span of control rises to 9 subordinates per manager (50 per cent increase) then we will only need 40 managers at the lowest level, 5 at the next, and a chief executive – a total of 46 managers, half as many as in 1970. But the number of managers' salaries we have saved is not the important point, the point is that we have cut out one level in the hierarchy – in 1970 there were 5, in 1980 there are 4. Why is this so important? Because, as we have seen, the pyramid is no longer able to give us the quick response to change that it used to give when subordinates obeyed instructions without question. Whereas an order could go down a five-level hierarchy in a matter of minutes, it now takes hours or days, partly because managers at each stage have to discuss each decision with their subordinates and partly because decisions take longer to make even without this discussion because they are now so much more difficult. Also, and equally important, slack occurs at the interface between a manager and a subordinate; cut the number of levels and we cut the slack.

If the pyramid is becoming of less value as an organisational structure for managers it might be asked why use it at all – why not design some new form or employ only the cell or the matrix? Perhaps this will come but the matrix only came into use in the late 1960s in a few organisations and the cell in fewer still; both will be highly controversial for at least a decade. The pyramid is still the only command structure tested by time.

There may be one new way to reduce the size of the pyramid still further and that is by removing from it every employee who does not need to be in it (i.e. those who are neither operators nor managers), namely the advisers. If one inspects the organisation chart of a company, for example, one usually finds that each manager has two types of subordinate, 'line' and 'staff' or executives and advisers. A works manager, for example, may have the following subordinates: two production managers (one for each of two major processes), an engineer, an accountant, a work study officer and a personnel adviser. Three of these men are executives and themselves have further subordinates in

193

line management, but the last three do not and are not line managers but staff advisers. Depending on circumstances it may be possible to take these three advisers (and others like them in the rest of the company) and place them in a management services department. This would leave the Works Manager with line managers only to supervise and, again depending on circumstances, his span of control could be restored to six subordinates by transferring to him three line executives from some other department. An example of how this might be done is shown in Fig. 53 – notice also that either the Sales Manager or the Works Manager becomes General Manager thus enriching his job.

There are many cogent reasons why advisers should not be located in the pyramid but rather in a special management services department:

(a) They are advisers, not managers, so why are they in the command structure at all? The answer is that there was nowhere else to put them because until recently the pyramid was the only known structure. While they remain in the pyramid they merely add to the number of people reporting to each manager.

(b) Their numbers are increasing rapidly; by the end of the 1970s advisers will easily outnumber the managers in most large organisations and may even outnumber the shop-floor workers. Their function in the organisation is to help managers to take decisions and to plan, to monitor confidence, to give specialist advice and in general to comment on what the organisation is doing and how well it is doing it – they take no active part in its operations. Perhaps they could do their job better and comment more objectively if they were outside the command structure altogether.

(c) Some of the newer specialists are essentially concerned with transdepartmental problems: the corporate planner, the financial adviser, the personnel adviser, the training officer, etc. Where in the pyramid should one place the computer manager, for example; should his boss be the chief accountant, the research director, the production manager? If the computer is to be used in only one of these departments the

194

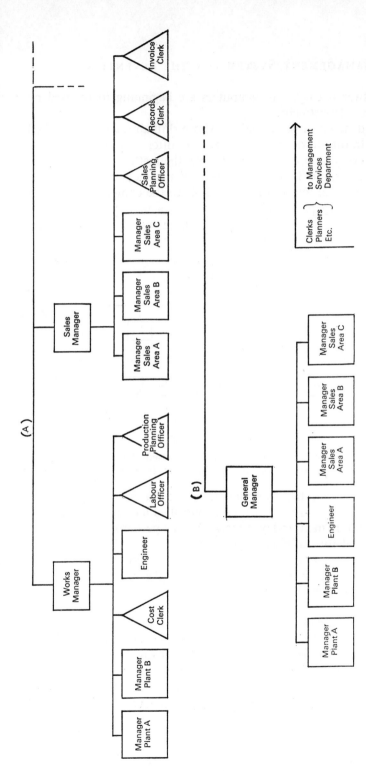

Fig 53: (A) Two senior managers each controlling a mix of line executives and staff advisers (B) One senior manager now controls six line executives

answer is easy, but computers are beginning to be used by every department.

(d) Even those specialists whose skill appears to be limited by tradition to one department can often be used by another. In many companies, for example, the method study expert is to be found in the production department where he may never be asked to apply his skills to the company's research laboratory procedures. If he was in a management services department he could be called upon by any section of the company requiring his skills.

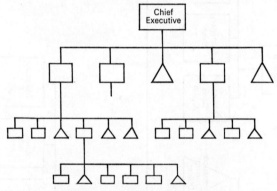

Fig 54: A typical traditional pyramid composed of both line managers (rectangle) and staff advisers (triangle)

Decades ago there were no advisers; if a manager controlled ten subordinates that meant he controlled ten line executives or ten fighting men, today it means he has perhaps six line executives and four advisers reporting to him – by 1980 it may be three and seven. So when the modern equivalent of a general gives an order it is not relayed in multiples of ten at each level in the pyramid but only in multiples of six. The pyramid has become so gorged with non-executives, the span of control is today so narrow that the pyramid of any large organisation has become a hindrance to action rather than a help. So the problem is this: during the 1970s the number of operators will decline due to automation in the office and factory, but the number of advisers will increase nearly as fast so that the number of managers (and therefore the number of levels in the pyramid

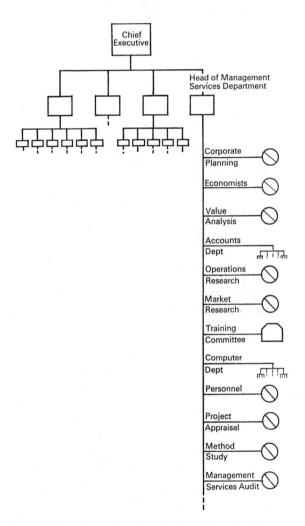

Fig 55: Organisation chart showing all the advisers having been placed in a management services department leaving a short squat pyramid composed of managers only

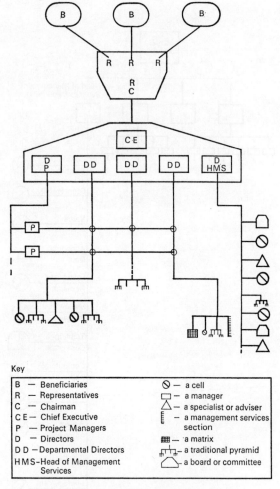

Key

B	— Beneficiaries	⊘ —	a cell
R	— Representatives	▭ —	a manager
C	— Chairman	△ —	a specialist or adviser
C E	— Chief Executive	Ɛ —	a management services
P	— Project Managers		section
D	— Directors	▦ —	a matrix
D D	—Departmental Directors	⊓⊓ —	a traditional pyramid
H M S	—Head of Management Services	⬠ —	a board or committee

Fig 56: A complete organisation chart

required to supervise these two classes of employee will decline only slowly. Where an organisation's output is increasing – as it usually will in the case of successful organisations – the number of levels in the pyramid will rise rapidly, and to absurd proportions in the case of very large organisations. Two solutions are offered: firstly the span of control exercised by each

198

manager must be increased (the consequent reduction in the intensity of supervision being in accordance with the movement towards wider discretion) and, secondly, as many advisers and advisory committees as possible should be taken out of the pyramid and placed in cells (or, for large groups of advisers in any specialism, in a small pyramid) in a management services department. The present situation is shown in Fig. 54, the proposed situation in Fig. 55.

Fig. 56 shows all three forms of organisation structure; matrix, cell, and pyramid. It looks like a Christmas Tree and is certainly very complicated. But, it is suggested, it is no more complicated than the traditional pyramid would be for the same organisation and it is certainly more logical; why should we think, when everything else is created in endless variety, that one ancient organisational form should suit us for every occasion?

A brief description of the job of the head of the management services department is necessary. It is to ensure that a sufficient number (and quality) of each type of adviser is available to the organisation. He decides whether to employ an adviser full time or part time or to use the services of an outside specialist organisation. He can decide this, and supervise all these people as well, on the basis of reports given to him by his own small audit section (referred to as management services audit section in Fig. 55) who receive reports concerning the quality of advice given by his staff to managers all over the pyramid and (since any adviser in the management services department may call upon any other for advice) from reports from his own staff as well. Discipline could be left largely or wholly to the cells themselves – if not now, perhaps later in the decade.

ORGANISATION STRUCTURES IN THE 1970s

A letter to *The Times** from five noted experts in public administration began, 'Fundamental changes in the local government system are not likely, and indeed ought not, to occur more than about once in a century'. Well, that is one view, but the principle we have adopted for MS 70 is directly opposite to this: MS 70

* 4 February 1970.

lays down that fundamental changes should *never* occur in an organisation structure but that, on the contrary, structures should change continuously in small, non-fundamental steps. This view results from taking account of the increasing rate of change in the environment in which managers work; this implies that any structure that is appropriate to an organisation in 1970 will have ceased to be appropriate by 1971 and it should be adjusted to suit the new conditions. One of the reasons this is not done is that the rules for designing a structure and for altering it in response to any given change were not known – better to leave well alone, therefore. But MS 70 provides the rules which show clearly the direction in which changes should be made and we can even describe the symptoms that begin to show themselves when a change is overdue. For example, we know that if the average span of control of the managers in a given organisation is shorter today than last year then the organisation will start to show the symptoms of a surfeit of supervision – subordinates develop a we-and-they attitude, start watching the clock, become less co-operative, resent new ideas, etc., because they feel they are becoming a mere cog in a wheel. Again, in an organisation that is growing we would expect to see far more service departments (personnel, etc.) including perhaps a project planning department and perhaps the matrix – if we did not we could expect to see such obvious symptoms of strain as the failure or late completion of the projects. Although there are now several different forms of organisation to choose from, the rules showing when to adopt which are fairly clear; the rules for increasing the span of control and reducing the number of levels in the pyramid are clear. This is not to suggest that it is ever easy in practice to make organisational changes – managers are human beings as we said before – but if the changes are made gradually and if the best moment for them is anticipated in advance ('When old George retires') and if we know broadly the design we are aiming for over the next few years, then these things become less difficult to do in the real world. The concept of a gradual planned movement towards a known goal is inherent in all parts of MS 70, but is nowhere more important than where people are concerned.

Let us end the chapter with some calculations to show what will happen to an organisation that ignores the warnings given here. Imagine a company, Hypothetics Ltd, which employed 1,000 factory and office workers in 1970 together with 200 advisers and whose average manager then controlled 6 subordinates – so there were 240 managers including the chief executive in a five-level hierarchy. Imagine that by 1980 Hypothetics Ltd have doubled output but have not improved productivity at all (so they will have 2,000 workers) and the number of advisers has risen to 600 (200 doubled plus 50 per cent). Now they need 522 managers in 6 levels (because the average span of control has not increased either) and this huge increase is certain to affect both their costs and the speed of response of the company to changes in the business environment. What could they have done? Firstly they could have used automation in the factory and office to keep the operators down to 1,000 by 1980 (output rising at 7 per cent per annum but productivity also rising by 7 per cent per annum.) They could have put most of the advisers (say 400) into cells in a management services department leaving, say, 200 still in the pyramid to be supervised in the normal way. They could have increased the span of control to 9. If they had planned to do all this steadily, gradually and continuously over the decade these might have been realistic, practical aims in the real world. Had they succeeded they would have needed only 153 managers (plus say 20 in the services department) in only 5 levels – and, it must be remembered, that Hypothetics' output has been growing at 7 per cent per annum. If organisations, especially large ones that are growing, are not to become crushed by the sheer lead weight of their management structure, something has got to be done.

Conclusion 5.1. During the 1970s the way in which managers manage organisations will change; the way in which they are structured within an organisation must also be changed.

Conclusion 5.2. All organisation structures consist of two parts – the beneficiaries' structure for representation of their views to the chief executive and the management structure. Both should always be consciously designed and redesigned frequently and as much care be given to the top half of the hour-glass as the lower half.

Conclusion 5.3. Where an organisation has few beneficiaries it is possible for them to use the personal form of representation in which there is very little slack. Larger organisations may use the group form and it may be necessary for some organisations to use the indirect form where slack is usually considerable. (Many versions of these and other forms exist but little formal research has been done.)

Conclusion 5.4. In the beneficiaries' structure slack can be reduced by appointing a monitor to advise them on the probability of the continued success of their organisation. Slack is increased where one man acts both as a beneficiaries' representative and a manager of the same organisation; this is true also where a man acts as chairman and chief executive.

Conclusion 5.5. The pyramid is an ideal command structure so long as (1) each man has one boss, (2) subordinates are obedient – where these conditions hold an organisation can respond rapidly to change. Both conditions will continue to be undermined during the 1970s leading to a decline in the pyramid and a rise in new structural forms for managers.

Conclusion 5.6. The cell, in which there is no official boss and no official subordinates, is one form that will come into use in the 1970s. In a cell employees organise the work and supervise themselves; it is appropriate to small organisations and small groups of employees.

Conclusion 5.7. The matrix will come into use in larger organisations and in departments or sections of large organisations. It is particularly appropriate for project management and for organisations having multicomplex activities. New multi-dimensional forms of planning and control will be developed for use with it.

Conclusion 5.8. The pyramid form will slowly decline, i.e.

in any given organisation fewer employees will be found in the pyramid as the decade progresses. This is partly due to Conclusion 5.5 but also to the effects of automation, the widening span of control and the growth of management services departments. In those larger organisations where the size of the pyramid is already an intolerable burden its decline will be rapid.

Conclusion 5.9. More organisations will form management services departments composed of a growing number and variety of specialists and advisers whose job is to advise or comment on the activities of the organisation. Many of these employees will be in cells except where there are large numbers of one specialisation when they will have to form a pyramid.

Conclusion 5.10. The head of this department will be responsible (to the chief executive) for ensuring that adequate advice is available to managers in any part of the organisation either from specialists employed in the management services department or from outside specialist organisations. He will evaluate the performance of these specialists by reports on the quality of their advice.

Chapter 11
MS 70

In each of the five previous chapters we discussed one of the five basic elements of MS 70 – the Four Steps and the Hierarchy. We came to several conclusions in each chapter and now we must put them all together and make sure that they fit into a coherent whole. Before we examine the conclusions we reached and before we try to fit them together perhaps we should just remind ourselves of what we are trying to do.

MS 70 – WHAT IS IT FOR?

Right back in Chapter 1 we made several points. Firstly we suggested that organisations were becoming more difficult to manage – few managers today would dispute that – but we added that this would go on indefinitely; management will continue to become more and more difficult as the years and decades roll on. Secondly, we expressed some discontent with the present state of the theory and practice of management; we complained that the specialist academics were so busy examining the bits and pieces of management in ever increasing detail that they never had time to put the bits back again and show us how they worked – they left the jigsaw puzzle scattered on the floor. We also complained that when a successful manager drew attention to a useful practical conclusion born of his experience it might have been valid when he learnt it but it could have become invalid within a matter of years. Thirdly we felt that the whole subject of management had become so weighed down with all the new knowledge and techniques that thousands of research workers in the subject keep churning out that the basic framework of management was in danger of collapse. It is rather like a man who owns a Ford Model T car

204

who, over the years, has fitted into it an automatic gear box, power steering, then a hydropneumatic trailing arm double pinion suspension. In other words, in Chapter 1 we suggested it was time to tow the whole groaning management vehicle back to the garage and redesign and rebuild it for the job it was going to have to do in the 1970s. So the purpose of MS 70 is to provide a new management system by which organisations can be better managed in the 1970s. We have tackled this job in three stages; firstly, in Chapters 2, 3 and 4 we ascertained what 'management' was; a four-step process carried out by managers who stand in some form of human relationship with each other – quite a complex arrangement as we saw in Fig 21.

Secondly, in order to ensure that our system was appropriate to the 1970s we had to predict what conditions would be like for managers in the 1970s. We did this in Chapter 5 and, sure enough, many of the trends we discussed there confirmed our worst fears about organisations becoming more difficult to manage. There was Trend Q – the ever increasing complexities of decision-making with growing penalties for being wrong; there was Trend H – the ever-growing size of large organisations (but a glimmer of light, too, because there will be more smaller organisations); then Trend J predicting that society would impose an ever-tightening band of demands on organisations – especially companies. There were Trends M and N suggesting that subordinates would increasingly resent the centralisation of power, or the officious use of authority and would become progressively more immune to penalty or reward from their boss. All this adds up to a management nightmare – and we still have to add Trend F which says that the rate of change will accelerate and Trend G, the bewildering increase in the variety of goods and services that organisations will have to provide!

So Chapter 5 confirmed the feeling expressed in Chapter 1 – that a new approach to management was needed in view of all these hostile trends. But Chapter 5 did something else as well; it revealed that not all the trends were hostile, only about half of them were. Suppose it was somehow possible to take the non-hostile trends and harness them, turn them to our account, use them to reinforce management? That is just the trick that we have been trying to pull of in MS 70 (and it is precisely the failure to play this trick that condemns so much management literature). There is no reason to think that these favourable trends, properly used, will be any less powerful aids to the manager than the hostile ones will be a hindrance to him. Consider some of them: Trend E, which suggests that managers can look forward to better educated subordinates who, one expects, will be more rational, more knowledgeable and if properly handled will contribute far more to the organisation than their predecessors. Then quantification, Trend K, will bring greater precision, less slack. The new specialists (Trend L), the computer (Trend C), improved communications (Trend B), the great banks of data being built up (Trend D) can all help the manager solve his problems, and some of them are powerful allies. The philosophy underlying MS 70, then, is that the 1970s contains ladders as well as snakes for the manager, there will be Goodies as well as Baddies in the film we are to see; let us design a system to combat the latter by arranging an alliance with the former. The words '*design* a system' are important; an organisation is a complex entity and it is not sufficient to allow its system of management to grow undirected – it has to be carefully designed, skilfully tailored to the needs of the organisation and for the environment in which it is to operate and, as we shall see in the next chapter, it has to be just as carefully introduced.

INTERNAL CONSISTENCY OF THE CONCLUSIONS

Over the past few chapters we have reached a large number of conclusions. Some of these turn out on inspection to be duplicates because we reached the same conclusion twice in different chapters. Others in later chapters supersede or are more comprehensive than some of the ones in earlier chapters. The crucial question here is whether any of them are in conflict with any others, for if they are it will make it impossible to complete MS 70 which is our aim in this chapter. Our aim is to bring all the conclusions together into a few simple but comprehensive statements which, when taken as a coherent whole form MS 70. Obviously, therefore, if any conclusions contradict any other the system will be internally inconsistent, at odds with itself and therefore useless even in theory let alone in practice. But these conclusions should be more than merely not contradictory, they should be mutually reinforcing – each should key into the other so strongly that when all are in position the structure should stand firm as rock.

Let us test some of them now. Conclusion 4.8 was recorded on page 169 as:

Depending on his level of confidence in achieving his target a manager will either do nothing, or take action to increase the chances of achieving the target or, if confidence is low, he will report impending failure to his boss.

This is merely a clarification of Conclusion 0.11 (page 40) which we reached much earlier before we changed 'Check Results' – to the wider description of Step 4 'Monitor Confidence'. There is no contradiction here, therefore. These two conclusions link with another – Conclusion 0.8 which says on page 38:

Once a manager has accepted a task from his boss he is not entitled to alter it without referring to his boss.

This is just another way of saying 'report impending failure to his boss' in Conclusion 4.8; so far, then, we have not found any statements contradictory to Conclusion 4.8. Here, however, is one that is mutually reinforcing. Conclusion 1.7 (page 76) is nothing to do with monitoring confidence and yet it contains the same concept of three targets. It says:

. . . targets. They can be set at three levels: (1) the result that represents failure and *must* be exceeded, (2) the result that the beneficiaries regard as satisfactory, and (3) the result that represents success.

and the same idea was repeated for managers in Conclusion 3.3 (page 147). So we have here a reinforcement; we have concluded not only that it is sensible to set a target at three levels but also that when a manager tests his confidence he decides what to do on the basis of these same three levels. Thus, if his boss has set him the task of increasing sales turnover, and if he has told him that an increase of 2 per cent is unacceptable,

4 per cent is O.K. and 6 per cent is excellent, then, when the manager comes to review his progress he will report to his boss, redouble his efforts or do nothing depending on his confidence of achieving 2, 4 or 6 per cent.

Consider now another set of conclusions; Conclusion 2.8 (page 113) says that ethical considerations will become important in selecting alternative ways of achieving a task. This is reinforced by Conclusion 3.9 which says that managers must ensure that subordinates do not use unethical methods, and is reinforced again in Conclusion 1.13 which says subordinates must not accept unethical instructions.

Take another set. In Conclusion 1.11 (page 76) we concluded there would be more management techniques for quantifying tasks; in Conclusion 2.7 (page 113) more techniques for evaluating alternatives; in Conclusions 4.9 and 4.13 (page 169) more techniques for testing confidence, and in Conclusions 5.8 and 5.9 (page 203) we concluded that special provisions would have to be made for all the experts and advisers in these techniques. The point here is this: if we had concluded that there would be a massive increase in the use of management techniques and if we had *not* made special provision for the inevitable increase in specialists, then MS 70 would have contained a serious flaw. It would be equally serious if we had omitted another consequence of the rise of these techniques – managers will have to learn about them, but (fortunately!) Conclusion 3.8 (page 148) draws attention to the need for training.

Now consider a much broader concept. Suppose we had said this about management in the 1970s (in fact most managers *would* say it): 'The job of the manager is going to become even more difficult in the 1970s and it follows that managers must take much more care and spend more time on everything they do. They must spend more time on making decisions, more on giving clear instructions and more on supervising the work of the subordinates. This means that more managers will be needed to run any given organisation in the 1970s compared with the 1960s.' As suggested, many managers do express this view and many organisations are behaving as if it were the only view – it will be interesting to see what happens to their pyramid structure during the 1970s! The criticisms we are levelling at this conclusion are (a) that it will result in a crushing superstructure of managers, and (b) that it takes no account of the trends that are favourable to managers in the 1970s – it ignores the idea of using the educated subordinate, it ignores wider discretion, it fails to envisage the use of the computer to help check results, etc. What we have said is diametrically opposite, MS 70 calls for fewer managers, not for more; we have agreed that managers must be much more careful with their decisions and that this will take more time (Conclusion 2.1) but giving instructions will take much *less* time (Conclusions 3.6, 3.7, 3.11, 3.15) and we have said that Monitoring Confidence will take *less* time (Conclusions 4.1, 4.2, 4.9) and we have said that *fewer* managers will be required (Conclusion 5.8). The idea of reducing the number of managers for any given organisation is one of the main themes running through MS 70; another, only slightly less pervasive, is the idea that managers will give fewer instructions to subordinates but each instruction will cover a longer time span (Conclusion 3.15). This is reinforced repeatedly in various ways in various conclusions: Conclusion 2.10 says there will be more long-range planning; Conclusion 1.8 refers to continuing tasks (which are so long-range one cannot see the end); Conclusion 2.9 refers to more forecasting; Conclusion 3.4 says that more instructions will emerge from planning, fewer from off-the-cuff decisions; Conclusion 3.8 says that subordinates must be better trained if they are to be left unsupervised for longer periods; Conclusion 3.12 includes venture management; Conclusion 4.6 discusses the problem of checking long-term results as do 4.7, 4.10, 4.11. They all point the same way, and all interlock.

These two major themes are also mutually reinforcing, it would not have made much sense if these two themes (simplified) were:

1. Fewer managers will be needed in the 1970s.
2. Managers will have to take more decisions and give instructions more often.

These are mutually incompatible. What we *have* said is:

1. Fewer managers will be needed in the 1970s.

209

2. They will take fewer (but bigger) decisions and give fewer instructions (each covering a longer time span).

If these two pervasive themes were the only threads to be woven into MS 70 our task in this book would have been much easier but it would still have been necessary to write it because these two themes are themselves not yet accepted by many managers. But there are several other major threads as well, and these have to be woven in without creating any inconsistencies or incompatibilities – on the contrary, each thread must strengthen the cloth. These other major threads include the problem of the beneficiaries and the part they should play in an organisation, the whole concept of wider discretion, the ever-escalating problem of taking decisions the consequences of which run through and interlink in wider discretion, giving instructions, monitoring confidence. Then there are the new forms of organisation to be considered, and we have had to bear in mind that the pyramid is crumbling, so we are trying to rebuild a system of management at the very moment in history when its traditional mainstay is sinking out of sight.

The question of compatibility is crucial; we only have to get one conclusion that is at odds with another and, since each interlocks with several others, a serious distortion could appear and so, when a manager tries to adopt MS 70 in practice he might create just the symptoms of stress in the organisation that we are trying so hard to avoid. In the belief that no such inconsistencies exist we will now state the principles of MS 70 in full.

MS 70 – THE FULL DESCRIPTION

What follows is a full description of MS 70 and therefore represents a highly distilled summary of all the conclusions we have reached and the discussions we have had in this book. In order to make the statement complete, we have also brought foward some practical conclusions that will be fully described in the next chapter.

Statement 1. The purpose and use of MS 70
MS 70 is a system of management for the 1970s. It is intended to act as a set of internally consistent and mutually reinforcing

rules (embodied in nine statements) to guide all those concerned with the management of any organisation in the 1970s (but not beyond). It is not suggested that these rules be instantly adopted in their entirety by any organisation – the rate of development and the starting base differs so much for each nation and each organisation that this is obviously not practical. The intention in any case is quite contrary to this; these rules should be adopted in small evolutionary (not revolutionary) stages as and when an opportunity occurs and this process may well take many years. It is important to plan the adoption of these rules because they are all interlinked and their balance must be maintained. The introduction of MS 70 could be made the responsibility of a project manager.

Statement 2. The role of the intended beneficiaries
The purpose of any organisation is to yield a benefit to someone – that is why it exists and if it fails to yield a satisfactory benefit it will cease to exist. It is necessary for beneficiaries, therefore, to identify themselves, to state the nature of the benefit they expect to receive and what volume is in their opinion satisfactory and what volume would represent failure. This they have to communicate to the chief executive. They must also monitor their confidence in the organisation's continuing ability to provide a satisfactory level of benefit.

Statement 3. The forms of organisation for beneficiaries and their representatives
To carry out these three activities they must forge strong links with the chief executive. Slack (i.e. the lack of strength and accuracy with which their views are represented to him) will increase progressively as they adopt the personal, group and indirect methods of representation. It is further increased if any representative is also a manager. It may be reduced if the senior representatives are formed into a Board and if there is a monitor. More attention must be given to this neglected half of the structure of organisations.

Statement 4. The forms of organisation for managers
Traditionally every member of an organisation – managers,

operators and advisers – were fitted into a single pyramid structure and each employee strictly observed the principle of agreed seniority. Advisers should be progressively removed from the main pyramid and formed into cells or small pyramids in a management services department. Managers and operators can also be formed into cells within the main pyramid which will decline in size (given constant output of goods and services) and the number of hierarchical levels will decline (due to automation and span of control). The matrix structure will be used for transdepartmental projects and in multicomplex organisations.

Statement 5. The role of the manager
Managers do four things: Steps 1, 2, 3, 4. They must be trained how to manage (i.e. how to take these steps and how to use the techniques relevant to each) as well as being trained in their particular job. Managers have both a boss and a subordinate so operators, advisers, beneficiaries are not managers nor is a manager when acting as an operator.

Statement 6. Step 1: 'agree to achieve a result'
For any given Task (whether Continuing or Project) a manager should be encouraged to make sure he has been correctly briefed by his boss (i.e. that his boss has correctly taken his Step 3) and should be satisfied that he is not being asked to do anything unethical. Having agreed to the instructions he cannot alter them without referring to his boss. He should be encouraged to participate in the deliberations and planning leading to the instructions he is given.

Statement 7. Step 2: 'select the best way to achieve it'
Having been asked to achieve a certain result the manager has to decide the best way to do this. Step 2 is becoming increasingly difficult because of complexity, size, penalty for error, the number of people to be consulted and the longer time span of decisions. The manager should take fewer decisions himself, delegating minor ones to subordinates, concentrating on the important ones. He should first decide how much time

212

and money to spend on deciding the best way of achieving a task, i.e. he should not search for the best possible way but only for a method that convinces him he should not look for a better one (Step 2a). He may then use many techniques as well as consulting subordinates and advisers to create a list of possible alternatives (Step 2b), failure to do so being pure bad management in the 1970s. He then (Step 2c) may use many techniques with the Sieve to evaluate each alternative and select the best, bearing in mind the strengths of the organisation and the fact that all forecasts are inaccurate, long-range forecasts especially. In Step 2d he should draw up an action plan but only in sufficient detail to eliminate misunderstandings amongst the subordinates who will carry it out. Any further detail they require for action can be planned by the subordinates themselves as part of a cascade of plans. (Planning is the elimination of alternatives in progressively greater detail before action is necessary; a plan is a set of instructions to subordinates.)

Statement 8. Step 3: 'give instructions'
There are five essential elements in any instruction and the way in which each is specified sets the whole tone of the manager-subordinate relationship. There will be a trend to expansive targets which require that: at Step 3a, the result to be achieved be quantified (preferably at three levels) clearly and verifiably, without superfluous figures, over longer time spans; the resources allocated at Step 3b to be stated in less detail – perhaps as only one monetary figure; the virtual abandonment of Step 3c – telling the subordinate how to do his job (except for ethical constraints); the manager must, however, say when he is going to check up on progress at Step 3d; unless they are large he is unlikely to mention penalties or rewards at Step 3e. By paying more attention to Step 3a managers can enormously reduce slack especially when instructions result from planning rather than from off-the-cuff decisions, when techniques of quantification are used, and if they reduce the number of instructions they give while increasing the time span of each. Some extra slack will occur (partly because of the reduction in Steps 3b, c and e)

213

but the increased use of Step 3x (wider discretion) will greatly improve the quality and realism of decisions at Step 2 as well as Step 3.

Improved communications should not be used to expand Step 3; they are much more valuable at Steps 2 and 4. Senior managers, chief executives and, in particular, beneficiaries (who also take Step 3) should note that some important tasks cannot be quantified yet, and that to set a project target for a continuing task leads straight to myopic management.

Statement 9. Step 4: '*monitor confidence*'
Having given instructions to his subordinates the manager then needs to gauge his confidence in the probability that his task will be achieved. One element in this is the progress being made by his subordinates towards their targets on which his own level of achievement depends; he will therefore check their results, but – subject to checking before the lead-time for action expires – less often than he used to and not until the figures are expected to be statistically significant (a calculation readily performed by computers which will, with improved communications, provide a comprehensive results service). He will apply the same considerations to checking progress in his own task which is the second element in confidence. The third element, the continuing validity of assumptions made at Step 2 when using the Sieve must also be checked for long-term tasks. So long as he is confident of achieving the 'satisfactory' or the 'success' level he need do nothing; if he believes that he will not achieve better than the Failure Plus level he must report to his boss. If he is not confident of achieving the 'satisfactory' level he will return to Steps 2 or 3 and probably enter the 'co-ordination' cycle. Operators and beneficiaries also take Step 4 but in respect of one set of results only (their own and the chief executive's respectively).

SOME MANAGEMENT MISCONCEPTIONS LAID BARE

The practical consequences of these nine statements will be dramatic – on the job of the chief executive, on Boards of

Governors and Directors, on the selection and training of managers, on computer programmes, on planning, on budgetary systems and so on. These practical consequences will be discussed in the final chapter.

To end this chapter we should discuss some misconceptions that managers and others hold to be true but which MS 70 suggests are false – if not today certainly by the end of the decade. Some of these we have already mentioned such as the idea that the chief executive is the top of the organisation – a misconception that is most evident among company employees, a view often encouraged by the managing director and his senior staff. Some managing directors take decisions which clearly imply that they are using the company as a vehicle for personal advancement or aggrandisement and they are able to do this because the beneficiaries have wholly inadequate links with him – they can get away with decisions which would be considered scandalous in, say, a charity or government department. Then we discovered that 'checking results' was an entirely adequate method of control for short-term tasks such as most managers perform today but that it would become an increasingly insufficient alarm system for the longer-term jobs that will form so much of a manager's work later in the decade. Not more than one in a hundred managers – or accountants – realise this; and we saw that 'managing by results', a very well known and widely respected phrase, would become a dangerous philosophy – if it is not already. We saw, too, that 'planning' is not just trying to fit together a sequence of actions, it is the process of eliminating alternative methods of achieving a given result with given resources. We saw that, for most practical purposes, those huge complex detailed plans covering the whole office wall were a mistake – plans should be simple instructions to subordinates showing them the framework within which their own plans must fit. We saw also that there was a great gaping hole in the planning process: the critically important pre-planning activity of creating alternatives. And associated with this is the misconception that a manager with a degree and a slide-rule can replace creativity. Again, the belief that subordinates will have to be more closely supervised as their jobs become more technical is commonly held today, but it is wrong – they will require less supervision because they will be better educated and better trained. Then the idea that there is no point in setting very long-term targets because we may not be alive to see the result – what nonsense! Then the idea that because one cannot forecast the long-term future one should not take long-term decisions – alas, though, we are going to have to take long-term decisions so we must take them knowing that our forecasts may be hopelessly wrong and so we will have to use sensitivity tests, the outcome matrix, decision theory; difficult techniques to handle they may be, but managers will learn to use them with the help of their advisers.

We have seen, too, the first cracks appear in the pyramid after countless thousands of years as the only way in which to arrange people in an organisation; with its collapse have come two new arrangements to be followed later by a kaleidoscope of new patterns in which a man can have no boss at all or a dozen – one of whom may be a computer! (Mercifully this will be very rare even by 1984.) We have predicted a surge of new advisers and can certainly foresee the organisation of the late 1970s where automation has cut the number of the operators in office and factory so that the advisers in the management services department exceed the number of managers and operators put together. We have predicted that ethical and social considerations will play a major part in decision-taking (a prediction that is certainly not made by many managers today).

All these conclusions deny, contradict or refute many of the cherished beliefs held today by a great many managers, advisers and even leading academics in management.

There are more of these heresies in MS 70, one of which, although purely academic, is interesting. MS 70 excludes the idea of 'maximising' –in fact we have denied it twice in two very different contexts – and this is important because economists and operations research workers both hold it as an important principle. We first denied it when we said that beneficiaries should tell their chief executive what level of benefit they considered to be satisfactory – we did not say that beneficiaries should tell him 'to maximise the level of benefit'. The main reason we did not do so was for the purely practical reason that beneficiaries can never *quantify* 'maximum' but can often

216

quantify 'satisfactory' – and can *always* quantify the level they consider to represent failure. Furthermore, and this is just as important, beneficiaries cannot verify whether the maximum benefit has been achieved (and so cannot say whether the chief executive has done what they asked him to do); they *can* say whether any level achieved is satisfactory. Just try this test: the shareholders of a company making a profit of £1m. in 1970 tell the chief executive to 'maximise profits by 1980'; in 1980 the profits are £1·1 m. Now, did he *maximise* them? We can't say. Did he produce *satisfactory* profits? We can say (No!). In devising MS 70 we have dared to suggest, then, that the extremely venerable concept of maximising is either wrong, or meaningless or of less practical value than the concept of 'satisfactory', not just for companies but for all organisations; and not just for beneficiaries, managers cannot verify whether subordinates have maximised anything either and so should also use the 'satisfactory' criterion when setting targets (or, better still, the 'success' criterion). In fact we have gone further and suggested that the easiest level of all to identify and quantify is not 'maximise', not 'success', not even 'satisfactory', but 'failure'. This can always be identified, and while beneficiaries and managers would never use it as a target they might well use it as a threat! (If it was not such a depressing philosophy we might offer a new aphorism: 'The job of the manager is the avoidance of failure; success is the prerogative of the entrepreneur!')

The second context in which we rejected the concept of maximising was at Step 2a. Here we concluded that managers should not search for the best possible method of achieving their task but only for the method that was good enough to convince them that it was not worth looking for a better one. The reason that this is an interesting conclusion is that operations research workers spend much time and ingenuity devising mathematical techniques to optimise decisions. MS 70 suggests they should not. This is the view taken here: time and money should not be spent on an ever closer approach to optimum unless the optimum, when found, is likely to justify the effort. We should bear in mind that every step nearer to optimum costs progressively more to take.

We must mention one other distinction between MS 70 and

current management philosophies. MS 70 suggests that one should set a target first and then look round for ways of achieving it – one should not, as most managers do today, decide to take some action and hope that one likes the result. We have preferred the approach of the man who decides he wants to go to London and then searches for the best route – rather than that of the man who decides to drive down a road because the surface looks smoother and then, when he arrives in Bristol ruefully realises that he would rather be in London. While the second man has saved himself the bother of clarifying his objective the first man has realised that there is a certain minimum target for any task, he has identified it and he has then searched for the best way of achieving it.

Chapter 12

MS 70 in Practice

In this final chapter we will attempt no further exposition or development of MS 70 itself – the nine Statements describe the completed system, there is no more to add. What we must do now is to draw some practical down-to-earth conclusions from it – which it is convenient to do in five sections. Firstly, we will ask how any organisation can tell whether it needs to adopt MS 70, what day-to-day events might reveal that the managers need to change their ways? What symptoms would we expect to see in an organisation that needs MS 70? Then, secondly, we will describe The Management Index. Thirdly, we must describe how MS 70 can be introduced, who should supervise its introduction, when should action be taken. Fourthly, we must describe some of the practical consequences of adopting MS 70, on managers, on training officers, on chief executives, etc. Finally, we wish to return to the question 'MS 70 – what is it for?' which we asked in Chapter 11 (page 204). The answer we gave then was 'to improve the management of organisations in the 1970s' which is correct but a far more fundamental and significant answer lies behind that one.

MS 70 – WHO NEEDS IT?

One of the major tenets behind MS 70 is that for an organisation to be successful many things have to be right; success very seldom comes through one stroke of genius, it comes because a good idea is harnessed to a well-devised organisation by a vigorous chief executive with an enthusiastic team who ... – and so on. Nor does failure often come from one misfortune or one major mistake – failure builds up from three or ten or fifty small, medium or large faults or failures. To put a nation's economy on a path of vigorous growth requires ten or a hundred faults to be corrected, it cannot be done by one wave of a wand. The decline of the Church in Europe has a dozen causes. And so on. Some small organisations, however, are successful because they have as their chief executive an entrepreneur – this is often their only cause of success and, while he retains full personal control, he will have no need of MS 70 or any other system. ('Entrepreneur' is used here to mean the dynamic leader of any organisation, not just a company – there are many such non-financial entrepreneurs: Dr Barnardo, Ralph Nader, Albert Schweitzer, etc.) Apart from these all too rare cases, all organisations will have to adopt MS 70 or something extremely similar and even these small entrepreneurial organisations will need it when their leader loses personal control, for when he does the organisation will have to be *managed*. This means that everything has to be right – the planning, the control, how the employees are treated, how decisions are made, the quality of their advisers, and so on through all the features that we have built into MS 70. So the answer to the question 'MS 70, who needs it?' is simple – all organisations need it except small ones with an active entrepreneur still in full personal control. This answers the question but perhaps is not very helpful – we want to know what symptoms an organisation might display that would convince us that MS 70 was really necessary. So let us give some examples from the every-day life of a manager – namely, the reader:

Somewhere on your desk you will find a report showing the actual cost of running your department last month compared with budget. (What ? You do not have a budgetary control system? You will certainly need one by 1980!) Look at this report and compare any actual cost with budget; let us say that it refers to overtime worked in the despatch department which was budgeted at £7,000 but was actually £8,000. Do you know if that difference is statistically significant? If not, how do you know whether or not to do something about it? (In 1980 you will certainly not have the time to waste wondering whether some figure is just a freak.)

Next, go and count the number of typists in the office. Are there any more than there were five years ago? Because by 1980

220

there must be *fewer* (unless the output of goods or services from your organisation is going to rise very fast – say 10 per cent per annum.) As a matter of interest, did you know how many typists there were five years ago; did anyone know, did the office manager know? If not it suggests that he has not been set a long-term productivity target and so one can confidently predict that the number of typists will creep up gradually over the years. But now forget the typists – what about shop floor workers' productivity, what about fuel efficiency, etc? Has anyone been set a long-term task in your organisation and is anyone checking their success over a long term?

Look out of the window; see those men cycling to work in their drab and dirty clothes? They work in a sewage farm; you wouldn't do that job for all the tea in China – and nor will they by 1980! Are there still any tea-in-China jobs in your organisation?

Is the Commonwealth a success? Perhaps you cannot answer and it doesn't matter. But can the Commonwealth answer – do the beneficiaries know what level of what benefit this organisation is supposed to yield to whom and what it is actually yielding? Is *your* organisation a success? How do you know?

When you were last on holiday did one of your colleagues take over your work? Or a subordinate?

Can you operate the terminal keyboard of a computer? Very few managers will get through the next decade without learning to do this.

Go to your filing cabinet and extract the papers relating to your last major decision; look through the list of assumptions you made. On the validity of these the validity of your decision depends. Now, did you apply a sensitivity test? Remember, this was a *major* decision!

Now the point of all these questions is this: most managers at most levels in most organisations (from a sewage works to the Commonwealth) would, in 1970, have failed every single one of these tests. No budgetary control, no statistical significance, no productivity targets, no wider discretion, no computer, no idea what a sensitivity test is: most managers would have scored 0 out of 10. But we predict that by 1980 any organisation whose

221

managers score 0 out of 10 will be dead! And we are saying that all these things – dozens of them – have got to be improved because management is going to become even more difficult; it is going to become more difficult for any organisation to be as effective in the 1970s as in the 1960s. And the best way to tackle this modernisation job on management is to identify the changes that must be made and put someone in charge of the whole modernisation project. And we are saying that this project is much the same in all organisations – the changes that all organisations must make are the ones in MS 70. By 1980 most organisations will have to score at least 8 out of 10 to stay alive.

THE MANAGEMENT INDEX

In the section above we asked a few questions at random. We are now going to introduce the Management Index which consists of rather a long list of questions which are designed to determine how much of MS 70 any organisation is currently using. The idea is this: most organisations answering this questionnaire early in the 1970s will produce a very low score – something like 20 to 30 per cent. But by the 1980s they will have to improve this to something over 80 per cent in Western-style democracies (U.S., Europe, etc.), rather lower elsewhere. So the management index (1) shows how far an organisation has to go from now to 1980, (2) if it asks itself these same questions every two years or so it can see what interim progress it has made in the introduction of MS 70 and how far it has still to go before 1980, (3) any obvious weakness in the management will be shown up by a poor score in a section of the questionnaire. Also (4) the management index can be used to compare the standard of management in one organisation against any other, and (5) to identify weaknesses in individual managers, i.e. it acts as a needs analysis for individual managers. Of course no great accuracy can be claimed for the figures that emerge (their value may be no higher than to confirm or deny a subjective feeling one may have about the quality of the management of an organisation) but it is put forward as a first-ever and therefore rather crude attempt to quantify this thing we call 'management'.

The rules are: in Part 1 (which contains questions to test the issues raised in Statements 1 to 5 in MS 70) one answers the questions for the *organisation as a whole*. In Part 2 (which tests Statements 6–9 in MS 70 and is therefore relevant to *individual* managers) the scorer should select a number of managers from each level in the hierarchy including from the very top levels and from the shop floor (or office floor) supervisors level. The chief executive must always be included. Insist that each manager selects his most important recent decision as the subject for the interview – he himself *must* agree that the decision was an important one – and ask him to answer the questions about that decision only. The scorer will have to use his own discretion on what points to award for partial answers; the maximum points for each complete answer is shown in the questionnaire where it will be seen that the maximum score possible in each Part is 100. Finally, add together all the points for the managers, divide by the number of managers interviewed and add the total points scored in Part 2 – then divide the grand total by 2. That is the Index Number (out of a maximum of 100) which, as mentioned above, will come out at around 20 to 30 for most organisations in the early 1970s but must be raised to around 80 by 1980.

We must make several comments about the Management Index before passing on to the next section of the chapter. Firstly, it must be emphasised that the questions in Part 2 are to be put to a manager concerning a decision that he himself admits was of great importance. This being so we must condemn him (by awarding no points) if, for example, he failed to notify his subordinates when he was going to check their results or failed to agree with them what results he expected to see, or if he failed to consider several alternatives, or failed to identify what might go wrong or what would happen if it did, or if he did not use some relevant management technique. In the earlier chapters of this book we said that a management system was rather like the wiring diagram for a radio set. The value of such a diagram is that by comparing it with the radio set we can tell at once why the set was not working – a wire has broken or a component has failed. By using MS 70 as the wiring diagram and comparing how a manager has taken an important decision

223

THE MANAGEMENT INDEX

PART 1 – FOR THE ORGANISATION AS A WHOLE (BASED ON STATEMENTS 1–5 OF MS 70), MAXIMUM POINTS 100.	Score
(Beneficiaries)	
Does the chief executive know exactly who is and who is not an intended beneficiary? [*Maximum 3 points*]	
Does he know what benefit they expect the organisation to yield to them and to other sections of society? [*5 pts*]	
Does he know what level of these benefits they consider satisfactory? [*3 pts*]	
Does he know what level they consider would represent failure, i.e. the level where they would seriously consider dismissing him or closing down the organisation? [*3 pts*]	
Has he agreed Rates and, if appropriate, Dates with them? [*4 pts*] (Most chief executives jobs are Continuing.)	
Do the beneficiaries (or their representatives) formally 'monitor confidence' at intervals that are sufficiently frequent to allow them to take corrective action in time to prevent the failure of the organisation? [*3 pts*]	
Are they now, at this moment, confident that the organisation will continue for some years to yield a satisfactory level of benefit? [*no points are awarded for the actual answer – but score up to 2 pts if the question can be answered, i.e. if the scorer knows that the beneficiaries know the answer, whether it is yes or no, then score up to 2 pts*]	
Do all the beneficiaries have direct personal contact with the chief executive? [*3 pts*]	
Do they have the group method of representation? [*3 pts*]	
Do they have the indirect method? [*1 pt*]	
Is there a board composed wholly or preponderantly of people who are solely beneficiaries or representatives? [*4 pts*]	
Does this board have a chairman or president who is their chief representative and not a manager? [*4 pts*]	
Is there any sort of official or unofficial Monitor? [*2 pts*]	
(Organisation)	
Is there an up-to-date organisation chart? [*4 pts*]	

Does every manager have a job description however brief? [*4 pts*]

Are all the operators, advisers and managers in the main organisational pyramid? [*1 pt*]

Does the organisation chart show any cells, i.e. is it officially recognised that a group of people are to be left to organise and supervise their work among themselves (e.g. typing pool with no senior typist)? [*4 pts*]

Are there any Project Managers? [*4 pts*]

Are there any matrix forms? [*4 pts*]

Is there a management services department? [*4 pts*]

Award points [*maximum 6 pts*] depending on how many advisers there are in the management services department compared with the number in the main executive pyramid.

Relative to output of goods or services (or some other criterion of size) are there now fewer managers (i.e. people with both a boss and a subordinate) than, say, 5 years ago? [*5 pts*]

Relative to output are there fewer hierarchical levels in the pyramid than 5 years ago? [*6 pts*]

Is there any employee whose sole or main job is to advise and help managers to select and train their subordinates? [*10 pts*]

Do managers use any of the recognised techniques for selecting employees (e.g. aptitude tests, intelligence tests, personality profile tests, etc.)? [*2 pts*]

Do they use any of the recognised techniques for identifying the training needs of their subordinates such as needs analysis? [*4 pts*]

Is there any senior employee whose sole or main job is to supervise the modernisation of the whole organisation (wider discretion, management techniques, decision-making procedures, etc.), i.e. a manager for the MS 70 project? [*6 pts*]

Part 1: TOTAL (*out of 100 maximum*)

	Score

PART 2 – FOR EACH MANAGER (BASED ON STATEMENTS 6–9 OF MS 70) MAXIMUM PTS 100

(Step 1)
Was this manager confident that he has understood clearly all 5 parts of the instruction that his boss gave him for this major and important task? Did events prove this confidence to be justified? [*5 pts*]

(Step 2)
Did this manager, realising how important the task was, ask himself how long he could allow himself, and what resources it was worth employing, in order to search for a better way of carrying it out? [*3 pts*]

Did he conduct a wide search for imaginative alternatives? Award points if he consulted his boss, several advisers in the organisation, several experts outside it, and, especially, his subordinates. Also award points for the use of any of the techniques for generating alternatives (e.g. brainstorming) [*6 pts*]

When evaluating these alternatives did he test each of them by the criterion of whether it would achieve the target rates and dates? [*2 pts*]

Did he also calculate whether each would demand less than the maximum resources given to him by his boss? [*2 pts*]

Did he also consider whether any of these alternatives should be ruled out on ethical grounds? [*2 pts*]

Did he take full account of the organisation's record of success or failure in carrying out the sort of activity called for by each of these alternatives, i.e. did he take account of the organisation's strengths and weaknesses? [*4 pts*]

Did he take full account of any trend or event that might occur during the lifetime of the task he had been given that would seriously affect its success or failure? [*5 pts*]

Did he include in his evaluations what might go wrong in the case of each alternative and did he calculate the consequences? Award extra points if he tried to estimate the probability of these things going wrong [*maximum of 5 pts*]

Did he make any contingency plans? [*2 pts*]

Did he, during these evaluations, consult his subordinates; award points only if there is evidence that they contributed ideas and knowledge to the decision? [*3 pts*]

Having selected the best alternative did he draw up a plan of action in sufficient detail for his immediate subordinates to understand what they were expected to do? Award more points if he encouraged any form of cascade planning, award fewer points if he included so much detail in his plan that the actions to be taken by his subordinates' subordinates were also fully specified [*4 pts*]

Did he ask his subordinates to help draw up his plan of action? [*2 pts*]

Award points, if, during Step 2 he used discounted cash flow, a computer, decision trees, decision theory, sensitivity tests, risk analysis, outcome matrix, network analysis, etc. [*5 pts*]

(Step 3)
Do each of his subordinates know what results he expects them to achieve and by when, i.e. have rates and dates been agreed? Has he made clear whether this is a continuing or a project task? [*3 pts*]

Has he made clear whether these targets are set at the failure level or the satisfactory level? [*2 pts*]

Has he described clearly what resources each subordinate has been allocated for their tasks? [*3 pts*]

Did he describe clearly how they were to tackle their tasks? [*1 pt*]

Did he warn them about the use of unethical methods? [*3 pts*]

Did he state clearly when he would first check their progress and was it agreed what results they would expect to see by then? [*4 pts*]

Was the timing of this checkpoint carefully designed so that it (a) cut down the frequency of supervision to a practical minimum, (b) allowed time for results that would be statistically significant to appear, and (c) gave time to take corrective action? [*4 pts*]

Did the subordinates know what penalties and rewards this manager would give for failure and success? Were these sufficiently large (bearing in mind how far away they were) to motivate them? [*2 pts*]

Did the manager set each subordinate an expansive target? Was the task itself or the resources or the method to be used overspecified so that intentionally or unintentionally the manager constricted the use of their initiative? Could the time span of their tasks have been increased? [*4 pts*]

Is there any indication that, when giving these instructions to his subordinates, the manager had made serious efforts to employ the ideas of wider discretion? Award points for use of each of the techniques in this field (fewer rules; reducing repetitive, dirty, menial jobs; increasing variety, complexity and time spans; group working; venture management; training; participation, etc.) [*10 pts*]

(Step 4)

For this particular task, did the manager have an adequate system for monitoring confidence; was there a system for reporting statistically tested results for each of his subordinate's tasks, for his own task and for testing the assumptions on which his decision was based? [*4 pts*]

Is there strong evidence that during the life span of this task this manager was monitoring, controlling and co-ordinating and taking corrective action? [*3 pts*]

Is there evidence that each time he took corrective action it was because (a) action *had* to be taken before statistically significant results were available, or (b) statistically significant results showed the task would probably not be completed, or (c) because the original assumptions were invalidated? [*5 pts*] Award no points if action was taken for any other reason.

Is this manager aware that single figures are useless; that forecasts should be accompanied by their probable errors, that targets should be set at two or three levels, that results should be accompanied by a measure of their significance? [*2 pts*]

Part 2: TOTAL (*out of 100 maximum*)

To calculate the Management Index: add the scores for all the managers and divide by the number of managers. To this figure add the score obtained in Part 1. Then divide this grand total by 2.

INDEX

227

we can see at once where he has gone wrong, which component he has left out, so to speak; the Management Index is like the report that an electrician might give the owner of the radio set after comparing it with the wiring diagram. So Part 2 of the questionnaire searches for management failures in each manager, Part 1 searches for failures in the organisation – where failures are found they can be put right by training the manager or by altering the organisation structure – both will take time to correct, however, hence the idea of a gradual evolutionary plan of modernisation.

Our second comment about the Management Index relates to the scoring system. It should be noted that if any question cannot be answered then no points should be given; because if it cannot be answered the relevant data is not being recorded; if it is not being recorded the management cannot think it important. For example, if it is not known whether there are now fewer managers per unit of output compared with a few years ago, then presumably this is not considered an important statistic and therefore it is right to award no points. Also relevant to the scoring system it should be noted that the score suggested for each answer does not necessarily reflect the importance of the question; thus four points are awarded to an organisation having cells and four points for having a management services department so it looks as if equal importance is attached to each – this is not so because up to another six points can be scored for a management services department in a later question. There are many other similar examples of this, some of which are intricately cross-related.

Our third comment is to reiterate the intended uses of the Management Index: to compare an organisation's present system of management with MS 70 so as to see where and how far it has to be changed before 1980; to check progress by repeating the questionnaire every year or two; to compare one organisation's system of management with another; and to identify weaknesses in both the system of management of an organisation and in the way any given manager manages (i.e. it can act as a needs analysis which will clearly indicate what training the manager needs in management skills and techniques).

Our final comment on the Index is this; it may be that the

most suitable person to act as scorer and interviewer for the Index is the monitor who, it was suggested on page 180 could, amongst other duties, make an occasional report to the beneficiaries as to the quality of the management of their organisation.

INTRODUCING MS 70 INTO AN ORGANISATION AND MAINTAINING ITS MOMENTUM

Earlier in this chapter we drew attention to the distinctly different ways in which success comes to an entrepreneur and how it comes to an organisation that has to be managed: the former succeeds because of his exceptional personality; the latter because the management have, by careful thought and prolonged labour, included all the right ingredients in the right proportions. We stressed the importance of both aspects – the ingredients must be right, the proportions must be right – but so far we have spent most of this book describing the ingredients that must go into an organisation if it is to be successful in the 1970s; several dozen are interwoven into MS 70. We have not discussed at length the fact that the balance of the mix of ingredients is also important, nor is there any need to discuss it at length since it is so obvious. We suggested above that a managed organisation will (with rare exceptions) only succeed if many features are right; it will fail only if many things are wrong. So, the training given to employees must be right, the decision-making procedure must be right, the beneficiaries must be strongly represented, and so on. But success is also dependent on their balance – too much training is as bad as too little, too much power in the beneficiaries' hands is as bad as too little and so on. All this is very obvious.

What is not so obvious is that because each of the ingredients of MS 70 are interlinked with others, if one alters one element (training, for example, or the beneficiaries' structure) then one must alter one or even a dozen elements linked to it – otherwise the balance is upset. Now this is clearly a major consideration when introducing MS 70 – it is useless to put right one feature without modifying all the features linked to it. Furthermore MS 70 is not designed as an instant therapy for current failings: its main purpose is to *prevent* things going wrong by gradually

229

modifying the organisation's system of management; the aim is gently to slide the organisation into the next decade rather than allow it to petrify for years until the strains become intolerable. But because of the importance of balance it is useless gradually modernising one feature of the system without modernising everything else – just as it is useless reducing the length of one leg of a table to lower its surface; one has to cut the same length from each of the four legs, or, in the case of MS 70, several dozen legs. In view of this complication, and because the introduction and supervision of MS 70 is clearly a transdepartmental project, it would be sensible to place one man in charge of the project – very large organisations would need a full-time man, medium sized could have a part timer, in small organisations either the chief executive or, again, a part timer or 'visitor'.

What one calls him is not too important (Management System Manager?); how he goes about his job is important. It is suggested that he starts by first fully understanding the philosophy behind MS 70, so that if he disagrees with any part of it, or if the 1970s do not develop as foreseen in Chapter 5, he can modify the system taking great care, of course, to ensure that if he alters one feature he also makes the consequential changes throughout. If he fails to do this he will destroy the balance and his system will contain just the sort of inbuilt stresses and strains that we have excluded from MS 70. Having fully understood the philosophy and having decided upon the system of management his organisation will need he should then test the organisation's score on the Management Index to give him some idea of how fast he will have to work. In particular, he should note at which section of the questionnaire the organisation showed a low or nil score. Then, thirdly, he should look for confirmatory symptoms. Finally, he should decide what to do and agree with his chief executive how it should be done. Let us look at some examples to illustrate this introductory process and then we can go on to consider how to maintain the momentum over a period of years.

Example 1
Imagine that a company has appointed a Management System Manager (MSM) and that he has decided to adopt MS 70 as his

blueprint – he is not going to make any changes to it in principle or in detail. Now he applies the questionnaire and the company's score is 28 per cent on the Index – quite a good score for the early 1970s but obviously there is some way to go before achieving the 80 + score that is suggested as appropriate for the end of the decade. But the MSM notices that the organisation scored particularly badly in the first section of Part 1. They scored 3 in the first question because the chief executive knew that the beneficiaries were the shareholders. But he was not sure what benefit they wanted – was it dividends or capital growth or growth in earnings per share? (He did have some idea what obligations they felt to other sections of society, however.) Nor was he quite sure what their idea of a satisfactory rate of growth was – should it be at 3 per cent per annum or 10 per cent? What would they consider 'failure'; bankruptcy, yes, but they would surely become restive if their dividend did not rise at all for, say, three years? So rates had not been agreed. Of course, this lack of a clear target was due to the shareholders having the indirect method of representation with no monitor and no board composed of beneficiaries. They only scored 9 out of 40, therefore, for the first section of Part 1.

Now, having made this discovery, what should the MSM do next? He could rush off and try to reorganise the beneficiaries – but this is a Herculean task. For one thing the chief executive, who is his boss we must remember, may not welcome an increase in the power of the beneficiaries, and for another there may be a more urgent fault to be corrected elsewhere in their management system. For these reasons we suggested above that before taking any action the MSM should next 'look for confirmatory symptoms'. This means that before he tries to correct this fault he should determine whether it is really causing any stresses; if it is he must do something about it at once, if not he can postpone it and include it as part of the long-term plan for the evolutionary modernisation of the management system. What 'confirmatory symptom' might he look for to see if this weakness needed urgent correction? Well, if the beneficiaries do not have strong links we would expect to see symptoms in three fields. Firstly, the organisation may have had a long period of relative stagnation at a level of achievement that is slightly above failure;

Q

if this is the case perhaps this fault should be corrected at once. (If the level of achievement is satisfactory there is obviously less urgency.) Secondly one may find that the organisation is diverting too much benefit to other sections of society (beyond the amount that society expects of a company) at the expense of the shareholders, or thirdly, that the managers are themselves diverting resources to their own ends. In these fields we might see the following symptoms:* the chief executive is using the company as a means of attaining a knighthood; a director who is keenly interested in amateur dramatics has persuaded the Board to subsidise the local theatre; the new factory has been sited in Manchester (rather than Liverpool) because of the predilection of a director for a certain strip-club in Manchester; a new product has been introduced, not because it is better than a competitor's product, but because it was invented by the Research Director. (As has been mentioned before some of these activities would be considered almost criminal if perpetrated by the senior staff of any other organisation such as a charity or a government department.) If the MSM sees any serious evidence of symptoms like these caused by the faulty beneficiaries' links then he may decide that this fault must be corrected at once.

His final step, then, is to propose solutions to this problem and supervise the necessary changes. But what solutions? Well, obviously he will consider recommending the appointment of a Board composed entirely or preponderantly of shareholders' representatives with no (or very few) executive directors, and he will certainly suggest that the Chairman or President is a representative and not a manager. His chances of getting these proposals through the chief executive are small compared with the likelihood of his being discreetly dismissed for proposing them, and it may be that he must either risk a fight (in which he might be backed by the beneficiaries) or wait until his opponents retire – this may not always be the wrong solution for, as we have stressed, MS 70 is a long-term project and if no serious harm is being done at present by this fault it would not be irresponsible to procrastinate. Another alternative, which the chief executive cannot so easily oppose is the appointment of a monitor by the beneficiaries. For any given situation there will

* All of which are taken direct from real life, of course – *author.*

be many solutions but it is hoped that one solution that will not be adopted for this particular problem of the beneficiaries' links is the German *Aufsichstrat* or Supervisory Board, which breaks at least two important tenets of MS 70. Firstly, its composition and procedure is laid down by law so that when changes are required the whole ponderous business of parliamentary democracy has to be invoked – according to MS 70 every feature of every management system requires frequent modification to keep it in tune with the rapidly changing world. Secondly the composition of these Aufsichstrat is two-thirds shareholders and one-third employees; MS 70 contains the view that, because of Trend J, all organisations are already under considerable pressure from all sections of society, so that it makes no sense to add to the employees' already considerable bargaining power in this way. (As it has turned out, however, many of the employees' representatives once elected to these *Aufsichstrat* tend promptly to forget who they are representing!) It is also questionable whether, having formed a Supervisory Board, any organisation is really in need of a second or Management Board or *Vorstad* as well. While MS 70 is non-commital here it is possible that in the 1980s an executive board in addition to a supervisory board (i.e. a two-tier system) will be found to be entirely unnecessary – but we must wait for MS 80 to find out. In Example 1, then, we show how a MSM in a company first adopted MS 70, then, by using the Management Index checked the real organisation against this wiring diagram, then decided whether or not to take immediate action by looking for confirmatory symptoms, and finally either took prompt action or delayed it, as part of his long-term plan depending upon the virulence of the symptoms.

Example 2

Imagine that a MSM is appointed to a regional government centre. When interviewing some of the managers in the Highways Department he notices that many of them attained very low scores for the questions in Part 2 on generating alternatives, evaluating them and using the various management techniques in this field. Now should he rush off and do something about this? No, for similar reasons to those suggested above in

233

Example 1: that there may be a more urgent fault elsewhere and he has no evidence that this fault has or will cause any decision to have been taken incorrectly. So he looks for symptoms, i.e. for evidence that this fault *is* having some really detrimental effects. He then learns that a new motorway bypass has recently been built to relieve the very bad traffic congestion in Northbridge; now if this major decision had been taken correctly and if no other major decision is to be taken soon then perhaps he can delay corrective action of this fault. So he decides to study how this latest major decision was taken to see if it reveals any serious symptoms. He discovers that the Northbridge bypass decision was taken by the regional government council of elected members who instructed the Highways Department manager 'to draw up plans for a three-lane motorway bypass for Northbridge'. (Notice incidentally that this was a constrictive task because they told him how to bypass Northbridge as well as that it should be bypassed.) Notice also that the manager was not invited to participate in the discussion of alternatives so the 'positive mode' of Management was absent. Several alternative routes were proposed at the time, of course, but the MSM discovered that no consideration was given to such alternatives as (a) not having a bypass at all, but instead using computer controlled one-way suburban ring routes; (b) having a bypass but not of motorway standard; (c) having a two-lane motorway and adding a third lane later. In particular, when discussing this last possibility he was told that a two-lane motorway was considered very briefly but was not pursued because a three-lane would cost only £12m. in 1970 whereas the cost of building a two-lane in 1970 and adding a third lane in 1978 would cost a total of £13m. – £9m. in 1970 and £4m. in 1978. Now as the MSM immediately recognised, the 1978 figure had not been discounted back to 1970 values and if that is done the net present value of the two-lane-plus-one-later alternative is £1m. *less* than the three-lane-now! In view of this (plus the fact that Southtown is likely to need a bypass soon) the MSM would presumably suggest an immediate training programme for the managers of this department, not only in discounted cash flow but in all the modern management techniques used throughout Step 2 of MS 70. In this example, then, this MSM went through

234

the same process as in Example 1 – this time there was clear evidence that urgent action was needed.

Example 3
Now consider the case of a MSM who discovers that a certain manager scores very high points in some sections of Part 2 and very low in others. Typical of one sort of manager is the one who scores well in those questions related to wider discretion – he consults his subordinates, he has set up a number of cells in his department, he sets expansive targets, he sets long-term tasks and checks results as seldom as possible. On the other hand he also scores very poorly on the questions relating to Step 4 – he sets up no adequate system for checking subordinates' results, there is no evidence that he is controlling or co-ordinating or taking corrective action. This is a manager who believes in *laissez-faire* and who would be categorised as being more concerned for people than for results.* (We do not wish to proliferate the jargon but it may be possible to draw a 'Management Profile' for any given manager from the marks he scores for each question in Part 2, and these profiles would almost certainly be found to fall into several distinct and recognisable categories; e.g., democratic, autocratic, decisive, imaginative, entrepreneurial, technique worshipper. In the same way an 'Organisation Profile' could be drawn up from the scores in each question in Part 1 where the profiles would be very different for the Police, The Women's Institute, the Coal Board, etc.) However, to return to this example: the question is whether the MSM should recommend any action over this particular manager who is clearly in danger of losing control of his department because his marks in some sections are too low and others far too high (yes, too high – the Management Index is intended to act as an indicator of progress towards an ideal in the late 1970s – this manager may be too far ahead of his time and placing too much faith in subordinates who are not yet mature enough or adequately trained to justify it). Again, this MSM should not take any action unless he can find evidence that the manager is likely to make a serious error of judgement. Quite

* It may be noted that the Management Index acts also as a Management Grid but covers a much wider field of enquiry.

235

clearly, if he consistently succeeds in achieving the targets set by his boss then there is no need to take action. If he does not, the causes of his failures are now very precisely identified, and the MSM may decide to recommend action.

Now these three examples were intended to illustrate how a Management Systems Manager could start the process of introducing MS 70. He should, where necessary, recommend prompt action but where possible should postpone action until he has decided his long-term programme. Only in this way can he be sure of maintaining a balanced organisation over the following few years; it will seldom be possible to achieve balance by merely correcting faults – all that will be achieved is the correction of the fault itself and this may even result in a less balanced system in the short term. Indeed it can be said that the management systems of most organisations are permanently out of balance partly because managers are unaware of the need for balance but also because any vigorous action to correct a fault tips the system out of balance again. Examples abound: a senior manager, realising that his team lacks creativity sends them on a course to learn the techniques of creativity (brain-storming, etc.) but neglects to send them on a further course to learn how to evaluate all the bright ideas they will be creating; a company decides to introduce new management techniques but fails to put the new specialists in a management service department, and fails to tell the managers what the techniques are for or how to use them; someone decides that all future managers must have university degrees but fails to ensure that their bosses apply the principles of wider discretion; a company introduces long-range planning but sets up no monitoring system – and so on *ad infinitum*. To correct all these imbalances takes years and, of course, as soon as everything is in balance it is immediately thrown out again by a senior manager taking a snap decision or by some unforeseen event. The maintenance of a smooth uninterrupted evolution towards MS 70 is impossible but the job of the MSM is to get as near as he can to this ideal. It must be remembered that in the 1970s the rate of change will be rapid and if the MSM falls behind in his programme the jump required to catch up may itself cause stresses in the organisation and this is quite apart from any

236

catching up on any backlog of inertia from the 1960s or 1950s. It is suggested that where the MSM can move towards MS 70 smoothly he should do so – he should ensure that a long-term programme of training for the managers in management techniques is drawn up and that progress is smoothly maintained. He can ensure smooth progress in other fields as well, the introduction of mathematical statistics into all computer result programmes, for example, or the gradual encouragement of wider discretion. Where smooth progress is difficult, however, is in changes to the organisation structure; here people are closely involved and human nature sometimes presents a formidable barrier – an organisation structure is, after all, a power structure. It is suggested, therefore, that each organisation change is planned in advance and that it takes place when a convenient moment occurs. Thus one would not sack or demote the typing pool supervisor just to make the typing pool into a cell – one can perfectly well wait, even for several years, until she can be moved to another job – in the meantime preparing the typists for added responsibility by adopting some of the other methods of wider discretion. Nor would one necessarily remove the advisers from a reluctant manager in the pyramid just for the sake of transferring them to a management services department; one can wait until the manager is ready to accept the change or is moved elsewhere. Conversely, when a manager leaves the organisation unexpectedly one should not instantly replace him, but first consider if this might be a good opportunity to increase some other manager's span of control by amalgamation of departments (as was illustrated in Fig. 53). By employing these simple tactics the MSM should be able to ensure that changes in the structural forms in which the managers are arranged not only keep pace with the rest of MS 70 but are appropriate for the range of activities that the organisation's long-range strategic plans predict that it will be carrying out.

The beneficiaries of any organisation are rather like the owner of a rally car preparing for a competition – he knows that he needs a skilled driver, that the route must be studied and refuelling sites, etc., chosen in advance, and that the car itself must be constructed and tuned for the conditions it will meet. The chief executive is the driver; the senior managers, aided

237

perhaps by a corporate planner, prepare the long-term strategy; the management systems manager is the chief mechanic who strengthens the suspension and widens the exhaust ports according to the conditions expected. Just as a car mechanic would not install a more powerful engine without improving transmission and brakes, so no MSM would encourage managers to delegate more to their subordinates without also ensuring that the subordinates could accept the wider responsibility; he would not encourage subordinates to generate bright ideas until he had encouraged their managers not to set constricting targets, and so on. The analogy with the car mechanic breaks down, however, when we remember that changes to organisations cannot be made in six hours or six days or six months; they may take six years. So it is no use in 1972 aiming to modernise an organisation to 1972 standards – one has to try to predict what a modern organisation will look like in 1978 and aim for that. So this is the job of the MSM: to decide whether to adopt MS 70 as it stands or to aim for a carefully modified version of it, to correct any urgent faults, to maintain a gradual balanced evolution* towards MS 70, monitoring progress all the way and occasionally testing confidence in the continued validity of the assumptions behind MS 70. How can we check whether the MSM is doing his job? By looking for the symptoms we could expect to see if he was not – low or inconsistent scores in the Management Index, faulty decisions, dearth of bright ideas, low morale, strikes, remoteness of the beneficiaries, etc. Any such symptom that does occur is a possible black mark against the MSM and he should certainly study the reasons behind such symptoms to discover what inconsistencies in the organisation could have caused them. After all, these are exactly the sort of symptoms which MS 70 is designed to prevent.†

We should note one final part of the MSM's job. One of the

* Not forgetting that occasionally he has to take a step backwards; either because he has gone too quickly (as the manager in Example 3 had done) or because the organisation faces an emergency and a temporary return to autocratic rule is called for.

† This is why we suggested in the footnote on page 6 that MS 70 was designed to act by a continuous systemic prophylaxis.

uses to which MS 70 can be put is a negative one: the principles we have built into it are intended as a comprehensive system of signposts to the future – *more* training, *longer* time spans, *wider* discretion – all these suggest the way in which the world is moving, the direction in which the arrow of time is pointing. Not only should the MSM try to ensure that his organisation moves in this way, he should also try to ensure that no permanent step is taken in the wrong direction. An engineer who designs a new machine that is even more boring to operate than the old one should be discouraged, for example.

THE PRACTICAL CONSEQUENCES OF MS 70

It is intended that MS 70 should have profound practical consequences on everyone connected with any organisation – on the beneficiaries, the chief executive, the managers, the advisers, the operators, and on all the various sections of society who are affected by the activities of the organisation. The aim is to create organisations that are precisely and purposefully aimed at achieving an accurately defined task, which do not have to neglect their obligations to others in order to achieve it, and which, furthermore, provide an expansive atmosphere in which employees can each live fuller lives. Few organisations meet these three criteria today; it should be our constant aim to design and redesign our organisations so that they do.

What should be the practical effects of introducing MS 70 on beneficiaries? The first effect is that they or their representatives will have to decide exactly what they want their organisation to achieve. Someone really must decide who is supposed to benefit from a prison, for example, is it society (and the benefit is to keep criminals out of circulation), or is it the prisoners (and the benefit is to help them to return to normal life)? If it is the former we need one sort of prison (such as those we already have!), if the latter, we need another sort. And having decided what prisons are for, the beneficiaries or their representatives must set up a system for monitoring confidence in achieving a quantified target – such as the escape rate or the rate of recidivism. And someone has to thump the table when the results are poor and demand a more imaginative approach; the beneficiaries from our prisons will never receive a satisfactory level of benefit unless we know who they are, the benefit is specified, a quantified target is set, a system of monitoring is developed and strong links are formed with the chief executive. Not until all five of these actions have been taken by the beneficiaries' representatives will appropriate action be taken by the management. All five – not just one or two. And is it not high time that shareholders in Britain told their chief executives what results they wanted? But again, all five, the same five, faults have to be corrected. If beneficiaries do take seriously the action suggested to them by MS 70 then they can be sure that at least someone is guarding their interest and, as soon as they lose confidence, they can insist that something is done, even if the only course left to them is to dismiss the chief executive. This, then, is the main practical effect on beneficiaries – they would have the means to insist on a satisfactory benefit. They might even receive more benefit due to the modernisation of the management mechanism but this would be a bonus and should not be attained at the expense of other sections of society – MS 70 is designed around the concept of achieving at least a 'satisfactory' benefit for the intended beneficiaries, the concept of 'maximum' benefit for them was rejected, remember.

What of the chief executive – how will he be affected? Both favourably and unfavourably; he will be given a clear brief by the beneficiaries so that at least he will know exactly what he is trying to do. But, to his already onerous duties will be added several more: a wider span of control, more advisers to listen to (including the MSM if the organisation is large enough to employ one full time or part time and, if it is not, the chief executive may have to be the MSM himself), more pressure from employees and the local community, more difficult decisions, etc. Apart from the material rewards (which will become far greater in the next decade) what can we do to ease the chief executive's burden? It is now considerable, it will become enormous. All he can do is to delegate more and more of his job by setting tasks to his immediate subordinates over longer and longer timespans; the solution is the same for him as for any other manager, only the scale is different. To be able to delegate in this way he must have faith in his subordinates; this means they must not only be skilled in the technicalities of their jobs and in the techniques of management but must be trustworthy. This means that character and personality, sadly neglected aspects in selection procedures today, will re-emerge as more important than paper qualifications. The chief executive's job, then, will polarise into four vital areas: (1) deciding the long-term strategy by which the organisation is most likely to achieve a satisfactory (not maximum) level of benefit and at the same time satisfactorily meet its obligations to society, (2) designing the management system that is best suited to the proposed strategy and the conditions in which the organisation will be working, (3) selecting and training his immediate subordinates, and (4) monitoring his confidence in (1) (2) and (3). He will have plenty of other things to do as well – dealing with emergencies, for example – but these four will become increasingly his major concern, and at present the first two receive little attention.

The effect of MS 70 on the average manager will be mainly favourable. He should find that he is asked to take increasingly larger decisions, is left to his own devices for longer, he will feel more confidence that his decision-making is based on sound principles, and he will enjoy a closer personal link with his boss and subordinates. He will probably spend much more time in discussion with experts and less time acting as an 'operator'. But he will have to master many of the techniques of management as well as the technicalities of his job; and the penalty for ignoring the rules of decision-making will rightly become severe – this does not mean he must never be wrong! It means that he must take important decisions by using the process we have called Step 2. He will have to learn to use a computer terminal, to ask it 'what would happen if?' questions, to resist the temptation to make frequent use of his video telephone to check up on his subordinates. And he may have to accustom himself to the idea of less dramatic promotions; there are two reasons for this. The first is that unless the organisation is expanding very fast it will require fewer managers, so as one retires or leaves it may be possible to amalgamate this job with another existing one rather than to promote a subordinate to fill it. The second reason is that we have proposed a system of continuous promotion – every step taken to give wider discretion is a promotion

241

in the sense that the manager will be less often supervised on tasks that are progressively larger and of greater timespan. Promotion is nothing more than a sudden increase in 'job content'; we are proposing that job contents should be progressively and gradually increased all the time – a sort of continuous promotion. Yes, it should be a good decade for managers.

It should be a very good decade for operators at shop floor and office floor. Towards the end of the 1960s the idea that all manual labour was dignified finally fell out of favour and the message has got home to managers – employees are entitled to be treated as though they were human. It is quite certain that during the 1970s there will be a scramble to eliminate dirty or repetitive or menial jobs (those members of society who are capable of doing no other type of job may find it harder to get work at all) and to enrich all unskilled, semi-skilled and skilled jobs. We can predict something else: several decades ago Henry Ford first used the mechanised assembly line where each man performed one simple repetitive job all day. At that time social conditions allowed us to look upon it as merely an ingenious solution to an engineering problem. Now it has become a nightmare. By 1984, we predict, not one Henry Ford type assembly line will exist in the Western-style democracies, not one. Instead, some new Henry Ford will have discovered how to assemble engineering products economically in such a way that men can work together as a group (probably in cells, without direct supervision). There really is now a possibility that strikes, absenteeism, militant and violent protest, accidents, complaints and the many other debilitating symptoms of social malaise that exists in many large organisations will be replaced by co-operation. Some time in the next decade or two we may even see more employees working not for material reward alone but because they enjoy constructing a new world, or because they wish to help other people to enjoy the existing one. There are now, and always have been, quite a few fortunate people who work because they are dedicated to what they are doing and because it is worthwhile; perhaps, one day, this luxury will be available to the mass of employees just as other material luxuries are now available to them. All this is still a long way off but the principles

242

of wider discretion and indeed many of the threads that run throughout MS 70 are intended as a step in this direction. One day, perhaps the greatest problem facing the designer of a management system will not be how to encourage employees to be creative but to contain their enthusiasm for work – i.e. the same problem that faces physicists who are still searching for a 'bottle' to contain nuclear plasma that is so hot that it will vaporise any known material!

As for the specialists, MS 70 implies there will be more of them, of course, but by separating them out into a management services department attention will be drawn to the fact that they are not managers and that their sole function is to advise – it is the manager's prerogative to accept or reject their advice. The rewards for giving good advice will grow; the penalties for poor advice will grow also and, as managers become accustomed to quantification, more advisers will be asked to quantify their advice and, as we have seen, figures can readily be checked; in other words managers will be able to check up on the quality of advice they are given. Many specialists will be given quantified targets, so here again their competence will be tested. Several new specialists may appear: experts in management systems, in generating alternatives, in the structural forms for beneficiaries and their representatives, in selection techniques that measure creativity, personality and character, in strategic planning and long-range forecasting, in cascade planning, in industrial sociology and psychology, in the quantification of 'intangibles' and opinions, in estimating probabilities and handling errors in forecasts, and in locating information. Small organisations which cannot justify employing full-time specialists in these and other fields will increasingly employ them part-time or use specialist consultants. Towards the end of the decade we may see some of the larger organisations closing down some of their own advisory sections and relying on contracts with organisations specialising in these fields – in other words much greater use will be made of consultants.

Training officers in organisations will have to be much more careful in selecting who should be trained in what – the cost of training will rise rapidly – and techniques such as needs analysis will have to be used; Part 2 of the Management Index is, as suggested above, an excellent device for identifying precisely where a manager's skill in management is weak. MS 70 clearly implies that managers must be trained in management as well as in the skills relevant to their particular job, and they must know what specialist techniques are available for each step in the management process so as to know when to call in which specialist. MS 70 also clearly implies that organisations will need fewer managers and more specialist advisers – a point that should be noted by those responsible for developing manpower plans for highly qualified employees.

The effect of MS 70 on the various groups of people and sections of society to whom all organisations also have obligations should be entirely favourable. Managers are already aware that ethics are an important consideration in many decisions and this element is built into the relevant parts of MS 70. There is no doubt that some organisations will have to set themselves quantified targets in these areas – companies with noisy or smelly or dusty processes will have to aim to reduce the nuisance to the local community at a rate that will satisfy them; cities will have to do the same for noise from cars and aircraft, smoke from houses and so on. The point is well taken today and needs no further discussion.

Finally there is the effect of MS 70 on the largest organisation of all – government. As a general rule the problems of management grow in proportion to the size of the organisation and no one can deny that most national governments illustrate this clearly. Governments have special additional problems, however, which help to make management even more difficult. Firstly there is the difficulty of quantifying tasks (probably a grossly over-exaggerated problem especially if one remembers that a task is the *result* one is trying to achieve and surely one must have some idea what that is! Cost-benefit and other techniques of quantification will certainly ease this problem during the decade.) Secondly there is the problem of ethics – for in a democracy the government, above all other organisations, must not be seen to provide a benefit to one section of the community at the expense of another – government is for the benefit of all. However, this problem, like the quantification problem, is not different in kind to the same problems facing all organisations –

it is only more severe. More severe also is the growing reluctance of educated citizens to be ordered about by petty officials, and their increasing resentment of detailed regulations and officious use of authority. We make this prediction: during the 1970s most Western-style governments will swing decisively towards decentralising detailed decision making. There will be a wholesale dismantling of petty rules and regulations (in accordance with the principles of wider discretion), such as the amount of cupboard space to be included in new houses, and when and where adults are allowed to consume alcohol. The idea of cascade planning will certainly have to be adopted by governments. They may have to improve the way their managers manage. But of all their problems none is so acute as their organisation structure where the pyramid may have a hundred levels, each criss-crossed by committees* and commissions in a labyrinth of incomprehensibility. Never was there a clearer case for some of the forms of management structure we have been discussing in MS 70.† Never was there a pyramid under such strain. It may be that national governments would achieve quite impressive scores on Part 2 of the Management Index (i.e. civil servants may not be bad managers by any standards of today) but in Part 1 the score would be such as to daunt any management systems manager! The study of structural forms of management for national governments has been so neglected and the symptoms of stress are so infinitely damaging to society that this problem deserves the highest priority.

ORGANISATIONS – WHAT ARE THEY FOR?

In attempting to design a system of management for the next decade we have discovered that there are half a dozen really

* Some of the committees are composed of *dozens* of members – a clear symptom of strain in an organisation.

† No doubt the cell, the matrix and the management services department would help considerably but it may be that a few organisations are so enormous (governments of some nations being among these) and the time it takes to alter their structures is so long, that they should consider going gradually but directly to some of the forms of organisation that we will not normally see until the 1980s. Unfortunately these, such as the possibility of a honeycomb, are completely unknown at present.

huge faults in the system of management at present being used in most organisations. Just consider them:

(a) Hardly any organisations (other than those run by an active entrepreneur) have any clear idea of what they are for. So great is the day-to-day pressure on managers that many have completely lost sight of the real aims of the organisation. If one asks a company executive what his organisation is trying to do he may say that it is to grow – but ask him 'growth of what' and 'growth at what rate'? and he does not know – nor does he know how fast his company has grown over the past five years or so, and this is tantamount to admitting that he knows neither the criterion by which to judge whether his company is successful, nor whether it has been successful, nor whether it is likely to be. Ask a chief of police or the Ministry of Education by what criteria they judge their success and whether they have, in the past five or ten years, been successful. Ask the Loamshire County Council, the Academy of Accountants, the local magistrates' court by what criteria they estimate their success or failure and they will not know – and even if they do know these criteria they will not know whether the records show their success or failure. No one can pretend that it is easy to state clearly what results each of these organisations should be geared to achieving, still less that it is easy to quantify them, but the fact remains that all organisations are established, often at great expense, to achieve a certain tangible down-to-earth real life practical result for the benefit of a certain well defined group of real life people.

(b) We have seen also how difficult it is becoming to take a decision. The growing size of organisations means that the consequences of a bad decision are enormous. But the complexity of facts, the inaccuracy of forecasts, the growing constraints of morality, the rate of change in society and technology, are all conspiring to make things more difficult for the manager. And yet, even though all this is well known, managers continue to take these decisions as though they were blessed with the flair of an entrepreneur – if they were

246

they would not be employed as managers but would be running their own organisations. There seems to be no alternative but to programme each manager to take important decisions in the strict sequence of steps outlined in Chapter 7 or something very like it.* They will have to develop the habit of asking themselves how much time to spend on each decision, they will have to use artificial methods of creativity, they will have to use the Sieve, they will have to plan.

(c) We have seen how every manager must give clear instructions to his subordinates – most managers today do this, but their instructions are usually clearest and most detailed in just the areas that make a subordinate feel constricted. There are five parts to any instruction: today the emphasis is on how the subordinate should do the job and what the penalties are if he does not do it properly; tomorrow the emphasis must be on what results he is to achieve. The whole infinitely powerful field of wider discretion is shut tight to many managers today. Nor do managers today realise that it is partly their responsibility to make sure they understand their boss's instructions (or rather, it is the responsibility of them both but the managers will get the blame if there is a misunderstanding!).

(d) Nor do managers today always take the trouble to check results (partly because they do not know what results to check) and thus they risk losing control of their subordinates. Tomorrow, if subordinates are to be given a longer lead, it will be essential to keep them under control and equally essential not to jerk the lead until it is really necessary – so the whole unfamiliar field of monitoring confidence becomes crucial for management.

* The thought of a 'programmed manager' sounds alarming – shades of robots and zombies! This is certainly not what we want, of course. What we want is that managers be trained to go about their management tasks (one of which is making decisions) in the same systematic way that any other professionals go about theirs.

(e) We saw also that the pyramid is creaking and cracking under the strain of being used in social conditions for which it was never designed; it was never intended to be used as a consultative structure but as a command structure. Nor is it valid where most of the efforts of most managements is devoted to change through transdepartmental projects.

(f) Finally, we have seen that there is something else wrong with organisations today; managers believe that their organisation can become successful overnight if only this or that or the other fault was corrected. This is, with rare exceptions, quite incorrect – one has to put right this *and* that *and* the other. Nor can this modernisation process be done at random. It makes no sense to introduce programme budgeting if one does not also introduce Project Managers. It makes no sense to encourage subordinates to be creative if their manager habitually sets constrictive targets. It is meaningless to set up a complex computer-communications instant-results service, if the flood of figures merely confuses the managers.

To put everything right takes years. If it takes years one has to aim to modernise to the standards appropriate years ahead.

This is what MS 70 is all about; it is a system of management designed to be appropriate for conditions that will exist towards the end of this decade; it is a design to work towards by careful evolutionary steps over a period that is sufficiently long to overcome the difficulties involved in such a journey, and to overcome the resistance to change that exists in all organisations. It is an attempt to draw attention to the fact that to achieve its purpose any organisation needs not only a suitable chief executive, not only the right strategy, not only to select the right products, the right services, the right market, not only an efficient factory or office, and all the thousand other things with which managers concern themselves. It needs also a system by which it can be managed. And that system must be *designed* for the job it has to do in the conditions in which it will be working. Everything else that man has ever invented has had to be designed for the specific purpose for which it is intended – a knife, a car, a house – so why not an organisation? The reason that organisations are not designed, the reason that they 'just grow', is that there exists at present no recognised job of 'Organisation Designer'; very, very few organisations have created a senior post (either part time or full time or 'visiting') for a man whose job is to ensure that the large number of really important features that make up an organisation are present, in good order and are in balance. Even if an organisation did create such a position they would find few people able to do the job because by education and training we are all specialists today – in production, in marketing, in atomic physics, in the design of computer systems, in office layout. Where are the experts in organisation design?

There are today many experts in corporate planning who can advise a company's chief executive on what products and markets to develop for the long-term future, there are economic advisers to suggest how a government could achieve economic growth. But where are men who, like a chief mechanic, can advise the chief executive on the design and construction of the organisation's machinery?

As with so many of man's inventions, organisations can be used to degrade or even destroy us, but they also can enrich the lives of those who benefit from them and those who work in them. In its finest form an organisation consists of a group of people working together in a fulfilling, creative and elevating partnership to meet the ends of another group of people – but doing so in such a way that all other sections of society can give it their warm approval. There are some like this. But most modern organisations, in particular some of the larger ones, seem to have wandered very far from this ideal. Most of the knowledge, if not all of it, by which their worst features can be cured is available. But someone in each organisation has to apply this knowledge carefully and systematically, patiently pressing and guiding it towards this goal. It may take many, many years but it is time to start.

Bibliography

ANSOFF, H. I., *Corporate Strategy*, McGraw-Hill, 1965.
ARGENTI, J., *Corporate Planning*, Allen & Unwin, 1968.
ARGENTI, J., *Management Techniques*, Allen & Unwin, 1969.
ARGYRIS, C., *Integrating the Individual and the Organisation*, Wiley, 1964.
AUDLEY, R. J., *Decision Making*, BBC. 1967.
BENNIS, W. G., *Changing Organisations*, McGraw-Hill, 1966.
BONO, E. DE, *Lateral Thinking*, J. Cape, 1967.
BOWYER, M., *The Will to Manage*.
BRABB, G. C., *Introduction to Quantitative Management*, Holt, Rinehart, Winston, 1968.
BRECH, E. F. L., *Management: its Nature and Significance*, Pitman, 1967.
CARLBERG, B. C., *Facing the Executive Challenge*, Pitman, 1967.
CASSON, J., *Using Words: Verbal Communication in Industry*, Shaw & Sons, 1968.
DALE, F., *Management: Theory and Practice*, McGraw-Hill, 1965.
DALE, E., *Organisation*, A.M.A., 1967.
DEARDEN, J., *Computers in Business Management*, Dow Jones Irwin, 1966.
DONALD, A. G., *Management Information and Systems*, Pergamon, 1967.
DRUCKER, P. F., *The Effective Executive*, Heinemann, 1967.
DRUCKER, P. F., *Managing for Results*, Heinemann, 1967.
FLETCHER, A., *Computer Science for Management*, Business Publications, 1967.
GALBRAITH, J., *The New Industrial State*, Houghton Miflin, 1968.
GELLERMAN, S. W., *Management by Motivation*, A.M.A., 1968.
HEIN, L. W., *The Quantitative Approach to Managerial Decisions*, Prentice Hall, 1967.

250

HERZBERG, F., *Work and the Nature of Man*, Staple Press, 1968.

HUMBLE, J., *Management by Objectives in Action*, McGraw-Hill, 1970.

KAHN, H. and WIENER, A. J., *Towards the Year 2000*, Macmillan, 1967.

KOESTLER, A., *The Act of Creation*, Hutchinson, 1964.

KOONTZ, M., *Principles of Management*, McGraw-Hill, 1968.

LEYTON, A. C., *The Art of Communication*, Pitman, 1968.

LIGHT, H. R., *The Nature of Management*, Pitman, 1968.

LIKERT, R., *The Human Organisation*, McGraw-Hill, 1967.

LUPTON, T., *Management and the Social Sciences*, Lyon Grant & Green, 1966.

MAYNARD, H. B., *Handbook of Business Administration*, McGraw-Hill, 1967.

MCGREGOR, D., *The Professional Manager*, McGraw-Hill, 1967.

NEWMAN, A. D. and ROWBOTTOM, R. W., *Organisation Analysis*, Heinemann, 1968.

PERRIGO, A. E. B., *Modern Managerial Techniques*, Van Norstrand, 1968.

RAWLINSON, J. G., *Creative Thinking and Brainstorming*, B.I.M., 1970.

REVANS, R. W., *The Theory of Practice in Management*, Macdonald, 1966.

ROSE, T. G., *Higher Control in Management*, Pitman, 1967.

SARGEAUNT, M. J., *Operational Research for Management*, Heineman, 1965.

STEWART, R., *Managers and their Jobs*, Macmillan, 1967.

STEWART, R., *The Reality of Management*, Pan, 1967.

VICKERS, SIR G., *The Art of Judgement: a Study of Policy Making*, Chapman & Hall, 1966.

WARREN, E. K., *Long Range Planning – the Executive Viewpoint*, Prentice Hall, 1966.

WILLS, G. and YEARSLEY, R., *Handbook of Management Technology*, Heinemann, 1967.

WOODWARD, J., *Industrial Organisation: Theory and Practice*, O.U.P., 1965.

251

Index

Advisers, *see* specialists
Agreed Seniority, 12–17, 35
Alternatives, 80–97, 143
Anarchy, 120, 139
Assembly line, 131, 242
Assumptions, continuing validity of, 162–5
Attitude Survey, 66
Auditor, 180
Aufsichstrat, 233
Authority, revolt against, 50, 119
Automation, 51, 191

Backlash, 47
Beneficiaries, 54–63, 151, 173–9, 239
Benefits, 55
Brainstorming, 96
Budgets, 190, 191

Cascade of tasks, 53
    Planning, *see* planning
Cell, 181–3
Chairman, 177
Change, 46, 95, 188, 200
Checkpoint, 118, 128, 158–9
Chief Executive, 34, 63–8, 122, 175–80, 240
Choice, *see* Variety
Co-determination, 233
Command, 181, 194
Communications, 43, 126, 136, 154
Computer, 44, 154–6
Confidence, 158, 161–5
Constrictive, *see* Target
Contingency Plan, 106
Co-ordination, 32, 186

Cost Benefit, 50, 244
Craftsmen, 135
Creativity, 86–97, 144, 146, 236

Decisions, 52, 78–114, 152
Democracy, 62, 138
Disaster detector, 105
Discounted cash flow, 97, 100, 234
Disintegrated Company, 137

Education, 45, 184
Efficiency, 123, 185
Entrepreneur, 217, 220, 246
Ethics, 100, 128, 180
Expansive, *see* Targets

Failure Plus, 68, 123
Family Tree, *see* Pyramid
Forecasting, 95, 101–6, 168
    errors in, 52, 105–6

Gap Analysis, 166
Glacier Project, 141
Government, 138, 190, 244
Group Representation, 177, 202
Group Work, 135, 183, 242

Hourglass, *see* Pyramid
Hunch, 102

Indicators, 66
Indirect Representation, 177, 202
Information, 45, 95
Initiative, 50, 72, 136, 139
Instructions, 115–49
    time span of, 137

Intended Beneficiaries, *see* Beneficiaries

Job Enrichment, 130, 134

Line and Staff, 193–6
Logic, 89–92

Management, basic elements of, 9–11
  business, 4
  failures, 2, 219
  Index, 7, 222–9, 235, 238
  missing link, 107, 143, 175
  myopic, 67, 214
  Positive Mode of, 88, 111, 234
  Profile, 235
  Techniques, 50, 102, 109, 208, 216, 236
  theory, 1, 204
Management Services Department, 192, 194–9, 236
Management Systems Manager, 229–38, 240
Manager, 16, 217, 241
  hierarchy of, *see* Pyramid
  and operators, 36, 40
Mathematics, 92
Matrix, 180, 183–91, 202, 212
Maximizing, 216–18
Monitor, 180, 202, 229
Morale Index, 71
Motivation, 120

Operators, 35, 242
  and managers, 36, 40
Organizations, attitudes to, 49, 55–8, 100
  basic elements of, 12–17
  Profile, 235
  size of, 48, 185, 188, 190
Outcome Matrix, *see* Pay Off Table

Participation, 141–3
Pay Off Table, 105
Penalties and Rewards, 12, 51, 116, 118, 119, 129–31

Personal Representation, 177, 202
Plan, 107–8
Planning, 107–14, 191
  cascade, 143
  detailed, 112, 125, 143
  enough, 166
Preference Curves, 66
Project, Manager, 186–8
  Task, *see* Task
  Transdepartmental, 186, 212
Promotion, 172, 241
Purpose, 54, 63, 117, 175,
Pyramid, Double ('Hourglass'), 60, 173, 175
  of managers, 16, 172, 180, 190–9
  representatives, 61, 173–80

Quantification, 49, 64–76, 102–3, 154

Rates and Dates, 67, 77, 121
Representatives, of beneficiaries, 60–2, 173–80, 231
Resources, 99, 123–6
Results, 70, 121–3
  checking 142, 150–61
Rewards, *see* Penalties
Risk, 104, 113
Rules and Regulations, 137, 245

Satisfactory, 56, 67–8, 117, 216
Selection Techniques, 127, 139, 144, 241
Sieve, 98–107
Significance, *see* Statistical
Slack, 53, 115, 176, 191, 193
Span of control, 192–8
Specialists, 50, 144, 180, 192–9, 243
Staff, *see* Line
Standard of Living, 51
Statistical Significance, 153–7
Strengths and Weaknesses, 101, 213
Subordinates, 31, 35, 146
Supervisory Board, 233
Surveys, 94
Symptoms, 230

INDEX

Targets, 64–5
  Constricting and Expansive, 74, 136
Tasks, cascade of, 53
  continuing and project, 31, 66
  dirty, repetitive and menial, 131–4, 242
Techniques, *see* Management
Terminal Cells, 187
Think Tank, 94, 96
Training, 45, 140, 241, 243

Transdepartmental, *see* Projects

Value Judgements, 66
Variety and choice, 47, 79, 85
  at work, 134
Venture management, 127, 136
Vorstad, 233

Weaknesses, *see* Strengths
Wider Discretion, 131–44
Wild men, 94